Gandhi

in a Canadian Context

Statue of Mahatma Gandhi at Vishnu Mandir, Richmond Hill, Ontario.
Photo by Alexander Damm

Gandhi

in a Canadian Context

Relationships between Mahatma Gandhi and Canada

Alex Damm, editor

WLU PRESS

WILFRID LAURIER
UNIVERSITY PRESS

LAURIER
Inspiring Lives.

Wilfrid Laurier University Press acknowledges the support of the Canada Council for the Arts for our publishing program. We acknowledge the financial support of the Government of Canada through the Canada Book Fund for our publishing activities. This work was supported by the Research Support Fund.

Canadä | Canada Council Conseil des arts for the Arts du Canada | ONTARIO ARTS COUNCIL CONSEIL DES ARTS DE L'ONTARIO an Ontario government agency un organisme du gouvernement de l'Ontario

Library and Archives Canada Cataloguing in Publication

Gandhi in a Canadian context : relationships between Mahatma Gandhi and Canada / Alex Damm, editor.

Based on a conference held at Wilfrid Laurier University in 2012.
Includes bibliographical references and index.
Issued in print and electronic formats.
ISBN 978-1-77112-235-1 (hardback).—ISBN 978-1-77112-259-7 (pdf).—ISBN 978-1-77112-260-3 (epub)

1. Gandhi, Mahatma, 1869–1948. 2. Gandhi, Mahatma, 1869–1948—Influence. 3. Gandhi, Mahatma, 1869–1948—Teachings. 4. Nonviolence. 5. Passive resistance. 6. Statesmen—India—Biography. 7. Canada—Social conditions. I. Damm, Alex, 1973-, author, editor

DS481.G3G35 2016   954.03'5092   C2016-903693-6
                                                   C2016-903694-4

Cover design by Martyn Schmoll. Text design by Mike Bechthold.

© 2017 Wilfrid Laurier University Press
Waterloo, Ontario, Canada
www.wlupress.wlu.ca

For Bryan Dare

Contents

Acknowledgements

I am grateful to many people for the encouragement and insight that helped me develop a modest collection of ideas into this book. Discussions with Michel Desjardins, Carol Duncan, Kay Koppedrayer, Meena Sharify-Funk, and Nathan Funk were instrumental in the initial stages of the project, as was the generous support of the Canadian Society for the Study of Religion (CSSR), under whose auspices most of this volume's essays were first presented at the conference "Gandhi in a Canadian Context" at the 2012 Congress for the Humanities and Social Sciences. Special thanks in this regard go to Michel Desjardins, Patricia Dold, Darlene Juschka, Richard Mann, Yasaman Munro, Rubina Ramji, and other current and/or erstwhile members of the CSSR executive. The Department of Religion and Culture at Wilfrid Laurier University, chaired by Carol Duncan, kindly contributed to hospitality at the event, and the event benefited further from the assistance of Nathan Ataide and Eveline Escoto.

For assistance in developing the conference papers into this volume, I very much appreciate the help of Patricia Dold as well as the wise suggestions by anonymous readers of the manuscript. The patience and support of Lisa Quinn, Blaire Comacchio, Siobhan McMenemy, and Rob Kohlmeier of Wilfrid Laurier University Press have been stellar, and I wish to thank the press for its interest in and dedication to this volume. My greatest good fortune has always been the support from, and the example set by, my parents Beverley and Alexis, and my partner Priya.

A Note on Abbreviations and Style

In this book, some authors have used the original, print edition of the *Collected Works of Mahatma Gandhi*, here abbreviated *CWMG* (100 volumes: Publications Division, Ministry of Information and Broadcasting, Government of India, 1955–94). These volumes are no longer in print. Other authors have used a revised edition of the *CWMG*, here abbreviated *eCWMG* (98 volumes: Publications Division, Ministry of Information and Broadcasting, Government of India, 1999). The revised edition sought to update and fill out the original edition. Significantly, its pagination differs from *CWMG*. There exist a limited number of print copies of this revised edition; contributors to this book have consulted its e-book version (i.e., online version), which is available at Gandhiserve.org, http://www.gandhiserve.org/e/cwmg/cwmg.htm. For a history of the publication of the *CWMG* and the debate surrounding the revised edition, see "CWMG Controversy" at http://www.gandhiserve.org/e/cwmg/cwmg_controversy.htm.

Except for already published materials, diacritical marks have been removed from Sanskrit and Hindi words in this volume. Many readers will not be familiar with the pronunciations these marks indicate, and the absence of such marks facilitates uniformity among the essays.

Introduction

Alex Damm

Driving along one of Canada's better-known roadways, Yonge Street, in Richmond Hill, Ontario, one cannot help but notice the larger-than-life statue of Mohandas K. Gandhi outside the Vishnu Mandir. In its size and verisimilitude, the statue is impressive, and it makes one think, if just for a moment, of what Gandhi means or symbolizes. It is not the only thought-provoking Gandhi image in this country. One sees similar representations of Gandhi in such places as Saskatoon, Quebec City (at the National Assembly), Hamilton (at Hamilton City Hall), and Ottawa (at Carleton University). Strikingly, mural images of Gandhi appear in two different schools within a short drive of my home in Peel Region, just outside Toronto. And in Moose Jaw, Saskatchewan, a United Church (St. Andrews) carries Gandhi's image in one of its stained-glass windows. Given their public locations, these statues and images cannot help but provoke curiosity about Gandhi in the Canadian observer's mind.

But there is more – in fact, these are only a few of the visible and intriguing links between the Mahatma and Canada. And however insignificant each link might seem, together they begin to suggest that we need to pay closer scholarly attention to the relationship between Gandhi and Canada. In the biographical study of Gandhi written by his friend the Reverend Charles F. Andrews, one notices that Andrews wrote part of the book in the east coast city of Halifax.[1] The 1997 critical edition of Gandhi's landmark treatise *Hind Swaraj* was edited by Anthony Parel, a long-time professor at the University of Calgary. In 2010, at a Wilfrid Laurier University convocation ceremony, the audience listened to Dr. Vera Good, an honorary degree recipient and former television producer with TV Ontario, the province's public television network. As a young woman, in January 1948, Good had attended Gandhi's prayer meetings at Birla House in Delhi, India.[2] And at Simon Fraser University in British Columbia, there is an annual Mahatma Gandhi Student Award. In my own experience, I have encountered fascinating hints of Gandhi in a Canadian context. In Toronto not long ago, I found a copy of a used book about him with a note dated March 1956, gifting the book to an instructor at the University of Toronto.[3] And links between Canada and Gandhi appear also in Gandhi's own writings, as the Mahatma certainly knew some things about Canada: he referred to cities like Saskatoon, Winnipeg, and Vancouver, and he had Canadian volunteers and supporters.

Surely, the casual Canadian observer of any of these images has taken a moment to consider what the image of Gandhi means. It is dangerous to generalize what an ordinary Canadian might think about Gandhi. But to anticipate one of the essays in this volume, I would hazard a guess that Gandhi's image – perhaps blended with memories of social studies classes, memorable aphorisms ("Be the change which you wish to see in the world"), and the 1982 Richard Attenborough film *Gandhi* – brings to mind a committed peace activist and a leader in India's independence movement.[4] Probably an average Canadian's reflection on Gandhi does not extend much beyond this, and while such reflection is certainly accurate as far as it goes, it is also limited.

We will return momentarily to address Canadians' limited awareness of Gandhi. First, though, let me note that the many images of Gandhi in Canadian contexts invite us more thoroughly to examine his place in Canadian experience. Certainly there are enough images at least to warrant further study of his place in Canadian experience. Canadian images of Mahatma Gandhi raise questions about his place here. Who, for instance, stands behind the raising of the many statues of Gandhi? Do these monuments imply active Canadian voluntarism along Gandhian lines? Is there emulation of Gandhi in religious communities? Do Canadians have an opportunity to learn critically about Gandhi at all? Are there issues in Canada today that parallel issues Gandhi had to address in the India of his own day? What themes in the study of Gandhi have occupied Canadian scholars? What is more, in Canada today there is ongoing writing about Gandhi (including his links to Canada), teaching about Gandhi, and activism inspired by Gandhi, yet reflection on Gandhi's connections to Canada has rarely been offered in published form.[5]

The immediate aim of this book, based on a conference held at Wilfrid Laurier University in 2012, is to examine connections between Gandhi and Canada. Its essays seek to explore the relationships – historical, educational, philosophical, and practical – between this country and India's foremost nationalist leader. This book's orientation is in the main academic, that is to say descriptive and analytical; most of the essays focus on the history and thought of Gandhi, or on Gandhi studies, each drawing attention to links between the Mahatma and Canada. Put another way, most of the essays do not primarily seek to apply Gandhian principles to contemporary Canadian issues, although many of them make soundings in that direction.

This book envisages two audiences. The first is an academic audience, namely Gandhi scholars and university students. As indicated, many of the essays pursue academic aspects of Gandhi, including his knowledge of Canada; his appreciation of Islam; his philosophical stance on violence and cowardice; and his place in Canadian post-secondary education. But at the same time, the book casts a wide net and addresses *all* educated readers, people who, for example, are intrigued by Canadian culture, history, and religion; people who want to know more about Gandhi in education; and people who seek to learn what possibilities exist for applying Gandhian insights to Canadian life. Admittedly, the last constituency will not find a detailed examination of how Gandhi might address contemporary Canadian issues (for example, building peaceful communities, environmental sustainability, and gender violence), and the authors hope that a comparable book might examine more thoroughly the application of Gandhian teachings to Canada today. Several essays, though, discuss or call for applications of Gandhian thought to Canada or by Canadians – a theme on which all of the book's contributors agree and to which I will return at the end of this essay. We consider this volume a first stage in a larger project of raising consciousness about Gandhi in this country.[6]

Not surprisingly, the contributors to this collection relate Gandhi to Canada in different ways that reflect their expertise and interests. Their essays fall into four thematic sections: (1) biography of Gandhi, (2) Gandhi's thought, (3) teaching about Gandhi and its impact on students, and (4) the importance of Gandhi in addressing contemporary social issues in Canada. The first section concerns Gandhi's own life. In "Mahatma Gandhi's Understanding of Canada," the editor discovers that Gandhi's awareness of Canada persisted over forty years. Moreover, elements of Gandhi's awareness evolved over time in response to his own changing career. Gandhi's evaluation of Canada was variously critical and appreciative, and his warmest comments were saved for Canadians who had contributed to his campaigning for *swaraj* (self-rule or independence). One lesson we take from study of Gandhi's references to Canada is that Canada was, in a small way, a force that supported his nationalist campaign.

The thought and philosophy of Gandhi is the focus of the following two essays. Each examines elements of Gandhi's thought and suggests how they are timely for contemporary Canada. In "A Dent in His Saintly Halo? Mahatma Gandhi's Intolerance Against Cowards," Scott Dunbar observes that for all Gandhi's belief in non-violence, he still regarded violence as superior to *fear*. Dunbar seeks to explain how Gandhi, a thoroughgoing spokesman for non-violence, could paradoxically advocate violence as a nobler behaviour than cowardice. For Dunbar, the answer lies in the Hindu culture in which Gandhi was raised, a culture in which bravery and fearlessness amount to arguably the most powerful virtues as expressed in such traditions as the *Bhagavad Gita*. Dunbar reminds us that Gandhi's non-violence was not quite as unconditional and total as we tend to think.

In "Gandhi and Islam: Their History and Implications for Canada Today," Ramin Jahanbegloo profiles what he calls *Gandhian Islam*. Surveying the numerous contacts between Gandhi and Islamic traditions, ranging from his collaboration with the Ali brothers in the *Khilafat* movement, to his fruitful alliances with such prominent Muslims as Abdul Ghaffar Khan and Maulana Azad, Jahanbegloo reveals the extent to which Gandhi was influenced by and was a contributor to principles of non-violence in Islam. In turn, Jahanbegloo reminds Canadian readers that precisely this Gandhian Islam, an authentic Islam that promotes non-violence, can be a model for Canadian Muslims and a valuable corrective to our media-influenced misunderstanding of Islam as a religion saturated with violence and conflict.

In the next several essays, the centre of gravity shifts to teaching about Gandhi in Canadian university education. Harold Coward's "Gandhi in Canadian Academic Religious Studies: An Overview" walks us methodically through Gandhi studies in their Canadian context. Coward provides a careful outline of Gandhian scholarship and university teaching about Gandhi in this country.[7] Beginning with scholarship, he documents the emergence over the past forty years of research interests on Gandhi, including three outstanding topics: Gandhi's relationship with religious traditions outside Hinduism, his contributions to non-violent co-operation and coexistence, and his political involvement with others in the nationalist movement. Coward also reveals an abiding interest in teaching about Gandhi in Canadian universities, from its origins in the 1960s through its expansion across the country to its present place in not only undergraduate but also advanced study. One leaves this essay with an impression that Gandhi studies are on a firm footing in Canada, although Coward cautions us that "course work is perhaps weaker than one would expect."

Continuing the discussion of Gandhi in education, Kay Koppedrayer and Anne Pearson provide two accounts of the impact of learning about Gandhi on Canadian students. After many years teaching a course on Gandhi at Wilfrid Laurier University, Koppedrayer ("Do Gandhi's Teachings Have Relevance Today?") surveyed former students and assessed the extent to which they remembered and believed that they had grown or developed through the study of Gandhi's life and ideas. The results are encouraging, for while some students admitted to limited recall or application of Gandhian principles, many had maintained an abiding admiration for Gandhi's values and indeed had taken it upon themselves to think in Gandhian terms when faced with situations that entail, for instance, conflict, sustainability, or harmonious relations among communities. Koppedrayer concludes that classroom learning about Gandhi is valuable: it affords students the opportunity to think dispassionately and critically about him, while also giving students who seek personal growth some valuable tools and ingredients.

In "The Gandhian-Inspired *Mahila Shanti Sena* Movement in India and Its Canadian Connection," Anne Pearson describes an organization to which she is deeply committed and that has had a similar impact on students. The *Mahila Shanti Sena* (or MSS) is a grassroots organization that began in the Indian state of Bihar over a decade ago and is composed almost entirely of women. The Sena gives women a leadership role in nonviolently addressing social issues ranging from spousal abuse and addiction on the one hand, to mobilization of government on the other. The Sena initially took up its work in India under the inspiration of Gandhian activist Acharya Ramamurti, but it has been helped from the start by the contributions of Canadians, including Rama Singh and Pearson. Today, Pearson coordinates volunteer placements of Canadian university students with MSS Canada (a branch of the MSS founded by Singh), strengthening it and raising consciousness of non-violent activism in Canada. Clearly, the fruit of the Sena has deep Canadian roots.

In "'Gandhi' in Canada in the Latter Part of the Twentieth Century," Paul Younger reflects on his decades of teaching a course on Gandhi at McMaster University, relating it to the changing Canadian scene and the changing composition of his classes. One of the fascinating conclusions Younger documents is that student concerns, and to some extent his own emphases in teaching, have been shaped by Canadian social concerns in the 1960s, 1970s, 1980s, 1990s, and 2000s. In the 1980s, for example, the particular class interest in Gandhi's vision of a pluralist (i.e., multi-ethnic and multi-religious) India reflected the emerging policy of Canadian multiculturalism, while in the previous decade, a new infusion of female students and new sensitivity to gender equity helped foster a strong interest in Gandhi's incorporation of women into his *satyagraha* and *sarvodaya* programs. As a seasoned scholar and teacher of Gandhi, Younger is well positioned to show how teaching can relate constructively to students' experiences, for instance by underscoring and problematizing them.

Finally, this volume turns briefly to consider Gandhi's relevance to Canadian communities today. This topic is taken up by Klaus Klostermaier and by Rama Singh. Klostermaier reflects on Gandhi's relevance in his essay "Mahatma Gandhi and Winnipeg, Manitoba." For Klostermaier, emulation of Gandhian principles is timely and necessary. Using instructive examples from his home city, he argues that several of Gandhi's teachings, including the need to cultivate Truth and non-violence, are deeply relevant, and that we should let compassion and service guide sound decisions and policy.

Rama Singh, who was instrumental in organizing the MSS, has launched a consciousness-raising activity through the Hamilton Gandhi Peace Festival. In "Who Speaks for the Conscience of Canada? Twenty Years of Hamilton's Gandhi Peace Festival: Local Lessons, Global Relevance," Singh discusses the aims, origins, and salient features of a public event dedicated to helping realize Gandhi's principles of *swaraj*, *satyagraha*, *sarvodaya*, and *ahimsa* (non-violence). Clarifying that the peace for which the festival stands must be defined broadly to include the equitable provision of security and other life necessities the world over, Singh reminds us that the festival is only the beginning; what is needed, he contends, are many like-minded people and communities, people who can act outside the limiting partisanship of politics and so "speak for the conscience of Canada." The Gandhi Peace Festival is an exercise in contemporary social change.

By this point, probably the reader has asked why this book appears in a series dedicated to the study of religion. What have Gandhi and Canada to do with religious studies? In point of fact, Gandhi has *everything* to do with religion: as Boyd Wilson reminds us, the Mahatma believed that all of the matters he felt were important to the society of his times, from proper diet, education, and economics to non-violent protest (*satyagraha*), self-reliance (*swaraj*), and good governance, were facets of or steps towards Truth, towards leading a life of Truth.[8] For Gandhi, Truth meant more than simply honesty – it was the manifestation of God's will. As he famously said, "Truth is God." So to analyze Gandhi's philosophy is to reflect on fundamentally religious matters. Gandhi felt that people should dedicate themselves to developing a life of Truth, a life that embraces and reflects the will of God, or *dharma*. Because Gandhi saw life through a religious lens, our discussion of Gandhi concerns religious principles. Gandhi's religious lens does not mean that we need constantly refer to the religious connotations of his ideas. We should remember, however, that for Gandhi, non-violent social change was a reflection of Truth – a reflection, to paraphrase Tillich, of ultimate concern.

Let me close by commenting briefly on this book's greater significance. For this, we return to the issue of Canadians' limited awareness of Gandhi. As we said earlier, this book's immediate goal is to help students and teachers better appreciate Gandhi's connections to Canada. But the book's ultimate goal – what we hope is its real significance – is to expand and motivate further Canadian study of Gandhi. Such study matters in two ways.

First, the academic study of Gandhi is a superb way of taking up issues that not only faced Gandhi's India but also face contemporary Canada. To examine Gandhi is to examine *Canadian* problems and potential solutions. Consider some topics that are already part of Canadian humanities curricula. Few of us would disagree that students need to assess the impact of consumer technologies, to understand that technologies often appeal to fleeting aesthetic pleasure and leave people less able to think for themselves, let alone understand the value of time and the essential virtues of patience and quietude. Few of us would disagree that we need to understand the tiresomely common phenomenon of financial gain for the few at the expense of the many, or the impact of colonialism on Canada's Native people, or the anti-democratic behaviour of many corporations and elected governments, or the question of Canada's international role as either "peacemaker" or "warrior nation." These are urgent topics. Crucially, they are also topics on which Gandhi reflected. Study of Gandhi proves the value of history for contemporary reflection. Whichever judgment students ultimately form of Gandhi, academic study of Gandhi deserves more attention.

Second, and related, we hold that Gandhi *matters to the well-being of Canada*. Gandhi's place in Canada is of not only academic but also moral significance, and this point deserves further comment. Gandhi's teachings about conflict resolution and non-violent direct action, about sustainability and interracial harmony, to take but a few examples, are worth applying in Canada today. Gandhi's teaching of *swaraj* or self-control entails living sustainably – for instance, consuming no more than what one needs for sustenance – instead of chasing the (commercially marketed) image of "happiness" that underlies today's markets for everything from automobiles and coffee to consumer technology. While this book is not asking readers necessarily to forgo coffee or car ownership, Gandhi's teachings on sustainability can help reduce consumption of finite natural resources and draw us away from the chimera that happiness is a function of luxury. A second illustration of Gandhi's contemporary value emerges in another element of *swaraj*: a call to respect non-European civilizations. In many ways, the

Europeans' treatment of Canada's Aboriginal people over the past five centuries resembles European behaviour in colonial India – behaviour often characterized by disrespect, inequality, disingenuousness, and theft. In *Hind Swaraj* (1910), Gandhi called upon Indians and Europeans alike to respect and indeed to imbibe traditional, pre-modern cultures. He held that Indians' adherence to traditional cultures, coupled with "passive resistance" to European culture and to the governments that upheld it, would *compel* Europeans to cease their exploitative policies.[9] Among Canadian Aboriginal people, non-violent assertions of tradition have already had a remarkable impact on white Canadians' perceptions of their dignity and treaty rights. The continued assertion of such tradition, nourished by Gandhian teaching and example, can further enhance the self-confidence of and equity owed to Canadian Aboriginal communities.

It would be unfair for us to forget that many Canadians are working consciously to refashion attitudes along more Gandhian lines. To take but one example, the Mahatma Gandhi Canadian Foundation for World Peace, in Edmonton, has developed fascinating and timely education projects on Gandhian themes for local high school youth. Such projects are a basis for building peaceful communities in which empathy and conflict resolution have a solid place. And for some time, a farm in Queens County, Nova Scotia, dedicated itself to sustainable and organic food production along lines that imitated the sustainability and self-reliance characteristic of Gandhi's *swaraj*. The farm, although it appears no longer to be in operation, showcased what real Canadians have done to emulate Gandhian teaching.[10] At the back of this book, you will find a list of readings and Gandhi-inspired associations in Canada that will help you learn more about these projects and perhaps apply Gandhian insights to social change.

Gandhi was a lifelong champion of *ahimsa*, non-violence, as a *summum bonum* of life and a way of seeing the world. It guided his approach to so many elements of life, including conflict resolution and the treatment of animals, political opponents, and the socially marginal.[11] Non-violence was Gandhi's charter. And it must become ours. We must affirm it, and we must go beyond affirmation to practise and to experiment with non-violence as a way of life. Non-violence can refashion our perceptions of others; it can heal our treatment of the natural world; it can adjust our attitude towards material goods; and it can transform our education. However we choose to use Gandhi's thought, to whatever extent, in religious or secular terms, and on whichever level, personal or social, the time has come for Canadians to take it more seriously: to discuss it, to critique and reshape and update it in places, but ultimately to act on it, in service of building a more harmonious society in which non-violence holds a deep and abiding place.

Notes

1 Andrews, *Mahatma Gandhi's Ideas*.

2 See "Spring Convocation 2010," wlu.ca.

3 The note reads: "Dear Dr. [Gordon] Murray: When Dr. Saini was here, we had written home for a copy of 'Gita' to present it to you. I am herewith enclosing you a copy of 'Gita.' I hope you will enjoy reading it. With regards, Yours Sincerely, M. Mehta." M. Mehta to Gordon Murray, 23 March 1956, editor's collection. The Gita to which Mehta refers is Desai, *The Gospel of Selfless Action*.

4 Kay Koppedrayer, "Do Gandhi's Teachings Have Relevance Today?," in this volume.

5 See the essay below by Harold Coward, "Gandhi in Canadian Academic Religious Studies: An Overview." To be sure, many studies of Gandhi have examined his relevance to the West generally (i.e., to Europe and North America), but there is little work on Canada in particular. For studies of Gandhi's place in other Western contexts, see, for example, Scalmer, *Gandhi in the West*; and Hardiman, *Gandhi in His Time and Ours*, 238–301. On the United States, see Leys and Rama Rao, *Gandhi and America's Educational Future*; Seshachari, *Gandhi and the American Scene*; and Danielson, *American Gandhi*. On the West generally and France in particular, see Markovits, *The Un-Gandhian Gandhi*, 13–39. And for numerous published reflections on the role and impact of Gandhi on African and Asian states, see the essays in Nanda, ed., *Mahatma Gandhi*.

6 The essays in this volume are written by Canadians or by academics who have made Canada their home. One of the book's subsidiary aims is to highlight Canadian Gandhi scholarship.

7 Coward's focus is scholarship and teaching in religious studies. Canadian scholars who work in other disciplines also have written about various facets of Gandhi. These scholars include Hans Bakker, who has published *Gandhi and the Gita* and *Towards a Just Civilization: A Gandhian Perspective on Human Rights and Development*. They also include Anthony Parel, who with Judith Brown has co-edited *The Cambridge Companion to Gandhi*, and who has edited a critical edition of Gandhi's *Hind Swaraj*; see Gandhi, *Hind Swaraj and Other Writings*). Moreover, the founding editor of the new *International Journal of Gandhi Studies*, Sushil Mittal, is Canadian. Mittal teaches at James Madison University in the United States.

8 Wilson, "Ultimacy as Unifier in Gandhi," 359.

9 Gandhi, *Hind Swaraj and Other Writings*, 117.

10 "The Real Gandhi Farm": Visit http://www.angelfire.com/clone2/gandhifarm.

11 On the paramount place of non-violence in Gandhi's thought, see, for example, Juergensmeyer, *Encyclopedia of Religion*; and Parekh, *Gandhi: A Very Short Introduction*, 92–110.

ॐ

Mahatma Gandhi's Understanding of Canada

Alex Damm

It might appear striking that over a century ago, Mohandas Gandhi could write with precision and confidence about Canada. Probably we are not accustomed to thinking about Gandhi as someone who knew or cared much about Canada, and there are good reasons for this. For one thing, Canada and Canadian affairs do not appear to be topics to which he paid much attention, a fact attested to by the dearth of references to this country in biographies of Gandhi and (as we will see) by the rather infrequent references in his own writing.[1] Gandhi had numerous pressing concerns in South Africa and India, where he developed and fought to defend his principles of *swaraj* (self-rule), *satyagraha* (non-violent resistance), and *sarvodaya* (universal uplift), and we cannot expect Canada to have loomed large in that regard. For another, Gandhi never visited Canada and had no direct personal connection to it. Moreover, he worked in a period well before people had access to the media we use today, such as television, radio, and the Internet, so there was relatively little opportunity for him to reflect on or involve himself in Canadian affairs.

But when we peruse Gandhi's writings, we find that Canada and Canadians have a small and enduring place in his thought. And this is the striking point. To be sure, Canada does not hold a *major* place in Gandhi's thought, but it certainly holds a place. And once a reader begins to see Gandhi refer to Canada, intriguing questions arise: What did Gandhi know about Canada? How did he characterize it? Was his view of the country and its peoples an informed one for the time in which he lived? And might Canada have played some role(s) in his reflections on India's *swaraj*, non-violence, and traditional civilization? In short, what was Gandhi's awareness of Canada? If we can discover more about Gandhi's understanding of this country, we might be able to deepen our understanding of Gandhi – for instance, of his principles and methods. We might also be able to learn whether Canada had a constructive role in shaping Gandhi's image of a responsible and authentic India. The topic certainly warrants attention.[2]

In this essay, I examine Gandhi's explicit references to Canada and Canadians in his *Collected Works*. Our study cannot reconstruct entirely Gandhi's understanding of Canada, for his printed words do not represent everything that he thought. Moreover, it has not been possible to identify every possible Canadian reference or subject in his writings. Our focus has more simply been on the words "Canada" and "Canadian" in these works. When we peruse them, we discover that there are at least fifty-three documents, mainly letters or newspaper articles, spanning the years 1902 to 1946, in which Gandhi explicitly engages Canada or Canadians; this averages approximately one reference each year during Gandhi's public career from about 1893 to 1948. There is some material, then, with which to reconstruct Gandhi's understanding of Canada, or at least to draw its contours.

From Gandhi's comments about Canada, there emerge some basic facts. For one thing, he envisioned Canada in a way that we would expect in the early twentieth century: he understood Canada as a British dominion that was politically loyal to Britain. To be sure, he did not always use the term "dominion." In fact, his terminology for Canada evolved a little: in the early 1900s, he referred to Canada as a "colony" or "self-governing colony" of Britain, while after about 1918, these terms gave way to the term "independence" – a subtle change suggesting a more autonomous country.[3] But the image of a British dominion was quite consistent. Moreover, as late as 1931 Gandhi characterized Canada as a cultural "daughter state" of Britain.[4] And we should not be surprised by this image, for a distinctly Canadian identity developed only gradually over the twentieth century; from Confederation through to the 1960s, Canadians were mainly from the United Kingdom and elsewhere in northern Europe and regarded themselves as essentially British subjects of the British Crown, though such a self-image changed slowly over that period.[5] Lest we forget this fact in light of our modern celebrations of a multicultural and autonomous Canada, we have much evidence to illustrate Canada's erstwhile formal and informal links with Britain. Until 1964, Canada's flag was the Red Ensign (and, for most of the preceding century, the Union flag);[6] its peoples bore mainly English names and imbibed English (British) education.[7] Indeed, there was no such thing as Canadian citizenship until 1947, and Canadian foreign policy and defence policy were (until the Statute of Westminster of 1931) essentially determined by the British Parliament.[8] Given these conditions, it is easy to see how Gandhi, in his day, would have described Canada as a British dominion and "daughter state."

For another thing, Gandhi's references to Canada tend to lack breadth or nuance. For example, Gandhi hardly ever refers to Canada's francophone population,[9] nor does he refer to Canada's Indigenous peoples. Perhaps his silence about such features of Canada is simply a function of limited knowledge of or interest in or access to information about Canada, for he rarely refers to other facets of Canadian life such as geography, history, arts, or culture.[10] Topics such as the French minority and Native Canadians would not likely have been discussed widely at the time in Canada, let alone internationally.[11] Moreover, we should not use present standards of justice for Aboriginal minorities to critique Gandhi. We must remember that he was a product of a late-nineteenth-century education that did not recognize Aboriginal rights as a subject worthy of attention.[12]

Be that as it may, our perusal of Gandhi's references to Canada brings to the surface significant themes in his understanding. Sometimes his references to Canada are tangential and insignificant.[13] That said, his writings do reveal two striking themes. The first concerns Canada, or more precisely the Canadian government; the second concerns the behaviour of individual Canadians.

Gandhi and Canada

A large proportion of Gandhi's reflections concern "Canada" in the abstract, especially its government and policies. When Gandhi refers to Canada, his focus is on the welfare of India and Indians within the British Empire. This should not be surprising, given Gandhi's lifelong work on behalf of Indian causes such as home rule. But there is a fascinating *development* in Gandhi's references to Canada. While he probably was not conscious of this development, it remains conspicuous. In writings essentially before 1917, Gandhi tends to refer to Canada when discussing the struggles that Indian immigrants face in the British Empire. After 1917, however, he begins to employ Canada more as a standard for envisioning India's independence. Below, I will show how Gandhi's discussion of Canada changes over time: early on (1902–16), his focus is on how Canada treats Indian immigrants; later (ca. 1917–46), he discusses Canada in the context of Indian home rule. I will also suggest that his references to Canada and his understanding of

Canada changed because his own role changed during this period, from advocacy for Indian immigrants towards directing the campaign for India's independence.

Canada's Discrimination against Indian Immigrants

It is well known that from 1891 to 1914, while Gandhi worked as a lawyer in South Africa, he dedicated himself increasingly to securing fair and equal treatment for Indian immigrants, vis-à-vis white settlers. His now famous ill treatment on a Durban-bound train in 1893, his consequent activism (such as lobbying and court litigation) to eliminate the economic barriers raised against Indian immigrants to South Africa, and his plan for *satyagraha* (1906) to protest the Asiatic Law Amendment Act, are well documented.[14] Also during this time, Gandhi founded and contributed energetically to a newspaper, *Indian Opinion*, as a vehicle for persuading Indians and whites to understand the need for legal equality in the Empire.[15]

Significantly, Gandhi sometimes mentions Canada in his *Indian Opinion* columns, and his discussion tends to concern Canada's poor treatment of Indian immigrants. Very often, he chastises Canada as one of many British colonies that treat Indian immigrants inequitably. To appreciate Gandhi's criticism of Canada, some context is necessary. In the late nineteenth and early twentieth centuries, many Indians immigrated to other British colonies for economic reasons. Many chose Canada, and most of these immigrants went to British Columbia, hoping to find work as labourers, for example, in the lumber mills.[16] According to Gandhi, as citizens of the British Empire they were entitled to immigrate to British territories to find a better livelihood.[17] But when they tried to settle in Canada, they encountered harassment by a government that feared them as a threat to the larger, white population, and that passed laws that were hostile to them. For example, they were forbidden to acquire trading licences,[18] and their wives were prevented from joining them.[19] Gandhi knew that the Canadian government had been deploying laws and various policies to make it harder for Indians to come to Canada.[20]

Gandhi's disappointment with Canada's unfair and restrictive immigration laws runs through his newspaper columns and other correspondence. The theme emerges repeatedly and clearly.[21] Much of his critique appears in various issues of *Indian Opinion* from the spring of 1908. In the first of a series of essays, titled "Indians in Canada" (25 April), he disdainfully observes that Indian immigrants were recently denied entry to Canada at Vancouver, including nearly 150 who had travelled on the SS *Monteagle* from Hong Kong. He places at least part of the blame on the Indians themselves, whom he believes should have engaged more directly in non-violent agitation against Canadian authorities to assert their rights as British subjects.[22] Here we see echoes of Gandhi's own *satyagraha* work in South Africa and intimations of his case in *Hind Swaraj* (1910) as it relates to Indians in India.

Gandhi's criticism of Canada continues in an essay of 9 May, in which he argues that the Canadian government has no right to prevent Indians from moving to British Columbia.[23] In this piece, however, Gandhi has stopped blaming the Indians for their plight. Indeed, he commends them, and reports a noticeable change:

> We learn from newspapers sent us by a friend from Winnipeg that Indians abroad are becoming more public-spirited everywhere ... [When] they were not allowed to land by the Canadian Government ... this led to a meeting by Indian settlers in Canada. Most of the participants were Sikhs. They met in a Sikh temple and showed great spirit. The meeting passed a resolution asserting that it would injure the cause of the British Empire if these Indians were forced to return.[24]

Gandhi's words express his conviction that Canada is not meeting its obligations as a part of the British Empire. He is pleased, though, to hear of the burgeoning self-confidence of the Indian immigrants in Vancouver[25] as they petition the British government to override Canada's immigration policy.[26] In this, we again hear echoes of Gandhi's views about the power of non-violent protest. Gandhi continues on these themes in his newspaper articles later in 1908, 1909, 1911, and 1913. In his 30 May 1908 article "Rhodesia Indians," for example, he explains that "the same harsh treatment that is our lot here [in South Africa] is being meted out to Indians in Canada."[27] By "harsh treatment" he is referring to the discriminatory immigration policies that Canada is applying against Indian immigrants.[28] Indeed, in an article of January 1913, Gandhi calls Canada one of the "worst offender[s]" among the colonies with regard to Indian immigrants.[29] His columns leave little doubt as to his frustration with the Canadian authorities and, sometimes, with the apathy of Indian immigrants themselves.

After Gandhi moved back to India at the beginning of 1915, he continued to criticize the discrimination facing Indians in Canada.[30] A particular and infamous incident concerned the steamship SS *Komagata Maru*. The previous year, Canadian authorities in Vancouver had prevented Indian passengers aboard the *Komagata Maru* from disembarking. Ultimately, the passengers had to return to Calcutta, the consequences of which included a riot and subsequent plotting against the British Raj that led to the Lahore Conspiracy Case.[31] It is no surprise, then, that by 1915, Gandhi had labelled Canada a place of many "hardships ... [of] our countrymen."[32] While he could report by 1929 that Sikhs in Vancouver were far more integrated and valued in that community, he observed that they had not yet been extended Canadian citizenship.[33]

Gandhi persistently criticizes Canadian immigration policy, and much of that criticism aims to raise awareness of discrimination in the British colonies, including Canada, with a view to overcoming it.[34] This last point merits repeating: Gandhi's discussion of Indian immigration to Canada does not stop at criticism – he seeks solutions to racist immigration policy, both by raising his readers' consciousness and by proposing tangible solutions. Sometimes he argues for lobbying Canada to change its ways;[35] other times, he argues for emulating Canadian-based Indians who are resisting racist immigration policies. By emulating the non-violent yet determined resistance of these Indians, other Indian immigrants will succeed in obtaining greater equality in matters such as licences and entry requirements. In mid-1908, for instance, Gandhi writes that "the Indians who have settled in Canada ... have started ... [a] journal in order to seek redress of their grievances. Their writing evidences great courage ... Indians in different parts of the world are waking up. If they cultivate unity, real courage and truthfulness, they may be assured of easy success" ("Rhodesia Indians," in *Indian Opinion*, 30 May 1908).[36]

We should note, finally, that there are times when Gandhi uses Canada as a tool for highlighting *India's* importance to the British Empire and for exhorting Britain to treat South African Indians fairly. Gandhi argues that within the Empire, India's trade with Britain trumps that with Canada, the implication being that Britain should protect the rights of Indian immigrants in South Africa.[37] In any case, for the most part, we can conclude that before 1917, Gandhi's references to Canada are usually critical and concern its Indian immigrants.[38]

Canada as a Yardstick for Self-Government

Beginning in 1917 and on through the 1940s – the decades during which Gandhi became a prominent leader in India's nationalist movement – his references to Canada shift. The change is conspicuous and noteworthy. To be sure, on a handful of occasions he continues to discuss Canada-bound Indian immigrants. But from 1917 onwards, his correspondence and newspaper columns change focus. He now looks to Canada as a sort of lens through which to envision the future independence of India; that is, he discusses Canada in the context of India's political future.

During the years 1917–18, Gandhi writes about Canada positively, as a country that provides a model for Indian self-government, for independence characterized by "partnership" with, not subservience to, Britain.

Gandhi knew that in some important respects, Canada was an autonomous country, a British dominion but essentially independent.[39] In this context, Gandhi mentions Canada as an example of the "real" independence to which India should aspire. Gandhi, then, appeals to the Canadian example to strengthen his argument for what India should become. It is not difficult to illustrate Gandhi's esteem for the Canadian model of dominion.[40] In the course of helping recruit for the British war effort in 1918, for instance, Gandhi spoke as follows:

> We would do well not to be content with a subordinate position in the Empire. It is a characteristic trait of the British that they would treat people who did so as beasts of burden. We can benefit by our connection with them only if we live as their friends or partners. They will protect the honour of their allies and be loyal to them unto death ... Why, then, should we think of breaking off our connection with them altogether? ... We aspire to *independence* ... on this basis. In this context, the examples of Australia and Canada are generally cited; we demand *a status like theirs*. They enjoy protection and, likewise, help in the defense effort. That is exactly what we want for ourselves.[41]

This admiration of Canada's dominion status recurs repeatedly in Gandhi's writings.

In the mid-1920s, though, Gandhi's assessment of Canada changes slightly. He contends more or less consistently that Canada's dominion status, with its functional independence, is permissible for India, but also that a fuller and more robust *total independence* is India's better option. Gandhi still seems to favour some association with Britain, seemingly under the symbol of the British Crown, but he now regards Canada's dominion status as something slightly less valuable than independence, a sort of second and tentative prize.[42] His clearest statement in this regard comes from an interview with a British journalist in the spring of 1924, and it is worth quoting in full:

> Home Rule, on the pattern of the Australian or Canadian constitutions, is not *swaraj*. Still, it will be infinitely superior to our present state of servitude. If Britain is unwilling to give to us complete independence, I would welcome and accept Home Rule. And I say India is certainly able to enter the British community of nations on that footing.[43]

Significantly, he adds:

> The whole of our demands can be compressed into one word, Retire! And if you are not yet willing to retire completely, give us at least the autonomy of your self-governing dominions [such as Canada] ... But if we are to

join the family of British nations, we demand a say, not only in our own affairs, but in those of the whole Empire, in proportion to our population. In other words, we shall expect the centre of Imperial interests to be shifted to India, as its most populous component. Any member of the Empire objecting to this change would have the remedy of leaving the Commonwealth of British nations.[44]

Gandhi is prioritizing full independence, indicating in his reference to "Empire" and "Commonwealth" that the British Crown would retain merely symbolic authority.[45]

While this assessment continues through 1931, as is evident in Gandhi's writings leading up to the second London Round Table conference on India's independence,[46] Gandhi's estimation of Canada as a model seems to have deteriorated further, for he now declares its dominion status unacceptable for India. In his commitment to "partnership" with Britain,[47] Gandhi no longer regards Canada's dominion status as even a secondary option. For however benign or insignificant this status might have seemed to observers at the time (or to us, today), Gandhi felt that such status was irreconcilable with genuine partnership – that is, with genuine equality between the United Kingdom and all of its former colonies.[48] Canada, for him, is no longer the model that it was.[49] By the 1940s, Gandhi clearly does not like the idea of symbolic British authority anywhere, preferring to envision all nations as a pure partnership.[50]

Gandhi's shifting image of Canada, from a nation of disappointing immigration restrictions to a nation that helped him imagine India's freedom, invites us to ask: Why did his understanding of Canada change? One key reason is the shift in Gandhi's own context and aims. Brown notes that prior to 1915, while living in South Africa, Gandhi had dedicated himself to ameliorating the status of Indian immigrants vis-à-vis the white citizens of South Africa.[51] He focused much of his attention on Indian immigrants' rights, and in this context it made sense for him to use Canada as an illustration how *not* to treat them.

After 1915, when Gandhi resettled in India, his focus changed from advocacy for immigrants to advocacy for *swaraj*,[52] although he had certainly anticipated working for *swaraj* during his South African years in his landmark book *Hind Swaraj* (1910).[53] Surely this new context helps explain why Gandhi began in 1917 to use Canada as a yardstick or gauge for envisioning the *swaraj* to which India should aspire. In short, Gandhi's changing life circumstances helped determine his changing discussion, and changing understanding, of Canada.[54]

Gandhi and Canadians

While Gandhi often mentioned Canada in his writings, he also often mentioned prominent individual Canadians. Almost without exception, he regarded these people positively: either he praised them, or he mentioned them as correspondents and friends and as supporters – financial and logistical – of his constructive work.[55] Gandhi's positive contacts with Canadians began early: he was a friend and correspondent of Sir William Wedderburn, who for some time was the Canadian Member of Parliament for Banff and who, both before and after his Canadian work, was a member of the Indian National Congress.[56] Also, in a 1908 issue of *Indian Opinion*, in a column titled "Lepers' Blessings," Gandhi praised the work carried out among Indian victims of leprosy by one "Mr. Anderson" from Canada.[57] In 1921, in his newspaper *Young India*, Gandhi praised foreign-born volunteers (including volunteers from Canada) who had come to India to support Indian *satyagraha* campaigns.[58] Some years later, in 1929 in his newspaper *Navajivan*, Gandhi spoke of a Ms. Helen Reed, who appears to have been Canadian and who was, says Gandhi, a "friend," who reported on a visit to Canada by Congress worker Sarojini Naidu.[59] Two years later, in 1931, after completing his momentous Salt March, he noted in a letter to Narandas Gandhi that he had received symbolic support in the form of a package of salt from an admirer in Canada.[60] Shortly afterwards, during the years 1934–36, Gandhi wrote affectionately about a Canadian woman, Mary Chesley, who had decided to come to India to assist in constructive work and to live as peasant Indians lived.[61] Gandhi was delighted with her efforts and lamented her passing in a memoriam in a May 1936 issue of his newspaper *Harijan*.[62] Finally, in 1942, Gandhi wrote a brief note to a Canadian whom he called "my dear Mildred." This correspondent, whom Gandhi had come to know while staying at Kingsley Hall in London during the Round Table conference,[63] had apparently donated money to Gandhi's ashram. In reply, Gandhi wrote: "Your contribution is welcome. Every copper tells when it becomes part of a heap."[64] In all, then, Gandhi had many positive contacts with Canadians, contacts that together hint at a high estimation of Canadian people.[65] These references do not imply that Gandhi was any less inclined to citizens of any other country. But his writings do suggest that he thought well of Canadians.

Summary

This chapter has shown that while Gandhi's references to Canada are few and the country's place in his thought is small, he did know something of the country and took some interest in it. He had a very clear image of Can-

ada as Britain's daughter state that was emulating some of the unfair practices in which Britain itself engaged. Moreover, while on the one hand he
envisaged Canada as a colony somewhat comparable to India, on the other
he indicated that Canada was receiving preferential treatment even though,
in his estimation, India was more economically valuable to Britain.[66]

Significantly, part of Gandhi's understanding of Canada evolved in tandem with his own life. During his work for Indian immigrants in South
Africa (1893–1914), he saw Canada as a disappointing if corrigible case of
colonial-era racism towards Indian immigrants. But later, during his years
in India, where he devoted so much energy to the independence movement
(1915–47), he came to see Canada more often as a gauge or aid for his vision
about independence. Gandhi's two images of Canada certainly coexisted in
his mind for at least some years; what changed around 1917 was their relative importance.[67]

What is more, Gandhi met and admired many individual Canadians, and this study reminds us that his reaction to Canada and Canadians
reflects something of the distinction he made elsewhere between political
institutions and individuals. In the same way that he could respect General
Smuts in South Africa and Lord Mountbatten in Britain, while remaining
critical of the racist policies in their respective countries, he could respect
individual Canadians while remaining critical of the Canadian state.

Finally, Gandhi's writings about Canadians remind us, in a small way,
that what Canadians do can matter a great deal abroad. Gandhi would no
doubt wish us to know that Canadian individuals can contribute to a more
harmonious, less violent world.

Notes

1 See, for example, Brown, *Gandhi*; R. Gandhi, *Mohandas*; and Payne, *The Life and Death
   of Mahatma Gandhi*. In the notes that follow, references to Gandhi's correspondence are
   frequent enough that I have omitted reference to his surname.

2 I have not found literature that focuses on Gandhi's views of Canada, having searched
   for these key terms in a university library catalogue, *Worldcat*, and in Pandiri, comp., *A
   Comprehensive, Annotated Bibliography on Mahatma Gandhi*. There are, however, discussions of Gandhi's awareness of Canada within studies of related topics. See, for example,
   Johnston, *The Voyage of the Komagata Maru*, 116–24. Also, for Gandhi's knowledge of the
   Vancouver-based nationalist Taraknath Das, see Parel, "Introduction," xxviii–xxix. See
   further the introductory comments in Harold Coward's essay in this volume.

3 For the early terms, see, for example, "Letter to W.S. Caine," 26 March 1902, *eCWMG* 2,
   449–50; "Johannesburg Letter," 26 January 1907, *eCWMG* 6, 244 ("British control ... is
   very slight"); "Indians in Canada [1]," in *Indian Opinion*, 25 April 1908, *eCWMG* 8, 281
   ("country," a term that does not seem to be in tension with "colony"); "Indians in Canada
   [2]," in *Indian Opinion*, 9 May 1908, *eCWMG* 8, 300; "The Sheriff's Meeting," in *Indian
   Opinion*, 10 August 1912, *eCWMG* 12, 231; "Speech on India and the Colonies at Bombay

Congress Session," 28 December 1915, *eCWMG* 15, 89–90 (Canada a "self-governing colony"); "Indian Colonial Emigration," in *The Indian Review*, 1 September 1917, *eCWMG* 16, 1 ("self-governing colony"); also cf. "Imperial Conference Resolutions," in *New India*, 15 August 1918, *eCWMG* 17, 193 (synonyms "colony" and "country"); and "The New High Commissioner and the Indians," in *Indian Opinion*, 1 May 1905, *eCWMG* 4, 266. For language that implies that Canada is more autonomous, see "Appeal for Enlistment" in *Mahadevbaini Diary*, vol. 4, 22 June 1918, *eCWMG* 17, 83 ("dominion"); "Speech at Ahmedabad," in *Prajabandhu*, 24 June 1918, *eCWMG* 17, 97; "Answers to Drew Pearson's Questions" (news clipping), 5 February 1924, *eCWMG* 27, 8 ("partnership ... with other parts of the Empire"); "A Good Beginning," in *Young India*, 6 December 1928, *eCWMG* 43, 306 ("dominion"); "Speech at Gujarat Vidyapith Convocation," 11 January 1930, *eCWMG* 48, 217; "Interview to 'Daily Herald,'" in *Bombay Chronicle*, 20 May 1930, *eCWMG* 49, 290; "Speech at Plenary Session of Round Table Conference," in *Indian Round Table Conference (Second Session): Proceedings of the Plenary Sessions*, 265–75, 1 December 1931, *eCWMG* 54, 224–25; and "Letter to Lord Samuel," 15 May 1943, *eCWMG* 83, 305. Nonetheless, in the course of arguing for Indian independence, Gandhi still characterizes Canada (accurately) as a unit without full autonomy from Britain: see "Interview to 'Stead's Review,'" in *The Searchlight*, 27 June 1924, *eCWMG* 27, 50–51; "Speech at Pembrooke College, Cambridge," in *Young India*, 19 November 1931, *eCWMG* 54, 122–23; "Speech at Plenary Session of Round Table Conference," 224–25; and "Letter to Lord Samuel," 305.

4 "Speech at Friends' House," 31 October 1931, *eCWMG* 54, 115 ("Canada is not considered to be in partnership with Great Britain. It is a daughter state. They represent the same civilization ..."); cf. "Interview to Evelyn Wrench," in *The Spectator*, 6 March 1941, *eCWMG* 81, 347.

5 One sees this shift in analyses of developing Canadian nationalism in several time periods. For the early twentieth century (to 1931) see Burnet, "Immigration and Ethnic Relations," 374; Behiels, "The Expansion of a Nation," 476–77; and Mathew, "Introduction," viii–ix. For the 1940s and 1950s, see Burnet, "Immigration and Ethnic Relations," 375; and Behiels, "The Expansion of a Nation," 494, 495. For the 1960s, see Behiels, "The Expansion of a Nation," 498–99; and Behiels and Mathew, "Introduction," ix–x.

6 See, for instance, Burnet, "Immigration and Ethnic Relations," 374; and (on immigration), Behiels, "The Expansion of a Nation," 498–99.

7 Burnet, "Immigration and Ethnic Relations," 374.

8 Behiels, "The Expansion of a Nation," 476–77.

9 He was, however, aware of the francophone population; see "From and About Sarojini Devi," in *Young India*, 30 May 1929, *eCWMG* 46, 60.

10 Gandhi occasionally discusses facets of Canadian life in the course of discussing Indian affairs. He refers, for instance, to the settlement of Dukhobours on the prairies ("Crusade against Non-Co-operation," in *Young India*, 4 August 1920, *eCWMG* 21, 117); to British trade with Canada ("Mr. Brodrick's Budget," in *Indian Opinion*, 22 July 1905, *eCWMG* 4, 362); and to a Canadian Governor General ("Lord Metcalfe," in *Indian Opinion*, 4 November 1905, *eCWMG* 4, 481). Cf. also note 4 above.

11 On Canadian awareness of Aboriginal people, see the work of Hulan (below). See also Newhouse, Voyageur, and Beavon, "Introduction," 5, 13; and Ruffo, "Why Native Literature?," 110, both quoted in Hulan, *Canadian Historical Writing*, 111–12. Still, some might argue that Gandhi's silence about Canadian Aboriginal peoples finds another explanation in his comparable silences about black South Africans (1891–1914) and towards India's Aboriginal peoples (1915–48). James Hunt explains that while Gandhi was sympathetic

to the causes of South African blacks, his sympathy was attenuated by the fact that the black and Indian communities faced distinct discriminatory problems – and perhaps more surprisingly – by a characteristically turn-of-the-century racist image of blacks (and those of mixed race) as a separate and lesser people. Once in India, observes David Hardiman, Gandhi sought to include Indian Aboriginal (*Adivasi*) communities in his nationalist work, but for most of his career he paid little attention to their distinctive culture and to the nature of the oppression they faced. See Hunt, *An American Looks at Gandhi*, 71–72, 76–77, 79, 87–88. Hunt believes that Gandhi's attitude began to change as he transitioned to India in 1915 (88–89). See also David Hardiman, *Gandhi in His Time and Ours*, 136–39, 142, 146, 147, 150.

12 For comments on the inbuilt ignorance of Aboriginal concerns and life in Western, colonial, or colonial-influenced education, see, for example (for British and later Canadian education), Battiste, "Enabling the Autumn Seed," 283; and (for colonial education generally) Dei and Doyle-Wood, "*Is We Who Haffi Ride Di Staam*," 159–60.

13 See, for instance, his letter to a member of the Canadian Baptist Mission regarding care of a crippled youth: "Letter to A. Gordon," 14 November 1928, *eCWMG* 43, 217.

14 Brown, *Gandhi*, 30–31, 33–34, 45, 50–51, 55–56. For the date of Gandhi's outlining *satyagraha* (1906), see Anthony J. Parel, "Principal Events in the Life of Mohandas Karamchand Gandhi," in Gandhi, ed. Parel, *Hind Swaraj and Other Writings*, lxvi.

15 Brown, *Gandhi*, 36, 42, 50, 52, 53.

16 For immigration generally and to Canada, see Johnston, *Voyage of the Komagata Maru*, 2–3; editor's note in *eCWMG* 8, 281n2 (citing contemporary comments by Rudyard Kipling); and Gandhi, "Speech on India and the Colonies," 90. On Indian emigration out of India and its motives, see also Brown, *Global South Asians*, 14–23, esp. 19–23.

17 See, for instance, "Letter to W.S. Caine," 449–51; "The New High Commissioner and the Indians," 266; "The Status of British Indians," in *Indian Opinion*, 6 January 1906, *eCWMG* 5, 57; and the notes below.

18 Gandhi, "Speech on India and the Colonies," 90; cf. Johnston, *Voyage of the Komagata Maru*, 3.

19 Gandhi's articles express particular concern about restrictions against immigration of labourers' wives. See Gandhi, "Speech on India and the Colonies," 90; and "Imperial Conference Resolutions," 194. For white British hostility towards Indians, see, for instance, "Speech on India and the Colonies," 89; as well as "Letter to W.S. Caine," 450; "Indians in Canada [3]," in *Indian Opinion*, 7 January 1911, *eCWMG* 11, 206; and the notes below.

20 For a British description of specific measures employed in Canada, see "India Office Memorandum for Imperial Conference," June 1911, *eCWMG* 12, 444.

21 Beginning in the aforementioned letter to Caine, dated 26 March 1902, 449–50. Gandhi here refers, for example, to unfairness in grants of licences to trade, to do business, in Canada (as well as in Australia and in Natal colony).

22 "Indians in Canada [1]," 281–82. Gandhi explains that the Canadian government has maliciously employed ostensibly benign laws, such as the "Continuous Journey" law, to prevent Indian immigration. This law required immigrants from a particular country to have travelled directly from that country (see editor's comments in n3). Again, Gandhi is thinking of the problematic behaviour of other colonies as well (282), and he has one eye on the British Imperial government in hopes that it will override Canadian immigration policy ("the eyes of the British are being opened" [282]).

23 "Indians in Canada [2]," 300. Once again, Gandhi alludes to other British territories as well.

24 Ibid.

25 Given that immigrants disembarked at the port of Vancouver, the assembly of Indians was likely there. This is the community to which Gandhi refers in later correspondence (see below) and to which the editors of *eCWMG* allude ("Indians in Canada [1]," 281n3).

26 "Indians in Canada [2]," 300; see also the editor's note here (n3).

27 "Rhodesia Indians," in *Indian Opinion*, 30 May 1908, *eCWMG* 8, 343–44.

28 Gandhi complains, for example, with reference to Rhodesia, that "even educated [Indian] persons are refused entry … if they are unemployed. If they can produce evidence of having found employment, the excuse is then advanced that the employment is unsatisfactory." He also continues to praise Indians' non-violent efforts to achieve equality. See "Rhodesia Indians," 343. For Canadian discrimination, cf. similarly his article "Vancouver Indians," in *Indian Opinion*, 9 January 1909, *eCWMG* 9, 240–41; and cf. further, as well as for Gandhi's frustration with Indians' own protest efforts, "Indians in Canada [3]," 206–7. (Gandhi here refers to earlier comments on the issue, in 1910 [see n1].) Further, on the discrimination problem in Canada and elsewhere, see "The Sheriff's Meeting," 230–31. According to the editors of *eCWMG* 10 (323n10), in late 1909 Gandhi had met one of the prominent leaders of this non-violent protest movement among Indians in British Columbia, Prof. Teja Singh. Gandhi's acquaintance with Professor Singh undoubtedly helped him learn more about Indian activities in Canada; he had already commented on Singh's work earlier in 1909 in "Vancouver Indians," 240–41.

29 Quotation from "England's Biggest Customer," in *Indian Opinion*, 18 January 1913, *eCWMG* 12, 380. Gandhi here lobbies the Imperial government to protect Indian immigrants' rights.

30 He continues to speak about other British colonies too, and the need for the British Imperial government to act over against the colonies; see his 1915 "Speech on India and the Colonies," 89–90; see also "Speech on 'The Secret of Satyagraha in South Africa,'" 27 July 1916, *eCWMG* 15, 241 (he also indicates Indian apathy in Canada here); and "Imperial Conference Resolutions," 193–94.

31 For Gandhi's assessment of the incident, see "Congress Report on the Punjab Disorders," March 1920, *eCWMG* 20, 25. For discussion of the *Komagata Maru* affair, see ibid. (and the editor's comments in n2); and Johnston, *Voyage of the Komagata Maru*, 24–26, 27–34, 37–91, 104–15; Gandhi also narrates in outline the events years later, in "Statement to the Press," in *Harijan*, 25 May 1938, *eCWMG* 73, 183–84.

32 "Speech on India and the Colonies," 89. Here again Gandhi speaks of Canada among other colonies and seeks to lobby the British government. Cf. "Speech on 'The Secret of Satyagraha in South Africa,'" 241. For a critique of "assisted emigration" from India to Crown colonies, see "Indian Colonial Emigration," 1–4.

33 "Sikhs in British Columbia," in *Young India*, 18 July 1929, *eCWMG* 6, 287–88: "The 'Komagata Maru' trouble is now a thing of the past. The British Columbians are ashamed of what happened and they do not in any way defend it." When Gandhi refers to citizenship, he must mean either Canadian citizenship (although such did not exist until 1947), or some other status at the time that granted rights to Indians in Canada.

34 "Letter to W.S. Caine," 449–51; "Rhodesia Indians," 343–44; "Vancouver Indians," 240–41; "The Sheriff's Meeting," 230–31 (and n1); "Speech on India and the Colonies," 89–90; "Imperial Conference Resolutions," 193–94; and "Indians in Canada [2]," 300. Gandhi's very use of such media as speeches and newspapers shows that he seeks to raise awareness of discrimination and so attenuate it.

35 "Letter to W.S. Caine," 450: "As to Australia and Canada, the remedy is to take up the proposed [anti-immigration] measures … and to attack the details."

36 Gandhi here as elsewhere is writing primarily to a South African audience in *Indian Opinion*, but no doubt he would appreciate readers overseas taking his columns to heart as well. Cf. "Vancouver Indians," 240–41. As for solutions, Gandhi points to the sheer motivational value of understanding discrimination in places such as Canada. See "Indians in Canada [1]," 282: "We must look upon the hardships caused by the movement against the Coloured persons in Canada and elsewhere as being beneficial [to us in the long run]." In a similar vein, Gandhi argues that Indians in India can compel change for Indians in other colonies by withholding their vast purchasing power. Doing so will force the Imperial government to exert pressure on colonies like Canada. See "England's Biggest Customer," 380.

37 See Gandhi's column "Mr. Brodrick and British Indians in the Transvaal," in *Indian Opinion*, 1 July 1905, *eCWMG* 4, 338–39; "Mr. Brodrick's Budget," 362–63; and "Letter to 'The Star,'" in *Indian Opinion*, 8 July 1905, *eCWMG* 4, 329. Cf. comments in 1906 by Gandhi's colleague, Sir Lepel Griffin, that India's contribution to Britain in the Boer War bears positive comparison to that of Canada. Accordingly, the British Imperial government should intervene in South Africa to protect the interests of Indian immigrants, just as it protects the peoples of Canada and other dominions: See "Deputation to Lord Elgin," 8 November 1906, *eCWMG* 6, 34. In this petition Griffin focuses on Indian immigrants to Transvaal colony (34).

38 Gandhi occasionally claims that Canada, its peoples, and its officials, even if appointed by the Imperial government, are fair and even-handed. See "The Status of British Indians," 58–59. Here (58) Gandhi speaks of Indian immigrants to various British colonies. Cf. his "Speech at Suppressed Classes Conference, Ahmedabad," 13 April 1921, *eCWMG* 23, 44.

39 See notes below. For this view late in Gandhi's life, see "Letter to Lord Samuel," 305.

40 Already in 1910, in his book *Hind Swaraj*, Gandhi had alluded to Canada's political stature as an independent British dominion, but his allusions appear noncommittal. See Gandhi, in Parel, ed., *Hind Swaraj and Other Writings*, 17–18 (cf. Parel's editorial note on lxxi). Clear reference to Canada as a model appears in 1917 in "Indian Colonial Emigration," 3.

41 Gandhi is speaking of military co-operation with (not domination by) Britain. "Speech at Nadiad," in *Gujarati*, 7 July 1918, *eCWMG* 17, 79–80 (italics added). For this esteem of Canada, cf. "Appeal for Enlistment," 83; and "Speech at Ahmedabad," 97 ("partners" within Empire). He adds on page 97: "We have to prove our fitness for swaraj." Cf. also "Criticism of Muslim Manifesto," in *Young India*, 7 July 1920, *eCWMG* 21, 17 ("Canada and Australia … have the power to secede. India has not").

42 In February 1924, Gandhi seems still to seek Dominion status as per Canada: See "Answer to Drew Pearson's Questions": "I still believe it possible for India to remain within the British Empire" (7) to which he adds: "A full partnership [in such Empire] for India with other parts of the Empire, just the same as Canada, South Africa and Australia enjoy. Nor shall we be satisfied until we obtain full citizens' rights throughout the British Dominions for all the King's subjects" (8). But Gandhi seems to clarify his stance in favour of independence, very shortly afterwards (in March 1924), in "Interview to 'Stead's Review'" (see n43, below).

43 "Interview to 'Stead's Review,'" 50–51.

44 Ibid., 52. Gandhi expresses similar sentiments in "A Good Beginning," 306 (305–6), indicating that complete independence is an ideal, and Dominion status secondary, and adding "the two are in no way incompatible provided of course dominion status for India

does not mean something quite different from what it means for South Africa or Canada." Cf. "Speech at Gujarat Vidyapith Convocation," 218, in which Gandhi accepts Dominion status in the sense of "virtual independen[ce]" as possessed by Canada. Here too he seems favourable to independence, using the word repeatedly (218–19). Cf. further "Interview to 'Daily Herald,'" 290, in which he prioritizes independence (adding that the Congress has already lobbied for such independence), rationalizing that "I have always heard that in England Dominion Status is understood to mean Independence, but by the Indian authorities it is not so understood."

45 Judith Brown writes that by 1929, Gandhi "would not make difficulty [for Britain] about an accommodation of the Dominion Status idea." See her *Gandhi and Civil Disobedience*, 42; cf. 36. This does not mean that Gandhi did not favour full independence; we have seen that he did. In any case, by 1931, following Gandhi's Salt March, "the Congress goal remained *purna swaraj* [complete independence]," and Gandhi "had maintained that independence did not necessarily mean dissociation from Britain, but might be association for mutual benefit at the will of both nations … He wanted a partnership between an equal India and Britain when he spoke of independence, though if he failed to secure that he would go for what he saw as the lower ideal of independence in isolation" (186, 187). Cf. 192. For Gandhi's references to "partnership" in and after 1917, see "Speech at Ahmedabad," 97; "Speech at Nadiad," 80; "Appeal for Enlistment," 83; "Criticism of Muslim Manifesto," 17; and "Answer to Drew Pearson's Questions," 8; and "Speech at Pembrooke College," 122.

46 In 1931, Gandhi would likely have known that as a Dominion, Canada was in essence wholly independent from Britain. In that year, Britain created the Statute of Westminster, a constitutional statute that granted Canada full autonomy in international trade and foreign policy (Canada had held such autonomy, *de facto*, since the Imperial Conference of 1926, on which see Behiels, "The Expansion of a Nation," 476–77). Given Gandhi's discussions about India with the British government in 1931 (on which see Brown, *Gandhi and Civil Disobedience*, 242–62), he was likely aware of the statute. At the least, he recalled having seen it briefly during Round Table meetings; see "Speech at Plenary Session of Round Table Conference," 224 (221–26). Moreover, Gandhi knew that Canada was a British dominion having full functioning independence: see "Interview to 'Daily Herald,'" 290; "Appeal for Enlistment," 83; and "A Good Beginning," 43. As late as 1943 he characterized Canada, rightly, as "virtually independent" ("Letter to Lord Samuel," 305).

47 "Speech at Pembrooke College," 122.

48 "Speech at Friends' House," 115–16; "Speech at Pembrooke College," 122–23 (Gandhi uses the term *equality* here); "Speech at Plenary Session of Round Table Conference," 224–25; cf. also "Interview to Associated Press of India," in *The Hindu*, 1 January 1932, *eCWMG* 54, 313. Indicative of Gandhi's desire for full independence are his equivocal remarks concerning symbolic British sovereignty. In 1931 he remarked that "there is a Crown, but how far I should be linked with the Crown I do not know." See "Speech at Friends' House," 116.

49 Although Gandhi remarked late in life that Canada is a "virtually independent entit[y]" ("Letter to Lord Samuel," 305), he commented in the 1930s that the very notion of Canada's independence was logically fallacious: "Canada is not considered to be in partnership with Great Britain. It is a daughter State. They represent the same civilization, same mode of life … Ours is a distinct civilization." See "Speech at Friends' House," 115; cf. similarly "Interview to Evelyn Wrench," 347. Canada has no true independence, and as such is a poor model for India.

50 Late in 1941, Gandhi advocated a global federation: "Why only a British Commonwealth? ... There should be, after the war, a commonwealth of all nations." See "Interview
to Evelyn Wrench," 347.

51 Brown, *Gandhi's Rise to Power*, 2–3, 10; cf. Brown, *Gandhi and Civil Disobedience*, xiii, xiv,
4.

52 Brown, *Gandhi's Rise to Power*, 1, 11–12, 14–15, 352, 359. Brown reminds us, though,
of two points. First, for Gandhi, India's *swaraj* through 1915 was more a cultural than a
political ideal (11–12). Second, "Gandhi ... saw no ... inconsistency between his old and
new activities. Before 1919 he had been merely a peripheral participant in politics, ven-
turing into that realm only when he felt he had to forward the causes which were his life's
work – the immediate service of his fellow men by righting 'wrongs' inflicted on them,
and the wider service of his country by promoting his ideal of true Swaraj ... where the
relationship of British and Indian would be one of partnership rather than subjection"
(354). Cf. Brown, *Gandhi and Civil Disobedience*, 4.

53 Brown, *Gandhi's Rise to Power*, 1, 11–12.

54 By 1929 (in an issue of *Young India*), Gandhi could also see that formerly racist immigration policy in Canada had given way to a more progressive attitude: "Sikhs in British
Columbia," 288.

55 Again, I have only observed individuals whom Gandhi or the editors of the *eCWMG*
explicitly note are Canadian. Gandhi reports from a letter by C.F. Andrews (1929) that
Canadians have responded very positively to the presence of and talks by Sarojini Naidu,
a Congress worker close to Gandhi who toured the United States and Canada. See "From
and About Sarojini Devi," 60.

56 On Wedderburn and his connection with Gandhi, see Parel, "Introduction," lxxiv; Gandhi, in Parel, ed., *Hind Swaraj and Other Writings*, 14. Granted, Wedderburn seems to
have had little lasting connection with Canada; but it remains interesting that Gandhi
dialogued with somebody so close to Canadian affairs. Cf. similarly the positive comments about Lord Minto (erstwhile Canadian Governor General) in "The Status of British Indians," 58–59.

57 "Lepers' Blessings," in *Indian Opinion*, 11 April 1908, *eCWMG* 8, 254. In 1920, in
his newspaper *Young India*, Gandhi notes that "the Dukhobours of Russia offered
non-co-operation, and a handful though they were, their grievances so deeply moved
the civilized world that Canada offered them a home where they form a prosperous community." See "Crusade against Non-Co-operation," 117; cf. "What the Scriptures Say," in
Navajivan, 8 August 1920, *eCWMG* 21, 127–28. In a sense, Gandhi's comments praise
the Canadian government's immigration policy towards the Dukhobours, over against its
policies towards Indians.

58 "Work in Jails," in *Young India*, 15 December 1921, *eCWMG* 25, 261. In 1928, Gandhi
negotiated with a member of the Canadian Baptist Mission at Vuyyuru, to help find
accommodation for a crippled boy; see "Letter to A. Gordon," 217.

59 "My Notes," in *Navajivan*, 10 February 1929, *eCWMG* 45, 41–42. Cf. report of the positive
response given in Canada to Sarojini Naidu: "From and About Sarojini Devi," 60.

60 "Letter to Narandas Gandhi," 12 January 1931, *eCWMG* 51, 25–26.

61 "Letter to Mary Chesley," 1 March 1935, *eCWMG* 66, 272 and n1 ("[a] Canadian Quaker");
cf. "Letter to F. Mary Barr," 16 July 1935, *eCWMG* 67, 256–57.

62 "In Memoriam," in *Harijan*, 23 May 1936; *eCWMG* 69, 29. In this obituary, Gandhi refers
to Chesley's having come from Canada (cf. similarly "Letter to F. Mary Barr," 24 May
1936, *eCWMG* 69, 32), although he refers to her as "an Englishwoman." Gandhi may be

equating "English" and "Canadian" here, but even if Chesley was born in England, she seems to have been, for some time at least, resident in Canada. In late 1941, Gandhi wrote a short, friendly note to the Canadian address of Sir Robert E. Holland; see "Letter to Sir Robert E. Holland," 28 September 1941, *eCWMG* 81, 130. It appears that Holland was for many years a member of the Indian Civil Service; whether he retired to Canada I am not sure. See "University of Cambridge Centre of South Asian Studies Archive," sasian.cam .ac.uk, http://www.sasian.cam.ac.uk/archive/papers/handlist/Handlist_H.htm.

63 "Letter to Mildred," 17 February 1942, *eCWMG* 82, 31n2.

64 Ibid., 31.

65 Gandhi is not so keen about a proposal by another Canadian correspondent (Edith Heney of Moose Jaw, Saskatchewan) to preach the Christian gospel to his ashram; see "Letter to Narandas Gandhi," 6 July 1931, *eCWMG* 53, 29.

66 See note 37, above.

67 On the whole, Gandhi's estimation of Canada as a nation or government seems modestly to have improved over time. This is to judge by evaluative comments later in the 1920s about Canadian immigration policy, and his references beginning in the 1920s to individual Canadian contributions to *Swaraj*.

ॐ

A Dent in His Saintly Halo?
Mahatma Gandhi's Intolerance
Against Cowards

Scott Daniel Dunbar

In his 1920 essay "The Doctrine of the Sword," Mohandas Karamchand Gandhi – better known as Mahatma Gandhi – asserted: "I do believe that where there is only a choice between cowardice and violence, I would advise violence."[1] Twenty-six years later, just two years before his death, Gandhi again stated: "Cowardice is impotence worse than violence … A coward is less than a man. He does not deserve to be a member of a society of men and women."[2] These strong statements, spanning decades of Gandhi's life, reveal a somewhat surprising invective against cowards in Gandhi's philosophy of non-violence, which illuminates a complex side of his personality that is neither well acknowledged nor well understood. In contrast to prevalent associations of Gandhi's life with non-violence and peace, this chapter examines the surprising fact that Gandhi denounced cowardice as worse than killing.[3]

Curiously, Gandhi's attitude towards cowards has not received much academic attention, suggesting that writers have been willing to overlook his odd statements as the idiosyncrasies of a "great thinker" rather than an integral part of his outlook; yet I contend that Gandhi's position on cowards was no idiosyncrasy at all, nor were repeated remarks about cowards anomalous in his writings. Rather, his strong stance was part of his comprehensive philosophy of *satyagraha* (meaning: "Truth-force") that shaped his life, thought and actions. I further contend that Gandhi's attitude towards cowards needs to be understood in light of his own self-understanding as a soldier of Truth-force and a warrior of non-violence. Gandhi saw himself as a peaceful warrior, no doubt, but as a warrior nonetheless. In his famous speech from Victoria Hall, given on 10 December 1931, he declared: "I regard myself as a soldier, as a soldier of peace."[4] In my assessment, Gandhi's self-designation as a soldier/warrior is the hermeneutical key to unlocking the meaning of his remarks about cowardice. Although he was – and still is – held up by many as a moral exemplar of peace, it is critically important to recognize that Gandhi never shirked from deploying militant terminology to advance his message: in fact, he embraced military language to further his aims by co-opting it into his philosophical discourse and political rhetoric. He shrewdly transmuted militant language into virtuous allegories of a higher spiritual struggle.[5]

This chapter makes a new contribution to Gandhian studies by probing the ethical tensions posed by the Mahatma's staunch advocacy of non-violence alongside his vitriolic condemnation of cowardice. In targeting this counterintuitive pattern in Gandhi's discourse, this paper problematizes prevalent assumptions about Gandhi found in Western popular culture, providing a helpful corrective for the study of Gandhi today. I suggest that Gandhi's negative rhetoric towards cowards has important implications for understanding the limits of non-violence in his philosophy of *satyagraha*. His vehement condemnation of cowards necessitates a re-evaluation of his level of commitment to non-violence because the Mahatma's inflammatory remarks arguably demonstrate a troubling pattern of intolerant, abusive, and even *violent* speech. Given the importance of "right speech" in *dharmic* religions, any consistent transgression of this ideal in Gandhian discourse is rightly a cause for concern and investigation.

Evidence of Gandhi's Intolerance against Cowards

It is important first to substantiate the claim that Gandhi's intolerant remarks were indeed a salient theme in his writings and not just a minor, insignificant point. Gandhi gave the issue of cowardice some serious consideration, working it carefully into his philosophy of action. To corroborate this position, I will quote several relevant remarks from Gandhi's numerous works covering decades of his life.

Writing in *Young India* in August 1920, Gandhi declared: "I do believe that, where there is only a choice between cowardice and violence, I would advise violence ... I would rather have India resort to arms in order to defend her honour than that she should, in a cowardly manner, become or remain a helpless witness to her own dishonour."[6] Later in that decade, Gandhi stated: "Non-violence and cowardice are contradictory terms. Non-violence is the greatest virtue, cowardice the greatest vice. Non-violence springs from love, cowardice from hate. Non-violence always suffers, cowardice would always inflict suffering. Perfect non-violence is the highest bravery."[7] In the 1930s, he added: "It is better to be violent, if there is violence in our breasts [hearts] than to put on the cloak of non-violence to cover impotence."[8] According to Gandhi, "a coward is incapable of exhibiting love; it is the prerogative of the brave."[9] Yet again in the 1940s, Gandhi asserted: "Cowardice is impotence worse than violence. The coward desires revenge but being afraid to die, he looks to others, maybe to the government of the day, to do the work of defense for him. A coward is less than a man. He does not deserve to be a member of a society of men and women."[10] All of these quotations demonstrate a deep loathing of cowards in Gandhi's thought. Such loathing was more than an isolated theme in his writing – it was entrenched in his mental outlook.

To add fuel to this vituperative fire, the following passage by Gandhi is worth quoting in full:

> I want both the Hindus and Mussalmans to cultivate the cool courage to die without killing. But if one has not that courage, I want him to cultivate the art of killing and being killed rather than, in a cowardly manner, flee from danger. For the latter, in spite of his flight, does commit mental *himsā* [violence] ... My creed of nonviolence is an extremely active force. It has no room for cowardice or even weakness. There is hope for a violent man to be some day non-violent, but there is none for a coward ... To run away from danger, instead of facing it, is to deny one's faith in man and God, even one's own self. It were better for one to drown oneself than live to declare such bankruptcy of faith.[11]

What are we to make of Gandhi's vociferous denunciation of cowards? His remarks certainly seem to challenge and even tarnish his widespread popular reputation for non-violence. The regularity of these statements, moreover, demonstrates that Gandhi's disdain for cowards was more than just an isolated incident or minor philosophical anomaly – it was a deep-rooted part of his outlook on life. Indeed, Gandhi's numerous denigrations are perhaps most shockingly expressed in his startling admission that *even the act of killing is better than cowardice.*[12]

I argue that Gandhi's stance on cowards reveals a tacit influence of Indian warrior ideals in his thinking, which raises questions about the role of *dharmic* warrior ethics in the construction of Gandhi's philosophy. I contend that Gandhi's negative position on cowards can be largely understood by looking at the rhetoric of "heroic" Hindu warrior values that strongly repudiate cowardice on the battlefield. I suggest that Gandhi's views on cowards are actually consistent with deep-rooted warrior ideals found in Indian culture that glorify bravery and denounce cowardice. These ideals reach beyond Hindu texts to encompass Jain and Buddhist discourse as well. Indeed, Gandhi's thought seems to have been shaped by India's ubiquitous martial metaphors concerning the disciplined quest for victory over rebirth and the conquering of desire, greed, and fear. Such metaphors imbued his thoughts about the struggle of non-violence to overcome injustice. Gandhi's negative rhetoric towards cowards can be largely understood by looking at this religio-cultural substratum of "heroic" warrior values that strongly abjure cowardice. It is no coincidence that Gandhi himself saw the human conscience as a battlefield, which demanded martial discipline to attain victory in one's own moral and spiritual struggles. The appropriation of military metaphors in Gandhian thought, however, gives rise to uncomfortable tensions in his ethics because his claim that violence is preferable to cowardice undermines the widely assumed paramount status of non-violence in his philosophy. While it may seem odd that Gandhi's renowned commitment to non-violence was trumped by the avoidance of cowardice, such a paradox finds resolution in the recognition that antipathy to cowardice (or, phrased positively, *a culture of fearlessness*) has deep spiritual and cultural roots in Indian society. And such antipathy to cowardice is deemed to be commensurate with the quest for Truth.

Five Hypotheses to Account for Gandhi's Aversion to Cowardice

How can Gandhi's intolerance towards cowards be explained? There are several possible hypotheses to account for Gandhi's remarks about cowards that reveal different ways of looking at the issue. This section examines various hypotheses and advocates the most plausible explanation. I have adopted an interdisciplinary approach to tease out multiple overlapping possibilities as well as their deeper heuristic implications.

The first reasonable hypothesis to account for Gandhi's intolerance towards cowards takes a *psychological approach* to understanding his remarks. It is conceivable that Gandhi's vituperative remarks may have derived from his childhood trauma of being taunted by bullies. In his autobiography, *The Story of My Experiments with Truth* (1927), Gandhi describes himself as a nervous child who suffered from intense shyness, which was exacerbated by the guilt felt over his father's death in what Gandhi considered to be shameful circumstances.[13] Gandhi also hints that he was subjected to verbal abuse by bullies.[14] His response to bullying was to run away from his tormentors; but Gandhi felt psychologically ashamed by his "flight reflex" to demeaning taunting. These factors may have contributed towards his disapproval of cowards later in life, since his strong views may have been a reflection of his own autobiographical angst in dealing with painful childhood memories of bullying. However, I do not think that Gandhi's antipathy towards cowards can be attributed merely to deep-rooted psychological feelings of guilt and/or shame. These factors may have played a role in his attitude but they were not likely the main variables. In my view, Gandhi's views on cowards should not be simply reduced to psychological trauma or lingering shame from his childhood.

A second, more probable hypothesis to account for Gandhi's statements on cowards points to the *political exigencies* that shaped his life and thought. Looking at matters in historical context, Gandhi faced immense political pressure to articulate a peaceful yet effective vision for the Indian nationalist movement in juxtaposition to the militant views of his contemporaries. Gandhi was both a politician and a religious figure so he was forced to respond to the verbal attacks of his political and religious critics who called his philosophy of non-violence a weapon of the weak.[15] In this light, Gandhi's harsh words denouncing cowards could have been a deliberate political tactic to co-opt the language of his foes to weaken their appeal. In the context of competing discourses of Indian nationalism, Gandhi's rhetoric may mainly have been polemical. After all, under British colonialism, Hindus were frequently ridiculed as weak and submissive. Indeed, scholarship on this issue by Sikata Banerjee (2005), Mrinalini Sinha (1995), and Heather Streets (2011) demonstrates that during colonial times, Hindus were depicted as cowardly and weak compared to Europeans. The colonial subservience of the Hindu population was attributed to the supposed effeminate qualities of Hindus.[16] Seizing upon such imaginary weakness and alleged lack of bravery, Indian nationalist figures such as V.D. Sarvarkar called for the militarization and masculinization of the Hindu nation.[17] In the context of the times, calls for Hindu bravery provided an impetus to nationalist organizations that espoused violent methods to overthrow British rule.

Looking at Gandhi's remarks in light of the historical context of India's nationalist struggle, wherein the discourse of aggression was commonly employed, it is not surprising that Gandhi tried to harness such language by denouncing cowards. He opposed any attempts to denigrate his philosophy of *satyagraha* as weak or cowardly, which helps explain his heated words in 1920, when he wrote: "I would risk violence a thousand times rather than risk the emasculation of a whole race."[18] His disdain for cowards can be seen as a shrewd political move – a tactic to transmute the discourse of his rivals and opponents. Here, we see the wily political side of Gandhi, who was known – even by his critics – to be a crafty politician. In this way, Gandhi mitigated the sting of his naysayers who thought that non-violence was an impotent strategy for achieving India's independence from British rule.

A third way to make sense of Gandhi's attitude towards cowards is to consider the impact of *scriptural influence* on Gandhi's thought. Although he honoured the scriptures of all the major world religions, Gandhi's favourite text was undoubtedly the *Bhagavad Gita*. One can certainly detect its profound impact on Gandhi's views of cowards. The *Gita* famously commands the virtuous warrior Arjuna to fight against his unrighteous cousins. The text insists that it is shameful for a warrior to flee from battle. Paralleling this teaching, Gandhi extolled his disciples to stand resolutely together against injustice, and to be brave in the face of violence for it is undoubtedly true that Gandhi's own remarks echo the *Gita*'s repudiation of cowardice. Numerous scriptural passages in the *Bhagavad Gita* convey the message that cowardice is deeply shameful. For instance, Lord Krishna criticizes Arjuna with "several cowardly labels to provoke him into action. He calls Arjuna ignoble (*anarya*), womanly (*kliba*), engaged in unprofitable action (*ajusta*) and dishonorable (*akirthikarana*)."[19] In another famous passage, Krishna declares: "If you will not fight this righteous war, then you will fail in your duty, lose your reputation, and incur sin. People will talk about your disgrace forever. To the honored, dishonor is worse than death" (*Gita* 2:33–34).[20] Of course, the *Bhagavad Gita* is only a small part of the much longer Indian epic known as the *Mahabharata*. And throughout this enormous corpus of materials, cowardice is resolutely denounced. As a case in point, the *Santiparva* (97, 20) stipulates that a soldier must never consider fleeing from the battlefield because "the gods … send calamities unto those who forsake their comrades in battle and come home with unwounded limbs."[21] Additionally, the text insists that those who seek to save their own lives by abandoning their comrades in war should be slain, burnt in a fire, or slaughtered like animals (*Santiparva*, 97, 21–22).[22] In case this message is not clear enough, the *Mahabharata* recounts the story of a mother, Vidula, who rebukes her *ksatriya* son because of his refusal to go to war. Finding him unwilling to fight, the mother exclaims:

> "Thou cannot be counted as a man. Thy features betray thee to be a eunuch!" She rebuked him. "Rise O coward! … You are neither man nor woman," she continued, "but only your mother's excreta. O let no woman bring forth such a son (as thou)." Thus chastened, the scales fell from the youth's eyes and he understood what his destiny must be [– that he must fight!]. (*Udyoda-parva*, 134)[23]

This compelling story, along with many other punctilious passages about cowardice in the Hindu scriptures, corroborates a long-standing Indian tradition of repugnance for cowardice among the warrior class, which appears to have deeply roused Gandhi's feelings and influenced his thinking.

A fourth way to look at the issue of cowardice is to consider it within a larger *socio-cultural framework* characterized by an ethos of South Asian warrior values. Viewed from a socio-cultural angle, warrior ideals carry significant weight in Indian society, even among ostensibly non-violent *dharmic* traditions such as Jainism and Buddhism. Both Gautama Buddha and Mahavira hailed from a caste of princely warriors; and even though these esteemed figures each embraced non-violence as the correct way of living, their continued articulation of martial notions of *conquering* rebirth, *victory* over ignorance and delusion, and the *eradication* of suffering helped shape a socio-cultural ethos that was not immune from the appeal of combative discourse or notions of spiritual bravery.

The bedrock of warrior values in Indian culture has Vedic roots, but the canopy of bellicose spiritual foliage arising from these roots covered more than Hindu sources. South Asian cultural resources from art, dramaturgy, classical mythology, politics, and architecture, among other forms, are replete with stories of righteous conquests in which an ethos of valour and honour influenced cultural ideals. Indeed, for millennia, respect for heroic warrior values circulated widely in symbiotic cultural discourses imbuing South Asian thinking. Within this socio-cultural milieu, the normative principle in *dharmic* traditions is that retreat in battles – both physical battles and metaphorical ones – is shameful.[24] The following story illustrates this attitude:

> [Once] a heroic mother heard the disquieting news that her son lost his courage in action and had fled in fear. If it were true [then] she expressed that she [w]ould cut off her breasts that had fed him with milk. With this determination she entered the battle-field with a sword in her hand and went on searching for her fallen son. When she saw her son's body cut in twain, she felt much more happy than when she gave birth to him.[25]

Gandhi was fed this type of diet of military heroic literature and folktales, not only from the aforementioned *Bhagavad Gita* – where cowardice is contemptible – but also through Indian art, drama, dance, and nationalistic patriotic song.

Looking at Gandhi's remarks within this larger socio-cultural perspective, one comes to appreciate that he was deeply influenced by cultural attitudes towards life in which cowardice was seen as an utter failure. Indic cultural patterns advocate spiritual struggles to combat negative selfish traits and to destroy unwholesome mind-states and delusions. Of course, Gandhi co-opted such warrior language into his own framework, within which respect for heroic warrior ideals remains implicit in the metamorphosis of combative discourse into spiritual notions *of swaraj* (self-rule). My analysis here offers ways to account for the ambivalent assertions in Gandhi's pronouncements about cowards vis-à-vis non-violence. His own view comes surprisingly close to the juridical polysemy in the classical Hindu rules of law (*niti*), which insist that one must not harm a retreating (or surrendering) soldier while simultaneously asserting that a fleeing solider deserves to die.[26] Gandhi, who was himself a lawyer, adopted an approach to cowards that was a double-edged sword: phrased positively, he encouraged bravery and courage on the spiritual path of non-violence; but conversely, he condemned the absence of these virtues as loathsome cowardice. An ethos of warrior language thus fueled the development of Gandhi's religio-political doctrines in significant ways that often go unrecognized. This militant framework for understanding his views (through the heuristic lens of cowards) does not fit well with modern images of Gandhi as a tolerant and non-violent champion; nevertheless, this suggestion accords with the tenor of Gandhi's own incongruities.

Finally, from a *philosophical perspective*, Gandhi's doctrine of *satyagraha* was incompatible with fear. The true *satyagrahi* had to confront his or her inner fear, defeat it, conquer it, in order to have no enemy. In that way, the true *satyagrahi* would have no weakness. And fear was one of the greatest weaknesses – especially the fear of death. Gandhi claimed that the non-violent activist, "like any soldier, had to be ready to die for the cause. And in fact, during India's struggle for independence, hundreds of Indians were killed by the British."[27] Whereas his opponents often treated Gandhi's approach to non-violence as merely a tactic for dealing with oppression, Gandhi saw it as a comprehensive framework for understanding human nature and spiritual living. Rather than seeing non-violence as some sort of "defensive" or "reactionary ethical response," he understood non-violence as a way of life and even the truthful nature of the divine itself.

Indeed, having no fear, being fearless, or fearlessness, is a common attribute associated with the divine in India.[28] India's philosophical and spiritual ethos expects the absence of fear as an advanced ideal associated with authentic gurus and realized devotees. Such a view is exemplified by the *Abhaya mudra* (meaning "fearlessness") frequently depicted in the sacred iconography of the Buddhas, Bodhisattvas, and Hindu gods. Indeed, a lack of fear is considered to be indicative of spiritual progress. Thus, the Buddha encouraged his disciples to overcome fear as they battled against the inner demons of the mind during meditation.[29] One must have no fear because if one has fear then one is still attached to unwholesome mind states. This celebrated concept of having "no-fear" seems to have played into Gandhi's own ethics because it necessitated banishing cowardice.[30] In this Indic philosophical context, cowardice is seen as incommensurate with the spiritual aspirant because fear represents a type of attachment that keeps one enslaved. A memorable saying illustrates this point rather well: While Abrahamic religions insist that the "Fear of God is the beginning of spiritual wisdom," in Gandhi's opinion, "Truth casts out all fear."[31]

Accordingly, Gandhi's ideal truthful warrior (the *satyagrahi*) must be fearless. The *satyagrahi* had to confront any fear of death and conquer it. This process was part of Gandhi's larger campaign of establishing self-rule (*swaraj*) for both India and spiritual practitioners everywhere. We must not forget that *swaraj* was not merely a political slogan to overthrow foreign rule; more importantly, it was a spiritual goal of self-transformation with the aim of ruling over one's senses and emotions, especially fear. Therefore, fearlessness was arguably the most important characteristic of an authentic *satyagrahi* and *Ahimsaka* (non-violent practitioner). And such considerations go to the philosophical roots of Gandhi's thinking. For as Koshelya Walli (1974) explains, when the *satyagrahi* confronts *Himsakas* (people of violence), "one needs to be fearless of the oppressors to be able to truly help the oppressed. A person cannot be afraid of someone and at the same time be truthful with that person. An *Ahimsaka* can also not be afraid of failure."[32] According to Gandhi, such fearlessness comes from having faith in the power of Truth = God. Thus, Gandhi saw fearlessness as the highest calling of the religious aspirant and spiritual warrior, exceeding non-violence in its philosophical importance.[33]

The Non-Absoluteness of Gandhi's Non-Violence

Gandhi's invective against cowards raises a number of problematic questions about the nature and scope of his non-violence. Why did Gandhi feel the need to embrace warrior language in his peacemaking initiatives when such language perpetuates a warrior mentality? Why do religious exemplars of peace adopt warrior metaphors? Does not such "spinning" of non-violence in the clothing of "bravery" and "fearlessness" give legitimacy to models of "religion as war and struggle"? And how does Gandhi's position on cowardice fit with his positive view of conscientious objectors? Such questions deserve more time and attention than can be afforded here, and I hope they will be taken up by others; nevertheless, the aforesaid ambiguities created by Gandhi's negative position on cowards can be accounted for, at least in part, by looking at the influence of Hindu scriptural ideals that strongly repudiate cowardice on life's physical, moral and spiritual battlefields. The overwhelming message found in Gandhi's writings, as well as in his lived personal example, was the interdependent mutuality of truth-force and non-violence. Violence was condoned only in exceptionally rare circumstances. One wonders then whether Gandhi's vehemence against cowards was primarily a tactic designed to have shock value for particular audiences, somewhat like a Zen *koan*? In light of this suggestion, Gandhi's remarks about cowards could be interpreted as performative and invocational rather than literal – a type of avidity to rouse the troops going into battles against injustice. Given the overall corpus of Gandhi's writings, as well as his actual lived example, it may be the case that his statements were not intended to be taken literally but were clarion calls for warrior-like devotion in the life of a *satyagrahi*. Certainly, his warrior path demanded a resolute willingness to die. This, itself, is a stark realization.

On the other hand, perhaps Westerners place too much emphasis on saintly stereotypes of Gandhi, never expecting him to have any angry, irritated, or intolerant feelings? This chapter shows that when faced with the choice between cowardice and violence, Gandhi demanded violence! His condemnation of cowardice challenges the predominantly peaceful representations of Gandhi found in popular culture. On the contrary, Gandhi's outspoken comments about cowards reveal a discernable dent in his saintly halo, thereby providing a counter-balance to the placid images of Gandhi in the popular imagination. His intolerance against cowards also reminds readers that saintly models of Gandhi are social constructs reflecting the apotheosis of favoured collective memories and disseminated ideals. Finding faults with the Mahatma takes him off his saintly pedestal and brings him back down to earth, which makes him more human and more real.

Logically, rejecting cowardice does not necessarily lead one to endorse violence. Although Gandhi's vociferous rejection of cowardice can be interpreted in light of various factors, such factors do not necessarily account for his allowance of violence. So why did Gandhi take the further step to actually permit violence? This important question deserves our attention and analysis.

In Gandhi's eyes, cowardice seems to have been a greater "evil" than violence. Perhaps he made this relative evaluation because, to him, cowardice represented living untruthfully. Gandhi cherished non-violence as the highest form of truthful living; yet by touting violence as better than cowardice, he suggested a clear sense of a hierarchy of right actions in his religio-political ethics. As a result, non-violence was not a moral absolute for Gandhi because *ahimsa* could be abrogated whenever moral cowardice was imminent. If cowardice arose then it needed to be banished and conquered as "untruth." Hence, contrary to the popular assumptions, *ahimsa* seems to have been a penultimate value for Gandhi. If this analysis is correct then Gandhian ethics should be rethought by scholars and admirers in light of his stubborn insistence on "heroic moral bravery" rather than commitment to complete non-violence.

The penultimate and non-absolute nature of non-violence in Gandhian ethics is not surprising given the fact that he actually permitted violence in a few famous circumstances. For instance, Gandhi allowed the euthanizing of animals (and theoretically people) for compassionate reasons to put an end to suffering.[34] He also "supported the British war effort in World War I, arguing that although he was opposed to war, if there had to be war, then it should be on the side of justice. Later, in 1929–30, he did not oppose violence to quell the Malabar Moplah uprising in India. And he backed Sardar Vallabhbhai Patel's deployment of troops to Kashmir in 1948."[35] Katherine Young notes, moreover, that when "his eldest son asked him what he should have done had he been present when Gandhi was almost fatally assaulted in 1908, Gandhi instructed his son that it would have been his duty to defend his father, by force if necessary."[36]

Again Young speaks for many readers when she asks, "How is this lack of complete and total support for non-violence to be explained? Some have argued that Gandhi was foremost a politician, not a *mahatma* ('Great Soul'/saint). If so, then this would make his ethic of nonviolence not absolutistic but rather pragmatic, contextual, and … it could be argued that these few situations in which Gandhi condoned violence were the exceptions that proved the rule."[37] Indeed, Gandhi admits this point: "Life itself involves some kind of violence and we have to choose the path of least violence … The strength to kill is not essential for self-defence; one ought to have the strength to die."[38] The above examples illustrate that Gandhi's commitment to non-violence was never absolute; his admonishment of cowards is consistent with this realization.

Conclusion

Mahatma Gandhi's invective, aversion, and intolerance against cowards is linked to his own self-image as a soldier of Truth and a leader of a movement of non-violent warriors who must overcome their fear of death by destroying all cowardice. Gandhi's exhortations for warrior-type bravery among his disciples, however, were accompanied by an uncomfortable permissiveness of verbal intolerance against cowards. Traditionally, Indian religions have glorified spiritual bravery and fearlessness, so Gandhi's polemic against cowards echoes classical *dharmic* notions of conquering fear, desire, greed, attachments and rebirth. Gandhi's brilliance, of course, was to transmute such religious notions into a philosophy of non-violent protest, living, and resistance; but he was not able (nor willing) to extract himself from deeply entrenched Indian notions that cowardice is shameful.

This culturally embedded archetype tempered his philosophical vision of non-violence and arguably caused moral tensions in his discourse.

In the end, one final critical question remains to be addressed: Is Gandhi's invective against cowards truly compatible with his comprehensive vision of *satyagraha*, or does it undermine his ethical integrity of non-violence by justifying verbal abuse towards cowards? Gandhi's numerous pronouncements throughout his lifetime demonstrate an intentional missive against cowards. The written evidence of this is incontrovertible. His intentions, however, are another matter.

Given the ubiquitous admiration, even adulation, of Gandhi in the West, his supporters may be tempted to dismiss Gandhi's recurring intolerance against cowards by reasoning that he "hated the sin but not the sinner." After all, it is well known that during the European period of colonial rule in India Gandhi never condemned the British *people* or *soldiers* as enemies of the Indian nation; rather, he viewed the institution of European colonialism as the culprit that subjugated peoples and exploited the Indian nation – a type of oppressive structural violence that needed to be challenged and dismantled.[39] For Gandhi, "there must be no enemy – only an adversary or opponent who has not yet been convinced of the truth. Fundamental to his philosophy was the distinction between [humans] and [their] deed[s]."[40] He writes in his autobiography that "whereas a good deed should call forth approbation and a wicked deed disapprobation, the doer of the deed, whether good or wicked, always deserves respect or pity as the case may be."[41] Therefore, one could make the alluring argument that Gandhi did not detest cowards, rather he detested cowardice.

However, I am not convinced by this argument. Although Gandhi claimed never to see anyone as his enemy, he certainly lost patience with so-called "cowards" in his ranks on his front lines. In fact, he specifically denounced cowards (not just the abstract idea of cowardice) with very harsh words, and even called off *satyagraha* campaigns as a result of alleged cowardly behaviour.[42] We ought to remember that Gandhi used his words thoughtfully and carefully. His repeated denouncements were not loose-lipped, ill-tempered utterances – mistakes that he later regretted. Although seemingly out of character, Gandhi's admonition of cowards was highly consistent with larger cultural patterns in Indian history, folklore, and society, which were never fully abandoned by Gandhi but strategically embraced in his rhetoric.

What are the lessons of this chapter for the study of Gandhi today? First, readers can discover a more accurate image of Gandhi by probing behind the wall of popular stereotypes and social constructions of saintliness. Westerners widely admire Gandhi as an archetype for peaceful change who embodies the hope that seemingly insurmountable conflicts can be overcome through non-violence. Gandhi has a favourable, even iconic, status among young people as an honest and ethical leader who advocated the incessant force of Truth. His steadfast commitment to non-violence in the face of adversity and injustice served to wash away animosity like the incessant force of the ocean's waves on a rocky shore; yet this peaceful, oceanic image of Gandhi is only one windswept narrative among others. Scholarship reminds us that such non-violent memories of the Mahatma are only part of the collective understanding of Gandhi.[43] Indeed, there are many stories about Gandhi, many perspectives on his life – many "Gandhis," so to speak. Around the globe, Gandhi and his ideas are viewed, represented, politicized, and even marketed in contrasting ways for disparate audiences, and such representations and audiences are not always favourable towards the man or his message. This particular chapter makes the person of Gandhi less of a saint on a pedestal and more of a human being by casting a spotlight on his discourse about cowards. I have sought to illuminate a more discomforting side of Gandhi's philosophy, not to criticize or judge, but simply to understand. For it is in the scholarly probing of stubborn shadows that one can readily glimpse the contours of the light. In this manner, Gandhi's grand ethical ideals become less abstract while lingering surface stereotypes are peeled away to show how Gandhi's words and his sanitized image are often at odds.[44]

At the same time, Gandhi's stance on cowardice has practical lessons for global citizens today because it reminds readers that – individually and collectively – people have a responsibility to speak up about social justice issues to help those in need. Gandhi insists that seekers of Truth should never shy away from voicing and defending their ethical convictions in a non-violent (but firm) way. He reminds readers to help the less fortunate, especially the poor, by using the following litmus test for all social action: "Whenever you are in doubt, or when the self becomes too much with you, apply the following test. Recall the face of the poorest and the weakest man [or woman] whom you may have seen, and ask yourself, if the step you contemplate is going to be of any use to him [or her]."[45] He exhorts people to conquer apathy towards helping others and to be free from fear, anxiety, and self-doubt. For Gandhi, each person's voice and actions really do count. His advice is echoed by his disciples, including Martin Luther King, Jr. who exclaimed, "We will have to repent in this generation not merely for the hateful words and actions of the bad people but for the appalling silence of the good people."[46] In a strange way, Gandhi's intolerance against cowards defends the aphorism that apathy in the face of evil – not violence – is the greatest sin.

Gandhi faced immense pressure to acknowledge religious bravery, courage, and fearlessness as a sign of patriotism while denouncing cowardly behaviour as disgraceful. Thus, it may seem odd that Gandhi's renowned commitment to non-violence was trumped by his intolerance for cowards, but it has been shown that aversion to cowardice has deep roots in Indian society, culture, philosophy, and religion. Therefore, Gandhi's views about cowardice arise from complex variables that can be fruitfully explored through an interdisciplinary analysis. His antipathy towards cowards ought to be situated in the larger context of an Indian socio-cultural milieu that admired heroic warrior ideals in religious and political discourse. Understanding the ethical amalgamation of Gandhi's non-violence with *dharmic* warrior ideals helps to explain his intolerant remarks against cowards and offers new insights into different ways of remembering and conceptualizing Gandhi today: his widely popular gentle face of truth-force ("*satyagraha* with a smile") or the more realistic, but less palatable, uncompromising face of intolerant truth-force ("*satyagraha* with a bite") exhibited tacitly in Gandhi's attitude towards cowards.

Notes

1　Gandhi, "The Doctrine of the Sword," in *Young India*, 11 August 1920, *CWMG* 18, 132.

2　Gandhi, "What to Do?," in *Harijan*, 15 September 1946, *eCWMG* 92, 143.

3　As a case in point, Gandhi asserted: "Better than cowardice is killing and being killed in battle." Gandhi, in Kumarappa, ed., *Hindu Dharma*, 156. Gandhi again remarked: "I have been repeating over and over again that he who cannot protect himself or his nearest and dearest or their honour by non-violently facing death may and ought to do so by violently dealing with the oppressor ... But a man who, when faced by danger, behaves like a mouse, is rightly called a coward." See Gandhi, *Non-Violence in Peace and War*, vol. 1, 77.

4　Gandhi, "Speech at Meeting," 10 December 1931, *eCWMG* 54, 282.

5　Gandhi interpreted the violence of the *Bhagavad Gita* as a metaphor for the inner struggle of the human conscience to promote righteousness. He wrote: "I do not believe that the Gita teaches violence for doing good. It is pre-eminently a description of the duel that goes on in our own hearts." See Gandhi, "Religious Authority for Non-Co-operation," in *Young India*, 25 August 1920, *eCWMG* 21, 200. Cf. Jordens, "Gandhi and the Bhagavadgita." However, Hindus such as Nathuram Godse and V.D. Sarvarkar rejected Gandhi's allegorical interpretation and embraced the *Gita* as a manifesto for justifying real violence. See Fernhout, "Combatting the Enemy."

6　Kibriya, *Gandhi and the Indian Freedom Struggle*, 72.

7　Gandhi, "Notes," in *Young India*, 31 October 1929, *eCWMG* 47, 340.

8　Gandhi, "Notes," in *Harijan*, 21 October 1939, *eCWMG* 77, 10.

9　Gandhi, in Andrews, ed., *Speeches and Writings of M.K. Gandhi*, 392.

10　Gandhi, "What to Do?" in *Harijan*, 15 September 1946, quoted in Kibriya, *Gandhi and the Indian Freedom Struggle*, 73.

11　Gandhi, "Between Cowardice and Violence."

12 In Gandhi's words, "Better than cowardice is killing and being killed in battle." Gandhi, in Kumarappa, ed., *Hindu Dharma*, 156. As noted above, Gandhi also stated: "I want both the Hindus and Mussalmans to cultivate the cool courage to die without killing. But if one has not that courage, I want him to cultivate the art of killing and being killed rather than, in a cowardly manner, flee from danger." Gandhi, "Between Cowardice and Violence."

13 Gandhi writes: "I used to be very shy and avoided all company. My books and my lessons were my sole companions. To be at school at the stroke of the hour and to run back home as soon as school closed – that was my daily habit. I literally ran back, because I could not bear to talk to anybody. I was even afraid lest anyone should poke fun at me." Gandhi, *An Autobiography*, 22. Regarding his childhood memories, Gandhi writes: "I was a coward. I used to be haunted by the fear of thieves, ghosts and serpents. I did not dare stir out of doors at night. Darkness was a terror to me. It was almost impossible for me to sleep in the dark, as I would imagine ghosts coming from one direction, thieves from another, and serpents from a third. I could not therefore bear to sleep without a light in the room. How could I disclose my fears to my wife – no child, but already at the threshold of youth – sleeping by my side? I knew that she had more courage than I, and I felt ashamed of myself." Gandhi, *An Autobiography*, 34.

14 Gandhi seems to hold himself partly to blame for his childhood bullying because he claims: "Bullies are always to be found where there are cowards." Gandhi, in *Young India*, 20 December 1928, quoted in Gandhi, "Bullying," 34. Susanne Hoeber Rudolph concurs that "Gandhi pictures himself as a shy, fearful and pathetic child ... Gandhi feared school and his schoolfellows." See Rudolph, *Gandhi*, 20.

15 Tendulkar, *Mahatma*, vol. 7, 331.

16 Banerjee, *Make me a Man!*; Sinha, *Colonial Masculinity*; Streets, *Martial Races*; cf. Kirpal and McDermott, *Encountering Kālī*, 185–86.

17 Gandhi's non-violent vision of India clashed with the construction of a militant Hindu identity fostered by Hindu thinkers who saw India as a state struggling to regain its cultural and historic pre-eminence. The foremost theorist in this ideological construction was Vinayak Damodar Savarkar (1883–1966), who coined the term *Hindutva* ("Hinduness") in the 1920s. The term became the new rallying cry for a self-assured belligerent Hindu identity. In *Hindutva: Who Is a Hindu?* (1923), Savarkar introduced the doctrine of *Hindutva*, which became a touchstone for the anti-Gandhi forces who plotted to assassinate the Mahatma. Therein, Savarkar called for Hindus to become militarized in the hope, writes Sofri, of achieving "Hindu racial superiority, and his dream of a great empire." See Sofri, *Gandhi and India*, 120. Savarkar's theory of *Hindutva* became one of the most influential ideologies in Indian nationalist discourse, giving rise to a volatile cocktail of militant organizations that collectively espoused *Hindutva* ideology. To understand this wave of militant Hindu antagonism towards Gandhi, we need to realize that Gandhi's enemies included several influential high-caste Hindus who rejected his ideas and tactics. Additionally, certain regions of India remained somewhat hostile to the spread of Gandhi's ideas due to their own histories of violent struggle. As Christophe Jaffrelot states: "Two large regions remained largely resistant to the message of Mahatma Gandhi: Maharashtra, the home of Nathuram Godse, as well as Bengal, from where Subash Chandra Bose, the President of Congress in 1939, did not hesitate to join Nazi Germany to fight against the British Empire." See Jaffrelot, "Delhi, 30 Janvier 1948," 64 (this is my translation of Jaffrelot's original French article). In Maharashtra, the Chitpavan Brahmins had a long, proud history of military struggle dating back to the seventeenth century, when they had served with Shivaji against Muslim aggression. Their

deeply entrenched tradition of militancy (and proud martial ethic) was antithetical to Gandhi's doctrine of *ahim sa* (non-violence). Moreover, the two principal conspirators behind Gandhi's assassination, who were hung for their actions – Nathuram Godse and Narayan Apte – were both Chitpavan Brahmins from Maharashtra, as was Savarkar, their ideological mentor. The Chitpavan Brahmins had a long history of supporting violence against alleged enemies of Brahminical Hinduism; see ibid., 66.

18 Gandhi, "Crusade against Non-Co-operation," in *Young India*, 4 August 1920, *eCWMG* 21, 117.

19 Young, "Hinduism," 285.

20 *The Bhagavad Gita*, trans. Ramanand Prasad (Fremont: American Gita Society, 1988).

21 *Santiparva* (97, 20), quoted in Chakravarti, *The Art of War*, 183.

22 Ibid.

23 *The Mahabharata, Udyoda-parva* (134), quoted in Aho, *Religious Mythology*, 75–79.

24 An exception to this standard would be the morally transgressive Hindu attitude of *kuṭa yuddha* (devious warfare), which advocated the view that retreat in battle is actually a wise, shrewd, and acceptable course of action to live to fight another day. Such "pragmatic" thinking influenced the tactics of Kautilya (ca. 300 BCE), author of the seminal *Arthasastra* ("Science of Politics and Administration"), and the adviser to Emperor Chandra Gupta, who reigned over northern India during the fourth century BCE. See Deshingkar, "Strategic Thinking," 357–58.

25 *Puram*, v. 277, cited in Dikshitar, *War in Ancient India*, 388.

26 *Mahabharata* 12.97, 21–22, quoted in Chakravarti, *Art of War*, 183.

27 Shepard, *Mahatma Gandhi and His Myths*.

28 Sharma, "Fearlessness," 49n2.

29 Premasiri, "The Place of Righteous War," 5.

30 Sharma, "Fearlessness," 38–39.

31 Of course, quotations are never as simple as they appear at first glance. A closer examination of the biblical corpus reveals a message about fear that seems to support Gandhi's position. Namely, 1 John 4:18 reads: "There is no fear in love, but perfect love casts out fear." *The Holy Bible*, RSV. The biblical quotation in the body of this essay is from Psalm 111:10.

32 Walli, *The Conception of Ahimsa*, xi.

33 Sharma expounds on this point in "Fearlessness," 35, 40.

34 In his Sabarmati Ashram, Gandhi was faced with the moral dilemma of whether to "put down" a maimed calf that could not be healed. His views on euthanasia were explained in the Gujarati weekly *Navjivan* in October 1928. The passage is worth quoting in full for its broader implications. Gandhi wrote: "A calf having been maimed lay in agony in the ashram. Whatever treatment and nursing was possible was given to it. The surgeon whose advice was sought in the matter declared the case to be past help and past hope. The suffering of the animal was so great that it could not even turn its side without excruciating pain. In the circumstances, I felt that humanity demanded that the agony should be ended by ending life itself. The matter was placed before the whole ashram ... Finally in all humility but with the cleanest of convictions I got in my presence a doctor to administer the calf a quietus by means of a poison injection. The whole thing was over in less than two minutes ... Would I apply to human beings the principle that I have enunciated in connection with the calf? Would I like it to be applied in my own case? My reply is 'yes' ... *Just as a surgeon does not commit himsa but practices the purest ahimsa when he wields his knife, one may find it necessary, under certain imperative circumstances, to go a*

step further and sever life from the body in the interest of the sufferer" [italics mine]. Gandhi, quoted in Tendulkar, *Mahatma*, vol. 2, 421–22. Cf. Gielen, "Mahātmā Gandhi's View on Euthanasia."

35 Nair, *Mahatma Gandhi*, 502.

36 Attenborough, *The Words of Gandhi*, 37–38.

37 Young, "Hinduism and the Ethics," 289.

38 Gandhi, "Between Cowardice and Violence."

39 It is true that Gandhi denounced certain behaviours, societal attitudes, and organizational structures such as untouchability, aggressive capitalistic models of economic exploitation, and European colonialism, as dangerous and wrong-headed. Today, such behaviours and organizational structures are often labelled as types of "structural violence" because they are seen to perpetuate forms of exploitation and oppression based on deeply embedded habituated systems of discrimination that have been built up over time as socialized dominant-group behaviours, which oppress certain classes or groups of people, often including women. See Johan Galtung, "Violence, Peace, and Peace Research"; and Vorobej, "Structural Violence."

40 Gandhi, quoted in "Gandhi on Nonviolence."

41 Gandhi, *An Autobiography*, 254.

42 Ramagundam, *Gandhi's Khadi*, 93.

43 For a good cross-section of contrarian opinions on Gandhi, see Coward, ed., *Indian Critiques of Gandhi*; cf. Nanda, *Gandhi and His Critics*.

44 This volume aptly demonstrates that Canadian scholars continue to investigate original issues surrounding Gandhi in new contexts and for new generations. In the process, if I may employ a popular Canadian expression, popular culture stereotypes of Gandhi are frozen for examination. My own consideration of Gandhi's intolerance against cowards offers a counterbalance to wholly irenic representations of the Mahatma in Western popular culture.

45 Gandhi, "A Note," August 1947, *eCWMG* 96, 311.

46 John J. Ansbro, *Martin Luther King, Jr.: The Making of a Mind* (Maryknoll: Orbis Books, 1985), 227.

ॐ

Gandhi and Islam: Their History and Implications for Canada Today

Ramin Jahanbegloo

The "violent Muslim fanatic" has emerged a dominant stereotype since 11 September 2001. This aligns with the generalizations about Islam as a faith motivated and practised by bloodlust and violence, and with prevailing misunderstandings and misevaluations of Muslim diversity. Muslim experiences of peacemaking and non-violence have been swamped by more powerful media-generated images of Islam as a religion of conflict and war. The challenge, then, is to generate an account for Canadians of the possibility of a *Gandhian* Islam, one whose ethical values such as tolerance and non-violence can be brought to bear on political issues. In promoting the paradigm of non-violence in Islam, Canadian Muslims can look back to the contemporary examples of Muslim leaders influenced by Gandhi, leaders like Khan Abdul Ghaffar Khan and Maulana Abul Kalam Azad. Through their readiness to collaborate with Gandhi, these prominent Muslims fostered a valuable legacy of non-violent Islam and helped us better understand the vision of a tolerant Islam that Gandhi shared with many of his Muslim contemporaries.

Gandhi first encountered Islam at a very early age. He was born in Gujarat, where the geography situates Hindus next to Muslims. His family had, therefore, great experience in dealing with Muslims as part of the local community in Porbandar. Muslims were frequent visitors to the Gandhi home, and one of Gandhi's closest childhood friends, who lived close to him and went to school with him, was a Muslim boy named Sheikh Mehtab. Mehtab, the son of a jailer employed by the British, had a very complex relationship with Gandhi, who describes him in his *Autobiography* as a young, hardy, and athletic man who kept him "under his thumb for more than ten years"[1] and who invited him to eat meat and to take up the cause of meat-eating as a way of ridding India of the colonial presence. Gandhi was warned by his mother and his eldest brother about Mehtab's evil influence on him, but he "claimed that the friendship was meant to reform Mehtab."[2] Although Gandhi failed to reform Mehtab, it is interesting nonetheless, and indicative of Gandhi's later ties with Muslims, that in the lifelong fight against British domination, he viewed Muslims "as friends and allies."[3]

The next significant phase of Gandhi's encounter with Muslims came during his years in South Africa, where in 1893 he began working as a lawyer for a Muslim merchant from Porbandar, Abdullah Sheth, who had built a business in Durban. During his long stay in South Africa and his first political experiences, Gandhi was able to forge close ties with Indian Muslims. He felt familiar with their cultural identity, and he shared a common life with them. "When I was in South Africa," he later recounted, "I came in close touch with Muslim brethren there … I was able to learn their habits, thoughts and aspirations … I had lived in the midst of Muslim friends for 20 years. They had treated me as a member of their family and told their wives and sisters that they need not observe *purdah* with me."[4]

It was Abdullah Sheth who suggested to Gandhi that he read Sale's translation of the Qur'an. That first reading developed his basic understanding of Islam, an understanding he would later strengthen when he read it a second time while incarcerated in a Transvaal prison in January 1908. By then, Gandhi had forged a broad resistance movement against racial discrimination in South Africa based largely on an alliance of Hindus and Indian Muslims. In his very first week in Pretoria, he had called a meeting at a Muslim merchant's house. "It was a largely Muslim gathering with 'a sprinkling of Hindus.'"[5] The bringing together of Hindus and Muslims in the Gandhian experience of *satyagraha* in South Africa was Gandhi's first important step towards the idea of communal harmony. This experience strengthened in him a powerful motivation to foster a joint commitment among Hindus and Muslims to truth and justice irrespective of their differences. By learning to navigate smoothly between different religious traditions and communities, Gandhi was able to convince his fellow Indians of the importance of interfaith solidarity. Gandhi had decided to affirm in South Africa that communal harmony and dialogue among religions was the only cure for violence and injustice. In this enterprise he was also helped by his readings of spiritual writers like Tolstoy. "We believe," asserted Gandhi, that

Tolstoy's teaching will win increasing appreciation with the passage of time … He pointed out that selfish priests, *Brahmins* and *Mullas* had distorted the teaching of Christianity and other religions and misled the people. What Tolstoy believed with special conviction was that in essence all religions held soul-force to be superior to brute force … There is no room in religion for anything other than compassion. A man of religion will not wish ill even to his enemy. Therefore, if people want to follow the path of religion, they must do nothing but good.[6]

There is no doubt that Gandhi's actions in South Africa and later in India were shaped by his conviction that all religious boundaries are arbitrary and false. That is why his view of religion brought into its fold people belonging to different religions. Although deeply religious by nature, Gandhi did not believe in rituals, customs, traditions, dogmas, and other formalities observed for the sake of religion. His religion, like that of Rabindranath Tagore, was not confined to temples, churches, books, rituals, and other outward forms. Thus his concept of religion was not bound by any dogmatic behaviours. Gandhi was convinced that doctrinaire approaches to religion do not help create inter-religious fellowship. Dogmatic religions do not promote creative dialogue. Religious dogmas directly or indirectly breed an attitude of dislike towards other religions. Gandhi's mission was to find common ground based on non-violence among religions. He wanted not only to humanize religion but also to moralize it. He would reject any religious doctrine that was in conflict with morality. In doing so, he would be challenging people of faith to recognize their religious hypocrisies. Gandhi argued that a person who believes in Truth and God cannot go to a mosque, synagogue, temple, or church one day, and the next day foster hatred and violence. He made no exception in the case of Islam. He did not hesitate to declare that "even the teachings themselves of the Koran cannot be exempt from criticism. Every true scripture only gains by criticism. After all we have no other guide but our reason to tell us what may be regarded as revealed and what may not be."[7] On another occasion, Gandhi completed this argument with an observation that takes us to heart of his position on religion and inter-religious dialogue: "My effort should never be to undermine another's faith but to make him [or her] a better follower of his [or her] own faith."[8]

Gandhi knew that independence could not come about by the efforts of the Hindus alone, so he involved the Indian Muslims in the struggle. Troubled by the "us versus them" divisions and mutual antipathy between Muslims and Hindus, he engaged in an open dialogue with Islam and the Muslims. He never accepted the argument that Hindus and Muslims were two separate elements in Indian society. That is why his willingness to go out of his way to win over Muslims to the Congress won him many friends and admirers among Muslims. In South Africa, "Gandhi had needed the wholehearted support of Muslim friends who went to jail with him, lived in his communities, supported him with funds, and generally made his victories possible."[9] On his return to India, Gandhi's increasing involvement with the Khilafat movement helped him secure political authority in the Indian Congress and strong legitimacy in the eyes of the British Raj. His involvement with the fervent believers in a pan-Islamic movement surprised most of his friends and followers, but "his stance was essentially a natural progression from the status he had prized in South Africa as spokesman for Muslim grievances, and from his championship of the Ali brothers during the war."[10] It is true that Muslim leaders like Abdul Bari, Maulana Azad, and the Ali brothers had launched and developed the Khilafat movement by the time Gandhi joined them in April 1918, but there is no shadow of a doubt that his arrival lent new strength to the agitation. He expressed his sympathy for the Muslims and the Khilafat movement at the Delhi Imperial War Conference in 1918, following this up with a letter to the Viceroy, Lord Chelmsford. "As a Hindu," he declared, "I cannot be indifferent to their cause. Their sorrows must be our sorrows."[11]

Gandhi's sympathy for the Khilafatists entailed more than simple fellowship: he was inviting the Muslim leaders to join his *satyagraha* and adopt non-violence. Moreover, by joining the Khilafat movement, Gandhi wanted to consolidate the bonds between Hindus and Muslims. Two years later, in a reply to Maganlal, who was troubled by his involvement with Muslims, Gandhi wrote: "If I had not joined the Khilafat movement, I think, I would have lost everything. In joining it I have followed what I especially regard as my dharma ... I am uniting Hindus and Muslims."[12] Anthony Parel points out that in *Hind Swaraj* Gandhi employs *dharma* as an ethical term for mutual assistance.[13] This, of course, was how Gandhi had approached the Muslim leaders in the Khilafat movement. He "treated the *Khilafat* as a 'Kamadhuk,' the mythical cow that gave whatever one asked of her."[14] Later Gandhi explained: "I have been telling Maulana Shaukat Ail [sic] all along that I was helping him to save his cow, i.e. the *Khilafat*, because I hoped to save my cow thereby."[15] Gandhi's emergence as a strong political ally and an inspirational leader in the Khilafat movement was not, however, a simple matter of a great number of Muslims being converted to his non-violent style of action. The Ali brothers were never totally converted to non-violence, although "as a gesture toward Hindus, Muhammad Ali stopped eating beef; departing from age-old practice, numerous Muslim homes celebrated Eid without beef."[16]

Gandhi's decision to align himself with the Muslims and the Khilafat movement had helped him reach broader groups in Indian society and to rise as a non-elitist leader in the Congress. The main division between Gandhi and the Khilafat leaders had to do with their differing attitudes towards violence. "The Muslim violence on the Malabar coast and the incipient violence of the extreme *Khilafat* leaders generated fear and resentment in other communities."[17] Many Muslim leaders, including Shuakat Ali and Jinnah, refused to accept non-violence as a moral absolute, although they accepted it as a temporary strategy to overcome the British. Jinnah was among the Muslim leaders of the Congress Party who in 1915 had welcomed Gandhi on his return from South Africa, but differences between them with regard to the non-cooperation campaign caused them to diverge early on. Jinnah, whose opposition to Gandhi's non-cooperation was well known to the British and to other members of the Congress Party, was especially perplexed that by 1920, the Congress, like most of Muslim India, had accepted Gandhi as their charismatic leader. "Your methods have already caused split and division in almost every institution that you have approached hitherto," stated Jinnah,

> and in the public life of the country not only amongst Hindus and Muslims but between Hindus and Hindus and Muslims and Muslims and even between fathers and sons; people generally are desperate all over the country and your extreme programme has for the moment struck the imagination mostly of the inexperienced youth and the ignorant and the illiterate. All this means complete disorganization and chaos. What the consequence of this may be, I shudder to contemplate ... I do not wish my countrymen to be dragged to the brink of a precipice in order to be shattered.[18]

It is true that Gandhi's Congress/Khilafat non-cooperation movement was partly responsible for Jinnah's skepticism and bitterness, but it also goes without saying that Jinnah's political style and the exaggerated "Britishness" he had adopted in his private and public life made it hard for him to compete with Gandhi's simplicity and transparency. It is absolutely clear that Jinnah's dream of an independent India did not go hand in hand with Hindu–Muslim unity. Generally speaking, although Jinnah pleaded for the Muslim cause before the Congress and the Hindu community throughout the years 1916 to 1938, he gradually gave up the idea of Hindu–Muslim unity and, in the decade before independence, advocated the exclusive cause of Muslim India. Jinnah's correspondence with Pandit Nehru in 1938 makes it clear that Jinnah had reached a dead end in his dealings with some of the leaders of the Congress. For Gandhi, Indian home rule and Hindu–

Muslim unity were not separate issues, whereas for Jinnah the opposite was true, as he told Gandhi:

> We maintain and hold that Muslims and Hindus are two major nations by any definition or test of a nation. We are a nation of a hundred million, and what is more, we are a nation with our own distinctive culture and civilization, language and literature, art and architecture, names and nomenclature, sense of values and proportion, legal laws and moral codes, customs and calendar, history and traditions, aptitudes and ambitions, in short we have our own distinctive outlook on life and of life. By all canons of international law we are a nation.[19]

Jinnah strongly resented it when the *swaraj* movement was related to the Khilafat. He was, in the words of Durga Das, "amazed that the Hindu leaders had not realized that this movement would encourage the Pan-Islamic sentiment."[20] Gandhi, however, saw in Khilafat an opportunity to seek Muslim cooperation in the *swaraj* movement. His political intentions in doing so were more democratic than theocratic. So it would be wrong to contend, as some analysts of Indian contemporary political history do, that Gandhi was "unwittingly responsible for jettisoning sane, secular, modernist leadership among the Muslims of India and foisting upon Indian Muslims, a theocratic orthodoxy of the Maulvis."[21] Jinnah, like Ambedkar, criticized Gandhi for insisting on the spiritualization of Indian politics. He disagreed with Gandhi's view that religious issues should be brought into the public sphere; in his own view, doing so would be a disaster as well as irrelevant to political matters in India. Yet Jinnah himself prioritized religion, and many of his critics saw him as a "communalist."[22] In other words, in his long political career, Muhammad Ali Jinnah clearly perceived Indian self-determination in terms of the Muslim community.

For Gandhi, it was quite the opposite: from his earliest writings in South Africa, he had replaced the divisive view of religion with a pluralist and tolerant one by equating religion with ethics. This, of course, was Gandhi's response to the spectre of the "Hindu raj" and to the cry of "Islam is in danger" that was widening the communal gulf in India and fostering a climate of hatred between Hindus and Muslims. For Gandhi, the difference between Hindus and Muslims was not solely about religion. It was also due, according to him, to the lack of truthfulness and transparency in the political realm. So as a social reformer, he believed strongly in the affinity between spirituality and politics. It is not surprising, then, that he chose to work with individuals whose primary interests were best defined in spiritual and ethical terms. He once declared that a true Muslim could not harm a Hindu and that a true Hindu could not harm a Muslim.[23] It was probably in this spirit that he developed a friendship with and a great esteem for both Maulana Azad and Khan Abdul Ghaffar Khan. In 1939, during his third visit to Ghaffar Khan, Gandhi declared: "If you dissect my heart, you will find that the prayer and spiritual striving for the attainment of Hindu–Muslim unity goes on there unceasingly all the twenty-four hours without even a moment's interruption whether I am awake or asleep ... The dream [of Hindu–Muslim unity] has filled my being since the earliest childhood."[24]

There is no shadow of doubt that Gandhi was influenced by the tolerant Islam of Ghaffar Khan and Maulana Azad and by their "soft reading" of the Qur'an, but it is also true that the spiritual teachings of the Mahatma and his political pragmatism captivated the minds of these two men. Azad was "the Muslim on whom Gandhi relied for advice" and was "a prominent example of the communal inclusiveness of Congress."[25] Without a doubt the evolution of Azad's outlook from pan-Islamic to secular nationalist was determined by his friendship and collaboration with Mahatma Gandhi and by the rise of communal problems in the Indian liberation movement. Through Gandhi, Azad learned that communal harmony would play an important role in the future of India and that in spite of religious, ethnic, and linguistic differences, India was one nation. Azad believed that the "two-nation theory" offered "no solution of the problem of one another's minorities, but only led to retribution and reprisals by introducing a system of mutual hostages."[26] Like Gandhi, Azad viewed Hindu–Muslim unity as necessary for the national reconstruction of India. In his famous address to the Agra session of the Khilafat Conference on 25 August 1921, he referred to Hindu–Muslim unity as a moral imperative for the future of India:

> If the Muslims of India would like to perform their best religious and Islamic duties ... then they must recognize that it is obligatory for the Muslims to be together with their Hindu brethren ... and it is my belief that the Muslims in India cannot perform their best duties, until in conformity within the injunctions of Islam, in all honesty, they establish unity and cooperation with the Hindus. This belief is based on the imperative spirit of Islam.[27]

Azad's entire argument was to present Muslims with the fact that the fundamental teaching of the Qur'an is mercy and forgiveness (*rahmat*). So it followed for him that these attributes of God should also be inculcated in humans. It is interesting to see up to what point Azad's *tafsir* (interpretation) of the Qur'an stays close to the text, while at the same time being inspired by the Sufi perception of God through *kashf* (personal revelation). Azad's faith in the essential unity of humanity and in the oneness of all religions stemmed essentially from the Sufi concept of "the unity of existence" (*wahdat-i-wujud*). Truth, for Azad, was one and the same everywhere. The mistake was to equate particular forms of Truth with Truth itself. Read from this angle, Azad's most important book, *Tarjuman-ul-Qur'an*, illustrates Azad's firm belief in tolerance and dialogue. In that book, Azad's idea of religious pluralism is expressed powerfully by the concept of oneness of faiths (*wahdat-i-Din*). For Azad, God as the "cherisher" and "nourisher" (*Rabb*) transcends all divisions of humanity by race, colour, and religion. It follows that the path of universal God (*Rabb-ul-Alameen*) is "the right path" (*Sirat-al-Mustaqeem*), which belongs to no particular religion. In another of his celebrated works, *Ghubar-i-Khatir*, Azad drew a parallel between the Sufi concept of "unity of existence" and the idea of pantheism as formulated in the *Upanishads*. If, at root, all religions reflected the same message, then, for Azad, there was no room for Hindu or Muslim communalism. As a champion of Indian nationalism and democracy, Azad sought a synthesis of modern secularism and spiritual traditionalism. He took his stand upon Truth by unifying the soul of Islam with the glory of his nation. "I am a Muslim and this fills me with pride," he proclaimed in his Presidential Address in 1942 at Ramgarh. "But in addition to these feelings, I am also the possessor of another, which has been created by the stark realities of my external life. The soul of Islam is not a barrier to this belief: in fact, it guides me in this path. I am proud to be an Indian."[28] Clearly, Azad viewed religious communalism as a serious obstacle to Indian solidarity. For him, Hindu communalism, like Muslim communalism, was a negation of pluralism and was not at all in tune with the concept of secular democracy. This is why he cautioned Indian Muslims against religious nationalism and suggested that the plurality of caste and communities made India a profoundly democratic country in terms of nation-building, however challenging the process might be. For him, secular nationalism could be an effective antidote to religious fanaticism in India if Indian political processes were guided and controlled by the political philosophy of secularism.

Non-violence was another ingredient in Azad's secular nationalism. He held that Islam was characterized by dialogue among faiths and the spirit of peace. According to him, non-violence served as an effective strategy in the struggle for independence. Yet unlike Gandhi, Azad did not believe in non-violence as an article of faith; for him, it was merely a matter of policy. It was not a moral absolute, but a useful expedient. That said, he was against any form of *religious* violence. In light of his religious humanism, Azad declared that there was no justification whatsoever for imposing one religion on another because the fundamentals of religion (*Din*) were one. Therefore, every individual had a right to follow his own religious path. In other words, Azad viewed religion from the broader perspective of a universal humanist and his entire philosophy was free from any form of religious dogma. It is in relation to this aspect of Azad's thought that a comment made by India's President Zakir Husain finds all its relevance. "In my opinion," he stated,

> the greatest service which the Maulana did was to teach people of every religion that there are two aspects of religion. One separates and creates hatred. This is the false aspect. The other, the true spirit of religion, brings people together; it creates understanding. It lies in the spirit of service, in sacrificing self for others. It implies belief in unity, in the essential unity of things.[29]

Azad owed his political inspiration to his knowledge of Islam. But as a defender of shared common values, he believed that religions were the common heritage of all mankind. His increasing receptivity to the messages of other faiths led him to recognize the humanist element in religion. This is why, for him, the outward forms of religion were useless without moral actions. In his view, religion was not supposed to dictate specific political actions, but to mould one's general principles in life. This is how he grew beyond the revivalism of the *Al-Hilal* period to manifest the real relevance of spirituality, as a moral imperative, to politics. His awareness of other religions also encouraged him to formulate the idea of a humanist coexistence of faiths. Azad's universal humanism drove him to oppose both Muslim and Hindu communalism, which saw no place for a genuinely religiously plural and democratic independent India. His plea for religious humanism and communal harmony was directly influenced by his political affinities with Gandhi and by his mystical reading of Islam. Azad wanted a unity between Muslims and Hindus in order for the independence movement to be politically effective: "He believed that constitutional forms could be devised for India in which the two communities could both thrive. He seems to have opted to follow Gandhi for much the same reason that most of the South African Muslims had done, namely that the Hindu activist seemed the most effective leader available in the struggle against white racism and [and] brutal imperialism. It was Gandhi's ability as an effective fighter that drew Azad to him."[30]

Gandhi's fruitful experiences with Muslims in South Africa and later with the Khilafat movement provided him with a new vision of Islam and its civilizational significance in India. In an address to the Congress Working Committee in 1942, he reiterated the importance of these issues:

> Hindu–Muslim unity is not a new thing. Millions of Hindus and Musulmans have sought after it. I consciously strove for its achievement from

my boyhood. While at school, I made it a point to cultivate the friendship of Muslim and Parsi co-students. I believed even at that tender age that the Hindus in India, if they wished to live in peace and amity with the other communities, should assiduously cultivate the virtue of neighborliness.[31]

This passage serves as a telling example of how Gandhi regarded Hindu–Muslim unity in the context of the independence struggle. He often used the Qur'an in tandem with the *Gita* or the *Ramayana* as an key text when shaping his religious consciousness. He even equated the struggle of the Prophet Muhammad with the mythical struggle of Rama against Ravana. It seems that Gandhi's personal interest in Islam was partly due to his fascination with the character of the Prophet Muhammad. He read and translated Washington Irving's *Life of Muhammad*. He was also introduced to the firm, vigorous, and courageous character of the Prophet by reading Thomas Carlyle's *Heroes and Hero Worship*. Gandhi wrote:

> My religion says that only he who is prepared to suffer can pray to God. Fasting and prayer are common injunctions in my religion. But I know of this sort of penance even in Islam. In the life of the Prophet, I have read that the Prophet often fasted and prayed, and forbade others to copy him. Someone asked him why he did not allow others to do things he himself was doing. "Because I live on food divine," he said. He achieved most of his great things by fasting and prayer. I learnt from him that only he can fast who has inexhaustible faith in God.[32]

Gandhi came to admire the Prophet Muhammad and to understand Islam as tolerant though reading Azad's commentary on the Qur'an and through his friendship and partnership with Khan Abdul Ghaffar Khan. While Azad initiated Gandhi into a Sufi understanding of Islam, Ghaffar Khan introduced him to the practical and pragmatic virtues of non-violent Islam. Azad and Ghaffar Khan were both in harmony with Gandhi's teachings about the oneness of faith and his distrust of religious fanaticism. Like his two Muslim companions, Gandhi was certain that Islam was essentially a tolerant religion and that the violent aspect of the Islamic tradition had been added only later, and only by some Muslims, to the basic principles of Islam. He affirmed:

> Though, in my opinion, nonviolence had a predominant place in the *Quran*, the thirteen hundred years of imperialistic expansion made the Mussalmans fighters as a body. They are, therefore, aggressive. Bullying is the natural excrescence of an aggressive spirit ...

I refuse to be lifted off my feet because of the scares that haunt us today. If Hindus would but believe in themselves and work in accordance with their traditions, they will have no reason to fear bullying. The moment they recommence the real spiritual training, the Mussalman will respond. He cannot help. If I can get together a band of young Hindus with faith in themselves, and, therefore, a faith in the Mussalmans, the band will become a shield for the weaker ones.[33]

Ghaffar Khan had convinced Gandhi that Muslims were capable of practising non-violence in politics and in social reforms. As for Gandhi, he was a true inspiration to Ghaffar Khan and his "Red Shirts" in their practice of non-violence among the Pashtoons. Ghaffar Khan's firm belief in the truth and effectiveness of non-violence came from the depths of his personal experience of Islam. For him, Islam was selfless service, faith, and love. And he emphasized that "without these one calling himself a Muslim is like a sounding brass and tinkling cymbal."[34] Just as Gandhi considered Hinduism to be based on non-violent *ahimsa*, so Abdul Ghaffar Khan reinterpreted his Islam to be based on non-violence. For both reformers, systematic non-violent social transformation was a matter of faith. "My non-violence has almost become a matter of faith with me," explained Ghaffar Khan:

I believed in Gandhi's ahimsa long before. But the unparalleled success of the experiment in my province has made me a confirmed champion of non-violence … Surely there is nothing surprising in a Muslim or a Pathan like me subscribing to this creed. It is not a new creed. It was followed fourteen hundred years ago by the Prophet, all the time he was in Mecca. And it has since been followed by all those who wanted to throw off the oppressor's yoke. But we had so far forgotten it that when Mahatma Gandhi placed it before us, we thought that he was sponsoring a new creed or a novel weapon.[35]

Many factors contributed to the popularity of the *Khudai Khidmatgars*. (Servants of God) Different sectors of Pashtoon society interpreted its program in their own way. As S.W.A. Shah puts it,

to the Pashtoon intelligentsia, it was a movement for the revival of Pashtoon culture with its distinct identity. To the smaller Khans, it was a movement that demanded political reforms for the province that would enfranchise them and give them a greater role in the governance. Its anti-colonial stand suited the majority of the anti-establishment *Ulema*, who always regarded British rule in the sub-continent as a "curse." For the peasants and other poor classes it was against their economic oppressors,

British imperialism and its agents the pro-British Nawabs, Khan Bahadurs and the big Khans.[36]

Ghaffar Khan's truthful character and his faithful and principled method of practising non-violence convinced the Pashtoons that the only cure for their blood feuds and their factionalism was to adopt non-violence and strictly adhere to it. According to J.S. Bright, a contemporary biographer of Ghaffar Khan,

> Ghaffar Khan is in complete accord with the principle of non-violence. But he has not borrowed his outlook from Mahatma Gandhi. He has reached it and reached it independently. Independently like a struggler after truth. No doubt, his deep study of Koran has influenced his doctrine of love ... Hence if Ghaffar Khan has arrived at the philosophy of non-violence, it is absolutely no wonder. Of the two, Ghaffar Khan and Mahatma Gandhi, my personal view is that the former has achieved a higher level of spirituality. The Khan has reached heaven, while the Pandit is firmly on the earth but ironically enough, the Mahatma is struggling in the air! Ghaffar Khan, like Shelley, has come from heaven to the earth, while Mahatma Gandhi, like Keats, is going from earth to the heaven. Hence, I do not understand why Ghaffar Khan should be called the Frontier Gandhi. There is no other reason except this[:] that the Mahatma was earlier in the field, more ambitious than spiritual, and has been able to capture, somehow or the other, a greater publicity. If we judge a person by spiritual qualities, Mahatma Gandhi should rather be called the Indian Khan than Ghaffar Khan the Frontier Gandhi: true, there the matter ends.[37]

Because of his proximity to Gandhi, Ghaffar Khan was accused by some of his close associates, including Mian Ahmad Shah, Abdul Akbar Khan Akbar, and Mohammad Akbar Khadim, of uniting the *Khudai Khidmatgars* with the Hindu-dominated Congress. Ghaffar Khan's response to his Pathan critics and to his future colleagues in the Indian Congress Party was as follows:

> I should like to make it clear that the non-violence I have believed in and preached to my brethren of the Khudai Khidmatgars is much wider. It affects all our life, and only this has permanent value. Unless we learn this lesson of non-violence fully we shall never do away with the deadly feuds which have been the curse of the people of the Frontier. Since we took to non-violence and the Khudai Khidmatgars pledged themselves to it, we have largely succeeded in ending these feuds. Non-violence has added greatly to the courage of the Pathans. Because they were previously addicted to violence far more than others, they have profited by non-violence much more. We shall never really and effectively defend ourselves

except through non-violence. Khudai Khidmatgars must, therefore, be what our name implies – pure servants of God and humanity – by laying down our own lives and never taking any life.[38]

Gandhi's response to this was as clear as always, confirming his belief in the non-violent essence of Islam. He wrote:

> I do not know how far the Khan Saheb has succeeded in carrying his message to his people. This I know that with him non-violence is a matter not of intellectual conviction but of intuitive faith. Nothing can therefore shake it. About his followers he cannot say how far they will adhere to it. But that does not worry him. He has to do his duty which he owes to them. The result he leaves to God. He derives his ahimsa from the Holy Koran.[39]

One can say that Ghaffar Khan succeeded as much as Mahatma Gandhi in his practice of non-violent action, when he turned the hardy Pathans towards the non-violent creed and away from the customary rough methods they had often used to settle their disputes with the government and among themselves. Of course, neither Maulana Azad nor Abdul Ghaffar Khan succeeded in convincing Muhammad Ali Jinnah to cease calling for the creation of Pakistan, which was an extremely violent process both for Muslims and Hindus. But such history illustrates how Islam has always been used for both non-violent and violent purposes. Gandhi understood this very well when he recognized that the violent version of Islam was not the true essence of this religion. A few years before the independence of India in 1947, he wrote in *Harijan*: "I have lived with and among Muslims not for one day but closely and almost uninterruptedly for twenty years. Not one Muslim taught me that Islam was an anti-Hindu religion."[40] In saying this he was confirming what he had said when he visited Abdul Ghaffar Khan at Peshawar in May 1938: "Islam ... believes in the brotherhood of man. But you will permit me to point out that it is not the brotherhood of Muslims only but universal brotherhood ... The Allah of Islam is the same as the God of Christians and the Ishwar of Hindus."[41]

In this respect, Gandhi's friendships and disputes with Indian Muslim leaders remain deeply instructive for Canadian Muslims today. Two Gandhian principles stand out here. First, what looms behind Gandhi's encounter with Islam and Muslims is the difficult question of self-transformation of every religion, particularly those that refuse an inter-religious dialogue. Gandhi required Muslims to recognize that Islam, like every other religion, was neither the whole truth nor nothing but the truth. That is why he rejected the notion that there was one privileged path to God, and that is why he encouraged inter-religious dialogue – it was so that individuals could see their faith in the critical reflections of another. One of his notable innovations was the interfaith prayer meeting, where texts of different religions were read and sung to a mixed audience. This provides evidence as to what sort of cultural pluralist Gandhi was. Second, for Gandhi, every sacred text, of whatever religion, reflected contradictory trends and impulses – sanctioning one thing, but also its opposite. Gandhi urged people to recover and reaffirm those trends that oppose violence and discrimination while promoting justice and non-violence. For him, a culture or a religious tradition that denied individual freedom in the name of unity or purity was coercive and unacceptable. When some women were stoned to death in Afghanistan for allegedly committing adultery, Gandhi criticized it, saying that "this particular form of penalty cannot be defended on the ground of its mere mention in the Koran." He added: "Every formula of every religion has in this age of reason to submit to the acid test of reason and universal justice if it is to ask for universal assent."[42]

In Canada as elsewhere, now is the right time for liberal and moderate Muslims to construct a new, *Gandhian* Islam, a religion that is compatible with the modern world and that is able to interact with the West and to coordinate itself with international norms. Two further and related Gandhian ideas invite emulation. The first is non-violent conflict resolution. In Islam, as in other great religions, there are fundamentalists and extremists who twist what is written in their holy book to justify their acts of violence and terrorism. Modern fundamentalism has positioned itself as a form of resistance to the secular and atheist world by reacting violently towards symbols of modernity such as commercial buildings, train stations, and subway systems. But it is in the interest of Islamic societies and Muslims in general to change the perception that Islam is a violent religion by changing how their societies often attempt to solve differences among themselves and with others. This is not at all hypocritical, nor is it to underestimate the civilizational potential of Islam, but it *is* a critical attitude. Those Muslims who resort to violence as a social and political means of solving conflict are placing their moral judgments and philosophical arguments on the same level as what they are rejecting as unjust and inhumane; and that in turn places them, by definition, at an equally low or even lower level of morality. And this is not a game on which to gamble; in Muslim countries that have embraced violence against their citizens or others, violations of individual liberties are a daily occurrence. Muslim countries today need to read Gandhi as a problematizer of both violence and modernity. Gandhi's harsh critiques of both tradition and modernity offer a theoretical terrain for a nonviolent critique of violence in Muslim theology and political philosophy. In other words, in order to develop an Islamic approach to non-violence that is dialogical and pluralistic, one needs to move beyond absolutist models of policy-making by building on contemporary models, *Gandhian* models, of peace and non-violence in the Muslim world. To return to figures such as Khan Abdul Ghaffar Khan and Maulana Azad would be to accept the Gandhian invitation to self-examination and self-criticism.

A second Gandhian idea that invites emulation is non-violent citizenship. Citizenship is a central concept in Canadian liberal democracy. For Gandhi, the problem of non-violent citizenship is not only to overcome egoism in the Western sense, but also to address the tension between citizenship as a local identity and a larger sense of unity organized around the idea of humanity. Gandhi inspires some very interesting thoughts about how we might create a community of dialogue by expanding human solidarity and moral togetherness. The very idea of a non-violent citizenship is inscribed in Gandhi's concept of a harmonious coexistence of diverse beliefs. As such, the problem that Gandhi poses for us is how to deal with politics in its inability to accommodate the presence of the *Other*. What Gandhi means by the idea of spiritualizing politics is that the true subject of the political is the citizen and not the state. In other words, in Gandhi's mind the citizen always stands higher than the state. But most of all, it means firm opposition to communalism of all kinds. So the real goal for a pluralist and non-violent public sphere in Canada is an engagement-influenced tolerance, a tolerance that is born out of constant communication and interaction between the secular and the religious. This will involve a struggle between those who wish to preserve the essence of their religious beliefs and those who seek deliberately to distort that essence so as to foster a theocratic element. To preserve and promote political pluralism in Canadian society, it is important for Canadian Muslims to learn from the experiences of Gandhi and the Muslim non-violent thinkers and activists like Ghaffar Khan and Maulana Azad, even though their experiences were far from perfect.

The results of emulating Gandhi are certainly unpredictable, but given the Gandhian view that no one possesses the whole truth and that truth emerges in a dialogical encounter among subjects, the making of a Gandhian Islam in Canada remains a welcome challenge.

Notes

1 Gandhi, "A Note," after 3 June 1940, *CWMG* 72, 127.
2 R. Gandhi, *Mohandas*, 15.
3 McDonough, *Gandhi's Responses to Islam*, 13.
4 Gandhi, quoted in Husain, *Gandhiji and Communal Unity*, 54, quoted in McDonough, *Gandhi's Responses to Islam*, 17.

5 R. Gandhi, *Mohandas*, 75.
6 Gandhi, "The Late Lamented Tolstoy the Great," in *Young India*, 26 November 1910, *CWMG* 10, 370, quoted in McDonough, *Gandhi's Responses to Islam*, 28–29.
7 Gandhi, "My Crime," in *Young India*, 5 March 1925, *eCWMG* 30, 336.
8 Gandhi, quoted in Tendulkar, *Mahatma*, vol. 2, 450.
9 McDonough, *Gandhi's Responses to Islam*, 39.
10 Brown, *Gandhi*, 140.
11 Gandhi, "Letter to Viceroy," 29 April 1918, *CWMG* 14, 379.
12 Gandhi, quoted in R. Gandhi, *Mohandas*, 245.
13 See Gandhi, in Parel, ed., *Hind Swaraj and Other Writings*, 42.
14 Qureishi, *Pan-Islam in British Indian Politics*, 104.
15 Gandhi, in *Young India*, 1924–26, 1927, quoted in Qureishi, *Pan-Islam in British Indian Politics*, 104.
16 R. Gandhi, *Mohandas*, 252.
17 Brown, *Gandhi*, 175.
18 Jinnah, quoted in Pirzada, ed., *Quaid's Correspondence*, 94.
19 Jinnah, quoted in Sherwani, ed., *Pakistan Resolution to Pakistan*, 78.
20 Das, *From Curzon to Nehru*, 353.
21 Karandikar, *Islam in India's Transition*, vii.
22 See Rauoof, *Meet Mr. Jinnah*, iii.
23 See Bhana and Vahed, *The Making of a Political Reformer*, 143.
24 Tendulkar, *Abdul Ghaffar Khan*, 291.
25 Brown, *Gandhi*, 309.
26 Azad, *India Wins Freedom*, 169.
27 Azad, quoted in Khan, "Portrait of a Great Patriot," 208–9.
28 Yusuf, "Maulana Abul Kalam Azad," 374.
29 Zakir Husain, quoted in Kabir, ed., *Maulana Azad*, 34.
30 McDonough, *Gandhi's Responses to Islam*, 77.
31 Gandhi, quoted in Tendulkar, *Mahatma*, vol. 6, 155.
32 Gandhi, *The Hindu–Muslim Unity*, 66.
33 Ibid., 47–49.
34 Tendulkar, *Abdul Ghaffar Khan*, 48.
35 Ibid., 93–94.
36 Shah, *Ethnicity, Islam and Nationalism*, 27–28.
37 Bright, *Frontier and Its Gandhi*, 103–4.
38 Abdul Ghaffar Khan, quoted by Gandhi in "Khan Saheb's Ahimsa," in *Harijan*, 21 July 1940, *eCWMG* 79, 2.
39 Gandhi, "Khan Saheb's Ahimsa," 2.
40 Gandhi, "A Baffling Situation," in *Harijan*, 4 May 1940, *CWMG* 78, 183, quoted in Gandhi, *Mohandas: A True Story*, 457.
41 Gandhi, "Speech at Islamia College, Peshawar," 4 May 1938, *eCWMG* 73, 143–45, quoted in R. Gandhi, *Mohandas*, 418.
42 Gandhi, "Notes," in *Young India*, 26 February 1925, *eCWMG* 30, 311.

Gandhi in Canadian Academic Religious Studies: An Overview

Harold Coward

For this book the editor asked me to research and write a chapter on "the Academic Study of Gandhi in Canada." To make the assignment manageable I have limited myself to Gandhi in Academic Religious Studies and divided my chapter into two parts:

1. Research on Gandhi by Canadian Religious Studies Scholars
2. Gandhi's Impact on Canadian Religious Studies Teaching

My approach is the very basic one of listing and describing the academic teaching, research, and publication on Gandhi that could be found for the period of roughly 1970 to the present. While the review of Gandhi research was somewhat systematic, the review of teaching is at best an informal survey dependent on my contacts in each Canadian Religious Studies department and their knowledge of the present along with, in a few cases (e.g., Paul Younger at McMaster, and Ron Neufeldt at the University of Calgary), memories of the past. Some departments such as those at York, Regina, and St. Mary's did not respond to my email request.

In doing my literature review, I encountered some interesting evidence of Gandhi's impact on Canada:

- A 1902 edition of *The Christian Century* carries a news item: Indian war veterans in BC met with the provincial cabinet asking for the vote and requesting that the province petition India for the release of Gandhi from prison.[1] While cabinet ministers supported the franchise request, they were not willing to support the petition for Gandhi's release because his primary purpose is the fostering of civil disobedience.

- Full-sized statues of Gandhi have been unveiled in Ottawa on the Carleton campus (with protests from Ambedkar followers) and in Winnipeg at the Canadian Museum of Human Rights (a gift from the Government of India).
- In Edmonton a Mahatma Gandhi Canadian Foundation for World Peace has been established with origins dating back to 1988, with the impetus coming from the Council of Indian Societies of Edmonton. The purpose of the foundation, now located at the University of Alberta, is to promote the ideals of non-violence in Alberta and Canadian educational institutions. The foundation offers a summer institute with education faculty credit courses on using a Gandhian perspective in the building of peaceful communities.
- The Canadian Bar Association, to mark the 2012 "Law Day" (15 April), released a poster with the question "What are lawyers capable of?" and highlighting "Mahatma Gandhi" (his glasses) "Philosopher, Philanthropist, Revolutionary."[2]

Research by Canadian Religious Studies Scholars

After a general search of the literature and a systematic search of the articles and book reviews in *Studies in Religion* from 1971 to 2011, volumes 1 to 40, it is evident that Canadian scholars of religious studies have made many contributions to the academic study of Gandhi. We will review these contributions by grouping them under the following headings:

- Gandhi and Religious Pluralism
- Gandhi and Politics
- Gandhi and Peacebuilding: Violence and Non-Violence

Gandhi and Religious Pluralism

This is one of the stronger areas of research on Gandhi by Canadian Religious Studies scholars and the international scholars whom they have engaged to take part in Canadian-led and funded projects. An early example in this regard is the article "Gandhi and Religious Pluralism" by the Australian scholar J.T.F. Jordens. It was written as part of a team-authored Social Sciences and Humanities Research Council of Canada (SSHRC) research project at the University of Calgary titled *Modern Indian Responses to Religious Pluralism*, led by Harold Coward and published by SUNY Press in 1987. Jordens describes how growing up in a household filled with Jaina, Muslim, and Hindu *bhakti* influences led the young Gandhi to take religious pluralism for granted. In South Africa (1884–1914), pluralism became a personal problem for him when pressure from close Christian friends to convert, and counsel from his trusted religious adviser, his Jain friend Raychand, led Gandhi to search out his own understanding of Hinduism and of religion in general. Under the influence of Raychand's Jaina *anekantavada* (no-one-view) teaching, and the Christian Edward Maitland's interpretation that the sacred scriptures of various religions were simply historical revelations of a basic universal revelation, Gandhi was led to his own understanding of religious pluralism – namely, that the various religions are but different spiritualization processes by which individuals are able to find perfection and realization of the common eternal truth. Back in India, Gandhi's statements on pluralism changed to an emphasis on tolerance – the various religions are like rivers that meet in the same ocean. Therefore, the various religions – Hinduism, Islam, Christianity, and so forth – must be tolerant of one another. Jordens notes that during this second period (1914–30), Gandhi views tolerance as rooted in the truth and non-violence that constitute the essence of Hinduism, of all other religions, and of religion itself.[3] In Gandhi's third pluralism period (1930–48), Jordens finds that Gandhi's focus shifts to equality. Jordens cites Gandhi as saying that the religions are all branches of the same tree. This Gandhi saw as an advance from "tolerance" to the position of equal respect for all religions.[4] To Gandhi the tree metaphor suggests equality or even identity in the essence of religions – religions are equal because at the root, at the trunk, they are really one. In essence, for Gandhi, there is but one true and perfect religion, and between its various branches there are no ultimately irreconcilable differences. The master key of non-violence may be used to get below the surface of apparent differences and to discover the underlying unity – the one truth from which all the branches grew.[5] The significance of this shift for Gandhi is that "after 1930 no single statement can be found affirming, or even suggesting the superiority of Hinduism, which he did refer to before that date."[6] Jordens doubts, however, that Gandhi's "individualistic normative concept of religion" and the "radical relativism" it implies would be widely acceptable.[7]

Klaus Klostermaier, in his 1971 *Studies in Religion* article on "Hindu–Christian Dialogue," goes into more depth regarding Christian influences on Gandhi. In his autobiography, says Klostermaier, Gandhi describes what contact with Christian friends, the Bible, and other Christian writers like Tolstoy meant to him. It brought him to a deeper understanding of and appreciation for his own Hindu scripture, especially the *Bhagavad Gita* and the *Ramayana*. Also, it freed him from religious bigotry and helped him see other religions as genuine paths to the same God, whom he worshipped.[8] In Klostermaier's view, the Sermon on the Mount, interpreted through Tol-

stoy and Ruskin, helped guide Gandhi's political career. Through his dialogue with Christians and his study of the Sermon on the Mount, Gandhi became sensitized to the unjust Hindu treatment of the Untouchables,
whom he renamed *Harijan* (Children of God) and cared for in his ashram.
While some Christian friends would call him a "Christian," Gandhi himself
wanted to be seen as a Hindu who was open to dialogue with Christians.[9]
However, when Gandhi put forth his understanding of all religions as equal
and as simply varieties of the one true universal religion, characterized by
non-violence, most Christians became skeptical.

Arvind Sharma carefully examines the suggestion of Christian influence on Gandhi's interpretation of the *Bhagavad Gita*. Counter to the suggestions of Christian influence from Jordens and Klostermaier (above),
Sharma argues that Gandhi's move to allegorical interpretation (instead of
the usual Hindu literal approach) was based on what he considered "internal evidence" provided by the *Mahabharata* and the *Bhagavad Gita* themselves. A careful reading of these texts shows that the focus is not on the
actual war on the plains of Kurukshetra, but rather on an imaginary battle
taking place in the human soul. Gandhi's move to an allegorical interpretation of the *Gita*, says Sharma, occurred quite early (1888–89) and thus
precedes his commitment to Jaina non-violence and Christian influence. In
line with traditional Hindu interpretation, Gandhi allows that the persons
described in the *Mahabharata* may be historical, but emphasizes the point
that the author of the *Mahabharata* uses them to drive home the spiritual
theme of an inner duel within the personality. Thus, Sharma seems correct
in his *Studies in Religion* article's conclusion that Gandhi moves to allegorical interpretation not because of Jaina or Christian influences but due to
internal evidence from the Hindu texts themselves.[10] In his book on Gandhi, Sharma states that the appeal of the New Testament "Sermon on the
Mount" for Gandhi was that it provided outside confirmation of what he
had already learned from the Hindu *Mahabharata* and *Bhagavad Gita*.[11]
This finding supports an earlier observation from Sharma on Hindu–Christian interaction by neo-Hindus such as Ram Mohan Roy, Vivekananda, and
Gandhi – namely, that while they were impressed with Christ's message as
confirmation of Hindu teachings, they were often negative towards institutional Christianity.[12]

The academic analysis of Hindu–Christian interaction, so often
sparked by Gandhi, was given a further boost in Canadian academic studies when SSHRC funded a research seminar led by Harold Coward and
held at the University of Calgary in 1987 with participants from Canada,
the United States, the United Kingdom, and India. The result was twofold:
the book *Hindu–Christian Dialogue: Perspectives and Encounters* (Orbis

Books, 1989); and the founding of *Journal of Hindu–Christian Studies*.[13] The book had a chapter on Gandhi, "Gandhi and the Christians: Dialogue in the Nationalist Era" by John Webster from United Theological College in Bangalore. In his chapter, Webster shows that during the years 1919 to 1939 the dialogue between Gandhi and the Christians focused on issues vital to both parties and to India as a whole – especially that of the Untouchables, which made the dialogue very intense. It was an issue over which the two sides differed profoundly on matters of principle, and thus had to oppose each other and potentially do each other harm. Webster writes that after independence, the Christian community in India remained encapsulated in this historic dialogue with Gandhi and seemed stuck in that bondage to the past.[14] The *Journal of Hindu–Christian Studies* (*JHCS*), with Harold Coward as editor, was founded in 1988 and housed first at the University of Calgary and then at the University of Victoria until Coward retired in 2002, at which point publication shifted to the University of Notre Dame in the United States. Now in its twenty-fourth volume, surprisingly the *JHCS* has had only one article on Gandhi, "Mahatma Gandhi: A Living Embodiment of Hindu–Christian Dialogue," by Professor Devadatta Dabholkar of Maharashtra.[15] Unlike Webster, Dabholkar presents a somewhat idealized Gandhi, one who lived an "inner Hindu–Christian Dialogue" as suggested by some of his speeches and writings. However, in the same issue, David Scott of United Theological College in Bangalore provides a critical response that identifies key Christian theological difference with Gandhi, especially his notion of *Swadeshi*, which runs the danger of closing the door on the free movement of the human spirit to *satya* (truth) and leading "the human spirit into bondage to relative reality, be it nation, religion or people."[16]

Too often it seems that scholarly assessments of Gandhi have given him a "halo" treatment. Except for B.R. Nanda's 1985 book *Gandhi and His Critics*, most studies have tended to see Gandhi as a saint. Nanda's book, in the wake of the Attenborough film, attempts to bring alive Gandhi's life as he experienced it, not as a saint but as the shrewd and obstinate opponent of the British rulers, the orthodox Hindus, older colleagues, and younger radicals (like Nehru) within the Congress Party. At the London Round Table meetings held to write a new constitution for India, as well as new rules for parliamentary elections, Gandhi was opposed by Ambedkar, the Untouchables' leader, along with leaders of the other religions – Christians, Muslims, and Sikhs. All found Gandhi both formidable and in his own way at times infuriating. What Nanda does not provide is a careful presentation and analysis of the critiques of Gandhi (and his responses to them) by the major figures and movements of the independence struggle between 1920 and 1948. To fill that gap in Gandhi scholarship, the Centre for Studies in Religion and Society at the University of Victoria, with major funding from SSHRC, put together an international team of scholars from Canada, the United Kingdom, and the United States, with over half from Canada. The results, *Indian Critiques of Gandhi*, edited by Harold Coward, were published by SUNY Press in 2003 and given a major review by Kay Koppedrayer in *Studies in Religion*.[17] In his chapter of that book, Timothy Gorringe explores the way Indian Christians and missionaries and Gandhi's close associate Reverend Charles Andrews interacted with Gandhi on issues such as caste, the Untouchables, his degree of militancy, the burning of foreign cloth, his self-righteousness, and his rejection of the body, which Gorringe says verged on Manichaeanism, in that it treated the body as an evil rather than a good. As Gorringe notes, Andrews "affirmed the goodness of marriage and disapproved of Gandhi's imposition of the vow of celibacy at his Sabarmati ashram."[18] Often Andrews found himself making common cause with Tagore in criticizing their friend Gandhi. While he had many and deep disagreements with Gandhi, Andrews's friendship for him was such that on his deathbed he was arranging for Dietrich Bonhoeffer to come and see Gandhi.[19]

In his independence strategy, Gandhi sought to incorporate minority groups such as the Muslims, Sikhs, and Untouchables within his Non-Cooperation movement. Roland Miller of the University of Regina examines what Indian Muslims thought of Gandhi. He found a range of responses, from the great appreciation of Khan Abdul Ghaffar Khan to the opposition of Mohammed Ali Jinnah, who accused Gandhi of causing split and division among Hindus and Muslims and between Hindus and Hindus, and Muslims and Muslims. Between these two extremes, Miller identifies four major categories of Muslim critiques: minor criticisms, disagreements over the doctrine of *ahimsa*, suspicions about the Hindu orientation of Gandhi's approach, and shifts in Gandhi's priorities when it came to accommodating Muslims. Miller's analysis deepens that offered by another Canadian scholar, Sheila McDonough, in her earlier book in which she traces Gandhi's responses to Islam from England through to the challenges in South Africa and India. McDonough suggests that Gandhi's understanding of and approach to Islam was Bhakti Sufi–inspired.[20] Miller observes that Muslim criticisms often arise from difficulties on Gandhi's part in comprehending the nature and interests of Muslims. But, says Miller, overall Muslim appreciation of Gandhi and his concern for their needs has exceeded and outlasted their critiques.[21]

As Nikky-Guninder Kaur Singh points out, similar problems developed in Gandhi's relations with the Sikhs. She focuses on an important Sikh group, the Shromani Gurdwara Prabhandak Committee (SGPC) and their sense of betrayal when Gandhi withheld support for their initiatives in the 1920s. Her analysis of the letters between Gandhi and the leadership of the SGPC shows that Gandhi's personal views and his own agenda led to a misunderstanding and mistrust of the SGPC project and even of Sikh teachings. For example, thinking that he was praising Guru Gobind Singh, Gandhi called him an "incarnation of God" – something that is anathema to Sikhs. Singh notes that Gandhi's saturation in inclusivist Hindu thought was so strong that he simply did not hear particular Sikh needs and demands. When Gandhi, in various ways, constantly lumped Sikhs together with Hindus rather than seeing them as separate, he was rejected by the Sikhs.[22]

Gandhi's relationship with the Untouchable communities of India from 1920 to 1948 is often cited by scholars, usually with a brief mention of Gandhi changing their name to *Harijan* or "Children of God" as an example of his concern for them. But as Coward's essay "Gandhi, Ambedkar, and Untouchability" shows, Gandhi's relationship with Untouchables and with Ambedkar, their leader, was complex and often filled with antagonism and mistrust. Throughout Gandhi's life, removing the evil of untouchability from Hinduism and India remained a major concern – although he and Ambedkar (himself an Untouchable) sharply disagreed on how that goal was to be achieved. Through a detailed study of their speeches, correspondence, and interactions, Coward shows how Gandhi's ideas of reconciliatory remaking of traditional caste structures ultimately proved unacceptable to both Untouchables and orthodox Hindus, whereas Ambedkar's approach of the rejection of caste and the assertion of political rights succeeded. Yet that success would not have been possible without Ambedkar's engagement with Gandhi throughout the independence struggle. But for Ambedkar's opposition to Gandhi at the London Round Table Conferences in 1930 and 1931, there would have been no need for Gandhi's Poona fast and his launch of the anti-untouchability campaign. Prior to the fast, Gandhi had opposed the entry of Untouchables to Hindu temples. But after the fast and hard negotiation with Ambedkar, Gandhi advocated opening the temples, wells, roads, and other public places to Untouchables. Also, Ambedkar's refusal to go along with Gandhi's patronizing *Harijan Sevak Sang* policy of serving Untouchables rather than politically empowering them helped Gandhi see that his narrow religious views of untouchability in the *varnashrama* context not only reinforced Harijan passivity but also betrayed his own political insight "that no system of oppression could be ended without the active involvement and consequent political education and organization of its victims."[23] Gandhi's blindness on this point rendered ineffective not only the Sevak Sang but also the Congress Party. Sharing Gandhi's philosophy of serving the Untouchables rather than challenging caste practice, Congress did little to get Untouchables into positions of political power. Ambedkar's withering critique of this approach seems to have caused Gandhi to start to doubt the wisdom of his thought and action.

Equality for Ambedkar did not mean equal status of the *varnas* but rather equality of economic, social, and political opportunity. Ambedkar, from the beginning, went much further than Gandhi in awakening Untouchables to their oppressed state and showing them how to obtain equality through education and the modern use of political and legal rights. After more than twenty-five years of unsuccessful struggle with Gandhi and the Hindus, Ambedkar concluded that the powerful inertia of the caste system was not changing – so he led his community to leave Hinduism for Buddhism and its view of equality. Yet it was Gandhi, as independence approached, who convinced Nehru, Patel, and other Congress leaders to include Ambedkar, the Untouchable, in India's first cabinet. As law minister and drafter of the new Constitution of India, Ambedkar was able to include many of the equality and justice rights for Untouchables that he had fought for (usually against Congress) throughout his life. Without Gandhi's intervention, it is unlikely that Ambedkar would have been given that opportunity. In 1948, shortly after Gandhi's death, when the Constituent Assembly finally voted to abolish untouchability and cries of "Victory to Mahatma Gandhi" rang out, Ambedkar may have felt that both in spite of and together with Gandhi, he had achieved something of his goal.[24]

In her fine study "Tagore and Gandhi," T.S. Rukmani identifies many similar points of debate during their long relationship from 1915 to 1941, the year of Tagore's death.[25] Usually known for his Nobel Prize for Literature, Tagore also pioneered social criticism and activism on behalf of women and the poor almost two decades earlier than Gandhi. As Rukmani puts it, "[Tagore] ... anticipated Gandhi in building a social consciousness in society. He cherished the independence of the self and the freedom of the mind above all else."[26] While Gandhi and Tagore had a lifelong admiration for each other, there were striking differences between their personalities and their ideas. Tagore's personality of a sophisticated, modern, literary gentleman contrasted sharply with Gandhi's dictatorial combination of maternalism and paternalism. In the realm of ideas and activism, while Gandhi focused on independence and nationalism through non-cooperation, Tagore immersed himself in international cooperation by bringing together the best of East and West. Gandhi's non-cooperation was rooted in a return to village life and its self-sufficient spinning of yarn, weaving one's own cloth (*khadi*), and burning foreign cloth/clothes. Like Ambedkar, Tagore was not enamoured of village life and strongly opposed Gandhi's burning of British-made clothes as an affront to India's poor. Rukmani notes that Tagore, in letters, plays, and articles (especially in *Young India*), "wrote against *charkha*, disagreed with Gandhi on the question of birth control, had reservations about the Poona Pact that Gandhi achieved through his fast in 1932, opposed his 1933 fast, and did not see eye to eye with Gandhi on the caste system."[27] Tagore, along with Nehru and others, condemned Gandhi's illogicality when he gave up his anti-untouchability campaign because of a 1934 earthquake in Bihar that Gandhi interpreted as a divine chastisement for Hindu sins against the Untouchables. Gandhi quit the anti-untouchability campaign among the Hindus and refocused his attention and energy on achieving independence from the British. Rukmani reports that in 1940, shortly before Tagore's death at the age of seventy-nine, Gandhi visited him at his Santiniketan University, approaching him as his *gurudev* seeking his blessing. Tagore feared for the future funding of Santiniketan and asked Gandhi to place it under his protection and assure it of permanence. Gandhi's respect for Tagore was such that he succeeded in getting the government of India to declare Santiniketan a national university with assured funding.[28]

Noel Salmond of Carleton University, in his *Studies in Religion* article examining Gandhi's unique position on the worship of images, breaks new ground.[29] Rather than castigating the practice of Hindu image worship as the British and the Arya and Brahmo Samaj had done before him, says Salmond, Gandhi defended the practice because of his commitment to religious pluralism – although he himself avoided images and temples. From his religious pluralism perspective, if "all religions are true" then there were no grounds to reject the practice of any one of them – so Gandhi "felt obliged to defend the liberty of others to pursue religion as they see fit."[30] In addition, says Salmond, Gandhi believed in the power and efficacy of the imaginal. "He saw images, symbols, and holy places as powerful human motivators, the life-blood of all religions … Despite his own aniconic sensibility, Gandhi regarded the sometimes crude and naïve forms of popular piety as preferable to the cold, intolerant certainty of the iconoclast."[31] Thus, Gandhi argued that all ranks of society, including the Untouchables, should have the freedom to enter temples and engage in image worship. Indeed, Gandhi went so far as to say that "the deity is only truly consecrated and installed – only truly present in the image – when all discrimination on the basis of caste is expunged."[32]

Gandhi and Politics

Indian Critiques of Gandhi includes several chapters on Gandhi's engagement with political figures active during India's independence struggle, namely, Nehru and Savarkar. Ronald Neufeldt (University of Calgary) provides a close analysis of the writings of V.D. Savarkar and his strong critique of Gandhi's rejection of the use of force, as well as his inclusive nationalism.[33] Savarkar's book, *Hindutva*, became the foundation for the Hindu Mahasabha (and Hindu nationalism) from the 1930s to the present, as well as the basis of its opposition to Gandhist (or Congress) approaches to the British, to India's fight for independence, to the process of nation-building, and to the place of minorities in India.[34] Gandhi began by supporting the Mahasabha's idea of organizing the Hindu community, but he soon criticized their tactics as vicious – especially in their rejection of non-violence. In return, Savarkar saw Gandhi as a significant, albeit misguided, adversary in the struggle for India's independence. Also at issue was the understanding of "nation." Neufeldt writes that for Savarkar, India was to be a Hindu state that all citizens viewed as a fatherland and holy land. There was no room for dual loyalties – that is, for loyalty to India and to an "alien" religion such as Islam or Christianity. This was especially true for Muslims, who, said Savarkar, had a theology that constantly pushed them to transform India into a Muslim state. With this in mind, Savarkar described Gandhi's idea of Muslim–Hindu unity as a "pipe dream."[35] Gandhi, by contrast, spoke in terms not of *Hindu* nationalism but of *Indian* nationalism, and an India that would accommodate the concerns and demands of its minorities. Gandhi believed in the possibility of a pan-Indian civilization that recognized diversity and multiple identities.[36]

In "The Convergence of Distinct Worlds," Robert Baird (Iowa) masterfully analyzes the mystery of what held Nehru (the rational, scientific-minded humanist) and Gandhi (the intuitive religious person) together.[37] They nurtured striking disagreements as well as personal differences, but they shared a commitment to a self-governing India. Nehru held that politics, economics, and social theory are governed by secular values in which religion has no place. He agreed with the distinction that Ambedkar had written into the constitution between the religious and the secular – two distinct realms with sharp boundaries. Nehru recognized that religions such as Hinduism and Islam sought to govern every aspect of human existence, and he argued that in the modern world that must change. As Baird puts it, "while Nehru fervently supported the freedom to 'profess, practice and propagate religion,' he also held that in the effort to maximize human freedom certain practices had to be curtailed if they limited the freedom of others."[38] In contrast, Gandhi saw all of life as a religious search. Therefore he could fast or engage in religious activities for political ends such as gaining independence. Throughout their long association in the Congress Party, the Nehru–Gandhi friendship never eroded, even though Nehru was successively adoring, angry, frustrated, and utterly confused with Gandhi.

It was the qualities of Gandhi that attracted the masses that held Nehru – his difference from other politicians in the way he spoke: quietly, gently, yet strongly and with in deadly earnestness. Gandhi's was a politics of action, and he seemed to speak the language of the masses and to carry them with him partly due to his strategy of non-violence (*satyagraha*), which for him was a religion for the elite *and* the masses. Whereas for Nehru, *satyagraha* was not unconditional, and not a religion, but rather something that seemed sound practical politics and therefore to be supported. Nehru was also frustrated by Gandhi's failure to articulate a clear basis for *satyagraha*, or something more than a vague meaning for *swaraj*. Gandhi's vagueness and intuitive approach was highly frustrating for the rational Nehru. Even more confusing and upsetting for him was Gandhi's use of fasts to reach a political agreement with Ambedkar and the Untouchables while incarcerated in the Poona prison in 1932. The intrusion of religion, in the form of a fast, into politics both angered and shook Nehru, who was also in prison at the time. But when Gandhi succeeded in getting Ambedkar to change his position from separate electorates for the Untouchables to a larger number of guaranteed seats (18 percent of the General Assembly seats), as long as they ran for election under the general electorate rather than under a separate rubric, Nehru was impressed. Ambedkar and Gandhi reached an agreement, the British accepted the revisions, and Nehru's relieved response to Gandhi was that he was a magician – but he worried that others might exploit his methods. When Gandhi again resorted to a fast the following year in trying to compel the orthodox Hindus to accept the Untouchables, this time without success, Nehru, having been asked for advice by Gandhi, replied saying, what can I say about matters that I do not understand? Baird comments that "Nehru continually vacillated between disapproval and disassociation and his desire not to hurt Gandhi. The very idea of a fast for some political end was abhorrent to Nehru."[39] Baird concludes that Nehru, wanting to build India on rational politics and economics governed by secular principles, had no desire to join Gandhi in his religious anti-technological and irrational pre-modern world. Yet they could join together in *satyagraha*, a program that enabled the weak and the poor to resist the strong. Nehru accepted it as a political expedient to be used in the march to independence, during which he and Gandhi were close comrades – so close that when they had to disagree, it was painful.[40]

In his book *Nationalism, Religion, and Ethics*, Gregory Baum of McGill University has a chapter titled "Mahatma Gandhi's Ethic of Nationalism."[41] Baum notes that Gandhi's nationalism in *Hind Swaraj* (*Indian Home Rule*) began with a criticism of modern European civilization as excessively focused on bodily welfare and material progress, with the result that virtue was extinguished and society collapsed into selfishness. India was superior, wrote Gandhi, because it was rooted in spirituality and doing one's duty by attaining mastery over one's mind and one's passions. Since the desires and cravings of humans are endless, they are never satisfied and are constantly frustrated. Thus, says Gandhi, our ancestors set a limit to our indulgences, realizing that happiness is largely a mental condition that comes from a life of discipline, wisdom, and compassion. Similarly, independence for India needed to be based on the self-rule of each citizen, *swaraj*. This was the "home rule" naturally enjoyed by Indian villagers, who lived modest, happy lives doing their duty even while at times suffering injustice – and this was an ethical achievement. This same self-rule by each citizen would provide a national basis for non-cooperation (*swadeshi*) and the path to independence, something that was the duty of every Indian. Baum observes that Gandhi rejected proposals – such as Savarkar's – for the gaining of independence through the use of arms because it could never achieve *swaraj* but only new forms of tyranny. By arming itself to fight Britain, India would inevitably become an industrial, technological society and so end up in the pitiable situation in which Europe had found itself – that is, it would become a Europeanized India.[42] So instead, the struggle for independence would have to be through the passive resistance of non-cooperation made possible by the self-rule of each citizen. This, says Baum, was Gandhi's basis for "ethical nationalism" – ethical because happiness in today's world demands self-restraint rather than endless consumption. Such discipline was also needed for success in the struggle for independence.[43] But, notes Baum, Gandhi did not fully recognize that if the independence struggle succeeded, the result would be the creation of a modern state that, as Nehru observed, went well beyond the Indian villages' capabilities. The modern state would need the power and institutions to impose and maintain a just and humane social order. Baum concludes: "Gandhi hoped, one supposes, that some form of democracy, not yet invented, would assure subsidiarity and decentralization."[44]

Michael Hawley (Mount Royal University, Calgary) introduces a new voice to Indian critiques of Gandhi. Sarvapalli Radhakrishnan viewed Gandhi as misguided and irrational, according to Hawley's analysis of his writings. On his first encounter with Gandhi, Radhakrishnan found him to be philosophically misguided and morally irresponsible. For Radhakrishnan, withholding clothing, education, and medical assistance was not only irrational but morally reprehensible.[45] As a young professor at Presidency College in Calcutta, Radhakrishnan had been strongly influenced by Tagore and his criticism of Gandhi's *swadeshi* ideas of village-based self-reliance. Like Tagore, Radhakrishnan rejected Gandhi's call for students to leave schools and burn foreign clothes. Indeed, Radhakrishnan viewed Gandhi's demonization of modern technology as wrong-headed.[46] During the struggle for independence, Radhakrishnan criticized Gandhi's reliance on non-violent resistance, arguing instead for active resistance. Yet from 1926 on, Radhakrishnan, following the lead of Tagore, publicly described Gandhi as a moral exemplar and a *mahatma* or "great soul," while retaining his criticism in private correspondence.[47] Unlike Gandhi, Radhakrishnan was not concerned about gaining support from the Indian masses; instead he articulated the ideal that he found in the *Upanisads* and in the methods of the ancient *rsis*.

Like Gandhi, George Grant (one of Canada's most original political philosophers) felt that modernity was something to be worried about because of its dehumanizing impact on society and life. In *Technology and Empire*, Grant vigorously expressed his concern about the dangers of technology and modernism. Grant knew of Gandhi and was influenced by his writings, especially *Hind Swaraj*. He expressed his admiration for Gandhi in Christian terms as one who, like Jesus, said, "Happy are those who hunger and thirst for justice's sake" (Matthew 5:6). That, in Grant's view, was what Gandhi had done.[48] Gandhi and Grant both judged society and its institutions against the "Perfections of God," which led many modern secular political philosophers to oppose them.[49] Grant, who described himself as a Tory and a Christian pacifist, agreed with Gandhi's teaching in *Hind Swaraj* that home rule is self-rule and that the way to it is by passive resistance through soul-force or love-force.[50] In *Technology and Empire*, Grant argued that science and technology were now focused on dominating both human and non-human nature. But unlike Gandhi, who called for a retreat to the village and for the rejection of modernity, Grant, following the French philosopher Jacques Ellul, said that technology was no longer something outside of us that we could choose to use for good or ill – most of us lived in a society and world in which technology increasingly dominated all existence. Politicians in both Canada and India (for example, Nehru) were so caught up in modernity that they did not see the limits of technology and mistakenly thought that it was promoting the liberation of humankind. While Gandhi as a spiritual saint could choose to live outside modernity in his village ashram, Grant thought that was not a possibility for most of us today or for society as a whole.[51] Thus Grant did highlight a difference between him and Gandhi, although they agreed that the problem with modernity was that its technology knew no limits outside of itself – and its secular assumption ignored the necessary criterion of divine truth. Having had the privilege of sitting in Grant's seminar as a doctoral student at McMaster and of being supervised by him, it is my view that it was not so much that he was influenced by Gandhi (and his Eastern views); it is more that he found in him "outside confirmation" of Grant's Western-based critique of European modernity and polity. But there was no doubt that Grant greatly admired Gandhi for his engaged spiritual saintliness, which challenged the powerful forces of modernity so heroically. And perhaps, as William Christian suggests, Grant may have agreed with Gandhi's statement from his *Autobiography*: "a perfect vision of Truth can only follow a complete realization of Ahimsa."[52]

Gandhi and Peacebuilding: Violence and Non-Violence

With funding from the Carnegie Corporation of New York, the Centre for Studies in Religion and Society (University of Victoria) put together an international team of scholars to research the obstacles and resources for peacebuilding in each of the major religions. Rajmohan Gandhi (Gandhi's grandson) came to Victoria to take part by focusing on "Hinduism and Peacebuilding," and wrote a fine chapter published in the resulting book, *Religion and Peacebuilding*, edited by Harold Coward and Gordon Smith.[53] Rajmohan frames his analysis within the recognition that Hinduism, from its founding texts onwards, evidences two opposing themes: revenge (war) and reconciliation (peace). The *Mahabharata*, he notes, can be used to justify war or to prove its unmitigated folly. "Yet ahimsa (nonviolence), kshama (forgiveness), and shanti (peace) are values mentioned with unequivocal favour in the Vedas, the Upanisads, the Gita, and the Mahabharata."[54] These two themes of violence and *ahimsa* may be traced through the history of India right up to the present.[55] This helps us contextualize our understandings of the Hindu nationalists and the followers of Mahatma Gandhi in Canada and the world today. As noted above, Gandhi's ideals of non-violence, forgiveness, and equality clash with Savarkar's *Hindutva* (Hindu nationalist) advocacy of retaliation and Hindu primacy. This of course led to the *Hindutva* champions labelling Gandhi as the enemy of the Hindus, which in turn led to his assassination in 1948. Rajmohan quotes Arvind Sharma, who says in his book *Our Religions* that the new Hindu fundamentalism places God rather than Gandhi on the pedestal and increasingly sees religious tolerance as a right that Hindus extend to one another within Hinduism but at the same time as a privilege that others such as Muslims and Christians (foreigners) must earn on clearly defined terms.[56] Followers of *Hindutva* at times claim religious authorization for war, revenge, and violence, citing the killings carried out in the epics and recommended in the *Gita*, and recalling history's wrongs. Gandhi, however, recommended a different, more difficult attitude: he said, "I cannot return evil for evil," and he required that both sides, Hindus and Muslims, admit their wrongs and ask for forgiveness. Rajmohan traces this Hindu peace-building ethic evoked by Gandhi through the *Vedas*, the Epics, the stories from the *Puranas* (mythological texts), and reconciliation events in history (for instance, as in the lives of *bhakti* [devotional] poets who bridged the divide between Muslims and Hindus). Also mentioned by Rajmohan, and discussed earlier in this chapter, is Gandhi's struggle with Ambedkar and the Untouchables, and his role in getting Nehru and other Congress colleagues to invite Ambedkar into the cabinet to chair the drafting of India's constitution – a peacebuilding exercise between Hindus and Untouchables for which credit is due to both Ambedkar and Gandhi.[57] Rajmohan notes that Hindu groups in India and Canada continue to stress Gandhian ethics, non-violence, reconciliation, and peacebuilding. These groups include the Brahma Kumaris, ISKCON (the International Society for Krishna Consciousness), the Ramakrishna Mission, and the Swaminarayan community.[58] Indeed, it seems that Gandhi is perhaps more discussed in Canadian courses on Hinduism. Michel Desjardins's review of Rajmohan's chapter calls it a gem – a finely nuanced picture of Gandhi's contribution to modern Indian politics and religion.[59]

Kay Koppedrayer (Wilfrid Laurier University), perhaps more than any other religious studies scholar in Canada, has maintained a consistent focus on Gandhi in her research (MA on Gandhi and Ambedkar, one book chapter and four journal articles all using Gandhi's early memoirs and his *Autobiography* as their subject matter). In her excellent article "Gandhi's *Autobiography* as Commentary on the *Bhagavad Gītā*," she returns to the Indian nationalists' use of the *Gita* as an authorization for war and violence. She shows how Gandhi's allegorical interpretation of war in the *Gita* was a response to nationalists who based their advocacy of violent means to overthrow the British government in India on their reading of the *Gita*.[60] Gandhi counter-posed his non-violent interpretation of the *Gita* against, for example, the views of Tilak on how to obtain self-governance from Britain by any means, including violence. In her carefully researched article, Koppedrayer adds to our understanding of Gandhi's non-violence by showing how he verified and developed his view of *ahimsa* in the course of writing his *Autobiography* in the 1920s as an exposition of the *Gita*. Gandhi contended that the function of violence is to obtain reform by any means, whereas the *Gita* counsels fearlessness, equanimity, and the acquisition of self-control. The *Gita*, verse 3.37, teaches that the main obstacle to personal spiritual growth, and social/political transformation, as found in Gandhi's vision of *swaraj*, is desire, anger, born of the quality of *rajas* (passion). In contrast to Tilak's call for violence towards the British based on a literal reading of the *Gita*, Gandhi described the battle between the Pandavas and the Kauravas as referring to the war within our bodies between the forces of good (Pandavas) and the forces of evil (Kauravas), and added that the forces of evil need to be destroyed – only then will we be pure enough within to successfully engage in non-violent passive-resistant political action. Koppedrayer shows how starting early in his life in South Africa, through his response to the Rowlatt Bills, to the Salt March in 1930, Gandhi's personal actions and political non-violent leadership were based in the *Gita*'s prescription of self-purification as a prerequisite for effective involvement in *satyagraha*. "Political transformation must be preceded by a state of internal non-cooperation with those same impulses as found in 'the evil system which the British Government represents' ... In your emancipation is the emancipation of India."[61] Koppedrayer clearly demonstrates how this approach of Gandhi's was present both in his expositions of the *Gita* and in his *Autobiography*, in which the purifying of his own life (all his passions for food, sex, and material possessions) led to the self-restraint needed for successful political action of the sort demonstrated during the Salt March. For himself and his followers, that success depended on inner purity or *swaraj* being realized as a precondition for outer political *swaraj* or national self-rule. Gandhi's personal and political strategy of non-violent passive resistance was founded in and sustained by his lifetime study of the *Gita*. As Koppedrayer points out, in the 1929 introduction to his translation of the *Gita*, Gandhi described *Anasaktiyoga* – a yoga that entails disciplined selfless action – as a corrective to Tilak's earlier *Gita* interpretation of using any means, including violence, to gain independence. Regarding the authority of his understanding and his application of the *Gita*, Gandhi made clear that it was not his own but came from his struggles with the voice within – *swaraj* emerged "through that struggle and the actions that follow ... when the teachings of restraint and purification are actualized."[62] Just as his *Autobiography* reveals his own inner struggle to apply the teachings of the *Gita*, so Gandhi prompts the listener or reader also to turn inward and discern, through struggles with the *Gita*, one's own right course of action and inner authoritative voice.

Paul Younger, in a 1987 book, examined the legacy of Mahatma Gandhi. The *Autobiography* idealizes the visionary idea of *satyagraha*; Younger, however, suggests that *satyagraha* was "not so much an idea as a demonstration-protest technique."[63] By trial and error, Gandhi found that peaceful protests and the acceptance of police brutality had two complementary effects: (1) they fostered radical solidarity within the otherwise scattered Indian community, and (2) they created a strong sense of guilt consciousness in the Christian rulers. Bringing all of this from South Africa, Gandhi appeared in India with this new idea of *satyagraha*, which he expounded as a *mahatma* who had suddenly arrived in their midst with the dress of a *sannyasi* or renunciant, and who wore a *dhoti* (leg-covering garment) and carried a walking stick, a dress exactly right for the occasion. Younger writes that the people immediately responded to this vision, as well as to his revolutionary idea and method of *satyagraha* for obtaining peaceful political action. It was as a seeker of order or *dharma* that Gandhi made his real impact on the Indian political system.[64]

Younger sets a recent discussion of Gandhi in the context of a course he has taught at McMaster University for the past thirty years. Limited to 150, the class contains a significant number of students with South Asian backgrounds who want to understand the role that violence and religion have played in South Asian societies. Younger examines Gandhi's contribution in terms of its reception by South Asian students in the context of Canada's multicultural society.[65] In an essay in the book *Teaching Religion and Violence*, Younger examines Gandhi's conversations with colonial authorities and his post-colonial contemporaries so as to help Canadian diaspora students figure out why India's post-colonial debates were so complicated, and why some groups still turn to violence long after the post-colonial era has begun. Focusing on the areas of society, religion, and politics, Younger examines the uniqueness of Gandhi's post-colonial contributions. He observes that his Canadian South Asian students see Gandhi's response to issues of the colonial era as "an interesting model for approaching the social controversies they do find themselves engaged with in the diaspora."[66] Against the colonizers' presentation of the colonized Others as "female" or "childlike," early-twentieth-century responses from leaders such as Tilak and Savarkar emphasized Indian manhood and martial character. By contrast, Gandhi ignored colonizers' efforts to stereotype Indians as weak and effeminate, instead insisting that "he had found the women around him to be stronger than the men and the heart of his political movement. In his view, women were no longer objects to be governed and protected in this way or that, but subjects leading the effort to define the political forms of the future."[67] In this way Gandhi not only undermined the colonial obsession with its masculinity and thus its natural right to use violence, but also Savarkar's idea that the way to free India from this British oppression was to outdo the colonizers with an even stronger show of violence.

Younger notes that for his students, Gandhi's identification with strong women rather than "male violence" comes as a surprise that relates to gender issues still alive within the Canadian diaspora community. Many students are surprised to see how effective Gandhi's post-colonial voice was with regard to the social and political issues involved in India's independence struggles. Gandhi succeeded in disarming the Orientalist critique of the colonizers by appealing not to India's martial heritage with its use of violence, but to its non-violent *ahimsa* heritage, which he located in his allegorical reading of the *Gita* and which manifested itself in the strength of South Asian women. What was required in society was not masculine force of the sort counselled by Tilak and Savarkar with its violence and strong anti-Muslim bias, but rather the *Gita*'s requirement that we all discipline our own passions. From such *swaraj* would come not only one's own personal freedom but also the freedom for all genders, races, and religions to live together peacefully in society. In this aspect of Gandhi, says Younger, South Asian students see a thoughtful model of post-colonial thinking and a way peacefully to pursue mutual understanding and respect in the society in which they now live. "In Canada, where there are now more or less equal numbers of Sikhs, Muslims, and Hindus, the discussions in the University are often about how all South Asian religious groups are developing into a common community."[68] While the *dhoti*-clad Gandhi might seem somewhat distant to these South Asian diaspora youth of Canada, says Younger, Gandhi does serve as a symbol for this newly emerging community in that he respected religious pluralism (especially with the Muslims), he encouraged intermarriage, and he was a pioneer of what is now called "'human rights' or 'minority rights.'"[69]

From the *Gita*, Gandhi adopted the view that it is the undisciplined person who resorts to violence. "To respond at a higher level is to respond with discipline and to invite a higher level of response from the opponent ... The religion Gandhi finds in the *Gita* is a religion of action, and it is only as one learns how that system of action works that one is able to initiate actions of non-violence or *satyagraha*."[70] Younger says that it is this aspect of Gandhi's teaching that the students, from every religious background, seem to like best. It leads them to ask if post-colonial religion is necessarily pluralistic, and to observe that Gandhi's style of post-colonial practice took for granted a religiously plural polity – one that he worked through with Nehru and Ambedkar to instill in the constitution of India as a new secular state. Younger concludes that for him and for his South Asian students, "the most important dimension of Gandhi's approach is that he saw religion as part of a social whole ... He did not use his energy to challenge arguments about the essence of Hinduism as they were put forward by either the British or [nationalists like Savarkar]."[71] Gandhi's vision for a post-colonial India with a healthy range of religious practices and an open form of community is one that Younger observes resonates well with Canada's South Asian diaspora students and the challenges they face in a twenty-first-century multicultural society.

Let us conclude our review of Canadian research on Gandhi with a brief look at a quite different article, titled "The Glow in the Eastern Sky: The Impact of Mahatma Gandhi on the Canadian Protestant Churches in the Interwar Years," published in *Journal of the Canadian Church Historical Society* in April 1990. The author, Robert A. Wright, explores the enchantment of Protestant clergy with Gandhi in the years between the First and Second World Wars.[72] By the late 1920s Gandhi's reputation among missionaries in India and clergy at home was that of a man of "Christ-like" virtue. As Wright puts it, "by forsaking all the luxuries of Western life – meat, alcohol, sex, money, material possessions, social status – and by promulgating an ethos of self-sacrificial pacifism, Gandhi seemed to have achieved an unparalleled evocation of the ascetic spirit of Christ."[73] Furthermore, in his dedication to India's poor and lower classes, Gandhi seemed to embody the "social gospel" that the well-off Canadian churches were by then abandoning. Although he had initially been rejected as a naive and vulgar Hindu, by the 1920s and 1930s his critique of Western Christianity (as contained in the books and speeches of E. Stanley Jones and C.F. Andrews) was striking sensitive nerves in Protestant Canada. In an age of big congregations, big choirs, big sermons, and big salaries, Gandhi provided a living example of what it meant to live like Christ, and he seemed to be offering hard advice for the re-establishment of values such as the social gospel. While there were pockets of strong opposition to Gandhi in the Canadian clergy – especially among those with an aversion to his politics – many agreed with a letter to *Canadian Churchman* (August 1934) that stated in part, "Does not Canada urgently need a Mahatma Gandhi? Does Canada possess a moral sense or a social conscience?"[74] In Wright's view, Gandhi's appeal to Canadian Protestant Churchmen in the 1920s and 1930s lay in his evocation of a spiritual and social gospel quality that seemed to be in decline in their churches. It was not that Canadians sought to infuse their Protestantism with Hindu insights. Rather, it was that Gandhi showed Canadians not a new vision of the Cross and the Kingdom of God, but a rediscovery of one that had become obscured by the materialism and pressures of modern church life. It also signalled a watershed in the militant apologetics of Protestant missions abroad.[75]

Gandhi's Impact on Canadian Religious Studies Teaching

Younger's analysis of the reception of Gandhi by students at McMaster leads us into the second part of this chapter, namely, an informal survey of the teaching of Gandhi in Canadian university religious studies departments in terms of courses, theses, conferences, and special lectures. Since I have mentioned Paul Younger, let us begin with his university.

McMaster University has one of the longest and strongest records of teaching Gandhi. As noted in Paul Younger's article (discussed earlier), the undergrad course "The Life, Work and Teachings of Mahatma Gandhi" has been taught there from the 1970s to the present and has attracted 100 to 200 students at a time. Also, Anne Pearson includes Gandhi in her "Indian Religious Tradition Course." For a while there was a course on Gandhi and Martin Luther King taught jointly by Graeme MacQueen and Paul Debar, but this was discontinued when MacQueen retired several years ago. Mac-Queen also taught Gandhi in Peace Studies for many years and was the leader of non-violent antiwar community action with a strong Gandhian element. At the graduate level, Younger and Debar co-taught a course on Tolstoy, Gandhi, and King for a few years. Younger supervised two MA theses on Gandhi. Kay Koppedrayer wrote an MA thesis "The Interplay of Ideas Behind the Question of Untouchability: The Interactions of the British, Ambedkar and Gandhi." McMaster organized a conference in 1969 to celebrate Gandhi's birth centennial with Canada Council funding and Suzanne Rudolph as keynote speaker. Annual Gandhi lectures have been held since 1996 under the sponsorship of the Centre for Peace Studies, with speakers from around the world.

At the University of Toronto, Religious Studies offers a course on violence and non-violence that has a component about Gandhi. Reid Locklin includes Gandhi in his courses on "Indian Christianity" and "Christianities of South Asia." The Toronto School of Theology has four courses that reference Gandhi: "Christianity and World Religions," "Religious Experience and the World's Religions," "Themes in Hindu Spirituality," and "Theology, Violence, and Peace," with much of the teaching by Michael Stoeber. Regarding theses, there was a PhD at the Centre for the Study of Religion on "Sarvodaya of Mahatma Gandhi: Realistic Utopia," by Thomas Vettickal (1998), and a ThD thesis at the University of St. Michael's College, "The Emerging Roman Catholic Liberation Theology in India: The Significance of Mahatma Gandhi" by Anthony Kozhuvanal.

Queen's University Religious Studies has three courses that include Gandhi. "The Hindu World" and a graduate course "Religion and Modernity" are both taught by Ellen Goldberg. William Morrow includes Gandhi in his "Religion and Violence" course, which is open to both graduate and undergraduate students.

At Carleton University there has been a flurry of activity on Gandhi, including the unveiling of a life-sized statue on campus. Noel Salmond has offered a senior undergraduate/graduate course on "Gandhi in India and the World" for the last two years. Chinnaiah Janman (History) is offering a course on "Gandhi and Ambedkar." These are the only stand-alone Gandhi courses, although over the years Gandhi has been included in the Asian religions surveys and in the courses on Hinduism. The Humanities Religion Program and the Mahatma Gandhi Society of Ottawa co-sponsored talks on Gandhi in 2006 (Rukmani), 2007 (Younger), and 2010 (Pattanaik).

Wilfrid Laurier University has a long-standing flagship course "Gandhi: Nonviolence and the Struggle for Freedom," first introduced by Emile Lang during the 1970s, with Kay Koppedrayer taking it over in 1988. It is now taught by Alex Damm both in the classroom and online. Courses on "Hinduism" and "Modern Indian Thought" have included sections on Gandhi, as has a graduate course on "India and the West." A recent course taught by Brent Hagerman on "Religion and Popular Culture" examined some popular representations of Gandhi. An MA research project by Mitra Bhikkhu examined Ambedkar with a side-inclusion of Gandhi. Koppedrayer notes that most of her publications have come out of her teaching of the Gandhi course. One of her courses includes a student project of living like Gandhi for a week, with the lesson plan published in *World History Bulletin* (2008) as "A Week in the Life of Mahatma Gandhi."[76]

At the University of Waterloo, Doris Jakobsh teaches Gandhi in her Hinduism course, and Nathan Funk includes some Gandhi content in the "Violence, Non-Violence and War" course. Jim Pankratz has a long-term project on "Gandhi and Mennonite Missionaries in India."

From Memorial University, Pat Dold reports that in her Hinduism course, Gandhi is studied as a modern reformer as well as a modern interpreter of the *Bhagavad Gita*. He is also included in a course on Asian religions and culture. In 2009 there were special lectures on Gandhi's relevance to the contemporary world by Pravin Seth, sponsored by the Shastri Indo-Canadian Institute.

At Acadia University, Bruce Matthews includes Gandhi in the "Introduction to World Religions."

In Montreal, at McGill University, Arvind Sharma teaches a long-standing course "Gandhi: Life and Thought." Gandhi is also discussed in "Hinduism and the East" and "Introduction to Hinduism" courses. At the University of Quebec at Montreal, Gandhi is included in the Hinduism course. At Concordia University, T.S. Rukmani teaches a course on "Gandhi, Colonialism and Beyond," and Gandhi is featured in the "Religion and Violence" course. There has been an MA thesis on "Conflict Resolution through Non-Violence" in which Gandhi is given prominence.

At the University of Manitoba, Klaus Klostermaier has included Gandhi in his graduate seminar "Masters of Spiritual Life" and has supervised a PhD thesis by Adela Torchia titled "Religion and Ecology: Gandhi's Khadi Spirit and Neo-Asceticism" (1996). In Klostermaier's *A Survey of Hindu-*

ism, there is a chapter on "Mahatma Gandhi: A 20th Century Karmayogi."[77] Klostermaier also published a book in German on the occasion of the Gandhi Centenary 1969, *Mahatma Gandhi: Freiheit ohne Gewalt* (*Freedom without Violence*), consisting of a biography and translations of his writings.[78]

The University of Calgary gives Gandhi major attention in four courses: "Introduction to Eastern Religions," "Introduction to Hinduism," "Religion and Modern India," and "Religion and Nationalism in Modern India." Ron Neufeldt has supervised a BA honours thesis, "Three Western Threads Spun by Gandhi," and an MA thesis, "Active Awakening: Swaraj in Gandhi's *Hind Swaraj* and in Savarkar's *The Indian War of Independence*." Neufeldt also presented a talk, "Civil Disobedience: Thoreau and Gandhi," in a Humanities Institute "Community Seminar."

At Calgary's Mount Royal University, there is a field school for students at Haridwar, India, which includes content on Gandhi. Courses taught by Michael Hawley that cover Gandhi include "Outstanding Lives: Gandhi," "Hinduism," and "Advanced Studies in Hinduism (the *Bhagavad Gita*)." Hawley's active research on Gandhi and the Sikhs is evident from his various publications.[79]

At the University of Victoria, Gandhi is taught by Martin Adam and Harold Coward in the introductory course "Hinduism, Buddhism, Sikhism and the Chinese Religions," and also in "Contemporary Religious Issues," which covers Gandhi, Ambedkar, and the Untouchables. Martin Adam also covers Gandhi in his course on "Religion and Violence." A guest lecture was given on "The Making of a Mahatma: Radhakrishnan on Gandhi" by Michael Hawley in 2001. Also at UVic, the Centre for Studies in Religion and Society hosted a major research project, "Indian Critiques of Gandhi," in 2001–3, led by Harold Coward with participating scholars from Canada, the United States, and the United Kingdom.

Conclusion

Our literature review of Gandhi research by religious studies scholars in Canada turned up a total of six books (by Klostermaier, Younger, Sharma, and Coward), thirteen chapters, and nine journal articles spread over three areas of religious pluralism: politics, violence, and peacebuilding. The largest area of research by Canadian scholars is that of "Gandhi and Religious Pluralism" with articles/chapters on Gandhi's approach to religion in general (Jordens), to Christians (Klostermaier, Gorringe, Sharma, Webster), to Muslims (Miller, McDonough), to Sikhs (Nikki Singh), to Untouchables (Coward), and to Tagore (Rukmani). Another strong area is "Gandhi and Politics," with fine chapters and articles on Gandhi and Nehru (Baird),

Savarkar (Neufeldt), Radhakrishnan (Hawley), and ethical nationalism (Baum). An outlier in the politics area was the chapter analyzing Gandhi's influence on the Canadian political philosopher George Grant (Christian). The third research area of Canadian scholars is that of Gandhi and violence/non-violence, with work on his *Gita* commentary and his *Autobiography* being crucial here (Koppedrayer, Sharma, R. Gandhi). With his recent chapter analyzing his Gandhi course and the resonance that South Asian students find between Gandhi and the role that violence and religion play in their experience in Canada's multicultural society, Paul Younger has opened a new and, I think, promising way of exploring Gandhi's potential impact and contribution to Canada today and for the future. Finally, two major SSHRC-funded research projects involving Gandhi have been conducted at the Centre for Studies in Religion and Society at the University of Victoria: *Indian Critiques of Gandhi* and *Religion and Peacebuilding*, with scholars from Canada, the United States, the United Kingdom, India, and Australia. Both projects have been led by Harold Coward.

Regarding teaching, our informal survey found long-standing courses dedicated to Gandhi at McMaster, McGill, and Wilfrid Laurier. Across the country, undergraduate courses involving Gandhi have included nine on Hinduism, six on modern India, seven on religion and violence, four in the context of introducing Eastern religions, and three on Gandhi and Christianity. At the graduate level, one course was offered at each of McMaster, Queen's, McGill, Carleton, Manitoba, and Calgary. With regard to theses at the MA level, three are reported at McMaster, one at Concordia, and three at Calgary. PhD theses on Gandhi have been completed at Toronto and Manitoba, and one ThD at the University of St. Michael's College, Toronto.

In conclusion, we could say that religious studies in Canada has a reasonably strong record of research on Gandhi, whereas undergraduate and graduate course work is perhaps weaker than one would expect. The long-term success from the 1970s to the present of the dedicated Gandhi courses at Wilfrid Laurier, McMaster, and McGill suggests that other departments should consider such offerings. And as Paul Younger's research paper demonstrates, such courses might well play an important role in communities that have a significant South Asian diaspora population – for example, Toronto. I know that I will be proposing such a Gandhi course for the University of Victoria.[80]

Notes

1 See *Christian Century* 60, no. 11 (1902), 333.
2 Visit http://www.cba.org/public.
3 Jordens, "Gandhi and Religious Pluralism," 9.

4 Ibid., 11.
5 Ibid., 12.
6 Ibid., 11.
7 Ibid., 15.
8 Klostermaier, "Hindu–Christian Dialogue," 92.
9 Ibid.
10 Sharma, "Accounting for Gandhi's Allegorical Interpretation of the Bhagavadgītā," 507.
11 Sharma, *A New Curve in the Ganges*, 85.
12 Sharma, ed., *Neo-Hindu Views of Christianity*.
13 See Coward, ed., *Hindu–Christian Dialogue*.
14 Webster, "Gandhi and the Christians."
15 Dabholkar, "Mahatma Gandhi."
16 Scott, "Response to Devadatta Debholkar," 28.
17 Koppedrayer, Review of *Indian Critiques of Gandhi*.
18 Gorringe, "Gandhi and the Christian Community," 162.
19 Ibid., 164.
20 McDonough, *Gandhi's Responses to Islam*, 108.
21 Miller, "Indian Muslim Critiques of Gandhi," 212.
22 Singh, "The Mahatma and the Sikhs," 189.
23 Coward, "Gandhi, Ambedkar, and Untouchability," 63.
24 Ibid., 64.
25 Rukmani, "Tagore and Gandhi."
26 Ibid., 109.
27 Ibid., 122.
28 Ibid., 124.
29 Salmond, "Both Iconoclast and Idolator."
30 Ibid., 389.
31 Ibid.
32 Ibid.
33 Neufeldt, "The Hindu Mahasabha and Gandhi."
34 Ibid., 132.
35 Ibid., 148.
36 Ibid., 149.
37 Baird, "The Convergence of Distinct Worlds."
38 Ibid., 19.
39 Ibid., 24.
40 Ibid., 37.
41 Baum, *Nationalism, Religion and Ethics*, 39–61.
42 Ibid., 46.
43 Ibid., 50.
44 Ibid., 61.
45 Hawley, "The Making of the Mahatma," 137.
46 Ibid., 139.
47 Ibid., 146.
48 Christian, "George Grant and Mahatma Gandhi," 16.
49 Baruna, *Gandhi and Grant*.
50 Ibid., 19.
51 Ibid., 26.

52 Ibid., 28.
53 R. Gandhi, "Hinduism and Peacebuilding."
54 Ibid., 49.
55 See R. Gandhi, *Revenge and Reconciliation*.
56 R. Gandhi, "Hinduism and Peacebuilding," 53.
57 Ibid., 64.
58 Ibid.
59 Desjardins, Review of *Religion and Peacebuilding*, 450.
60 Koppedrayer, "Gandhi's *Autobiography*," 71n6.
61 Ibid., 53.
62 Ibid., 63.
63 Younger, *From Ashoka to Rajiv*, 65.
64 Ibid., 66.
65 Younger, "M.K. Gandhi."
66 Ibid., 271.
67 Ibid., 272.
68 Ibid., 288.
69 Ibid.
70 Ibid., 280.
71 Ibid., 289.
72 Wright, "The Glow in the Eastern Sky."
73 Ibid., 10.
74 Ibid., 13.
75 Ibid., 18-9.
76 Koppedrayer, "A Week in the Life."
77 Klostermaier, *A Survey of Hinduism*.
78 Klostermaier, *Mahatma Gandhi*.
79 Hawley, "M.K. Gandhi and the Sikhs"; Hawley, "Getting Past Orientalism."
80 Thanks are due to June Thomson, our centre's librarian, for her invaluable assistance in the literature search.

Do Gandhi's Teachings
Have Relevance Today?

Kay Koppedrayer

Does knowledge of Mahatma Gandhi matter? The chapter that follows rests on this pivotal question.

Knowledge of Gandhi

Make reference to Gandhi in any conversation, and virtually everyone within earshot can conjure up some image of who he was and what he accomplished. Much of what results is impressionistic, gained from popular culture. Quotations from Gandhi appear on various websites supporting non-violence, vegetarian lifestyles, peace, inter-religious dialogue, and a range of other causes. References to Gandhi show up in all manner of places. The symbolic power of his image has continued to be put to all kinds of uses, even for purposes that Gandhi himself would have been unlikely to support, as seen in Apple's "Dare to Be Different" advertising campaign of the late 1990s. Conscripting Gandhi in its technology war with Microsoft, Apple relied on the ubiquitous photo of his sitting behind a spinning wheel to convey a message of quiet conviction, of going against the grain, of participation in a social movement, of whatever. The impact came with the juxtaposition of image and ad copy: Gandhi was now promoting the use not just of new technology, but of a particular brand, despite the many antagonisms against technology that he voiced over his lifetime. That ad campaign was, in Salman Rushdie's words, a testimony to how the idea of Gandhi had become "a part of the available stock of cultural symbols, an image that can be borrowed, used, distorted, reinvented to fit many different purposes" (1998).[1]

In other words, knowledge of Gandhi is not necessarily knowledge – deep knowledge, informed knowledge, measured knowledge – of Gandhi. Comprehending his thought and his lifelong activism shows a different level of understanding than does recognizing or reacting to it. Returning to the pivotal question of this chapter, my interest is in a fuller and deeper understanding of Gandhi and his teachings, and whether or not (or in what ways) it informs the lives of those who have that understanding. I was wondering if learning about Gandhi had any lasting impact on those who did have it. Did they continue to find his teachings inspirational? Did they find his social and political thought relevant? Did they ever apply or implement Gandhi's teachings? Those were the concerns underpinning my question, "Does knowledge of Gandhi matter?"

To pursue this line of inquiry, I designed a case study drawn from my teaching experience. During my twenty-two years of employment (1987–2009) at Wilfrid Laurier University in Waterloo, Ontario, I regularly taught a third-year course on Gandhi's life and teachings. I had inherited the course from my predecessor, and I approached it with some hesitation in my first year of teaching. Within a couple of weeks that first year, I recognized its potential. A course on Gandhi entails study of a nexus of historical processes and movements, prompting students to reflect not only on Gandhi's activism but also on colonialism, state formation in South Africa and on the Indian Subcontinent, the circulation of religious thought, conflict mediation, non-violence, personal formation, and more. One can cover a lot of ground without losing focus by keeping Gandhi as the focal point. For that reason I grew to love the course; indeed, I developed a deeper respect for Gandhi's life work and thought the longer I taught it. The course was popular enough for it to remain on the books throughout my teaching career and afterwards. In fact, in 2011 the department added an online iteration of the course for distance learners.

Given its long lifespan, the course has had a river of students pass through it, a couple of generations by my reckoning. Those students' interest in Gandhi has varied, reflecting Canada's changing demographics as well as trends in social, political, and environmental activism and students' lifestyles. Documenting those changing trends would be fruitful work, but for another chapter. My concern was different. My pivotal question, "Does knowledge of Gandhi matter?" was now in a more refined form: "Have Gandhi's teachings had any lasting impact on people who as university students spent part of a term thinking about him?"

Based on the study I conducted, the answer to that question is a qualified yes. With a couple of exceptions, former students that I contacted enumerated the different ways that Gandhian thought remains important to them, particularly his views on conflict transformation. In the paragraphs that follow I present the results of my case study, outlining the methods I used to contact former students, the questions I presented to them, and the responses they gave. I will flesh out the explanations they provided to gauge how a selected group of Canadians have found Gandhi's teachings to be relevant. Their reflections suggest that although Gandhi was from another place, and certainly from another time, his teachings continue to speak to attentive listeners, in both expected and unexpected ways.

The Case Study

The design of the case study was straightforward. I contacted former students and posed to them a set of open-ended questions. The questions were short and to the point:

1. What do you recall from the course, if anything, about Gandhi? About his teachings? If nothing, please say so, as nul responses are also important.
2. Did anything you learn about Gandhi or his teachings have any lasting impact on you? If so, how so? (For example, do you still ponder over some of his ideas? Or do you continue to find his courage inspiring?)
3. Have you ever drawn upon or applied any of Gandhi's teachings (for instance, techniques of conflict transformation, ideas of non-violence, vegetarianism, or the like) in your life? If so, please provide examples.
4. Anything you would like to add?

In order from one to three, the questions addressed retention of material (What information, if any, did one remember?), integration (Did Gandhi's teachings have any impact?), and application (Did the respondent ever draw from Gandhi's teachings in real-life situations?). These are primary objectives of good pedagogy. Former students might well have been able to recall details of Gandhi's life or the contours of his moral and political activism. Perhaps they might even have been able to discuss those things at length at a cocktail party or some other such venue. They may well have been able to undertake an analysis of Gandhi's philosophy, but whether or not any of it was ever taken to heart is a different matter altogether, hence questions two and three. The first question related to "knowledge of," the other questions addressed impact.

The probe behind question two related to imagination, as in whether or not anything of his teachings, his life, or his moral example had captured students' imaginations. Through the wording of the question, I sought to differentiate between Gandhi's lived experiences (his life, the moral example that he set, his actions, and so on) and his teachings (non-violence, *satyagraha*, and so on). I included the example, "Do you continue to ponder …," because I also wondered whether any learning continued long after the university classes were over. As for question three, its concern was relevance: When all things were said and done, did the former students find Gandhi's teachings to have any relevance for them? Here I was hoping that the responses would allow further clarifications as to different forms of relevance. I had at least three types in mind: application or selective appropriation of certain elements of Gandhi's teachings; instrumental use or implementation of some techniques or attitudes; and integration – that is, having one's outlook informed by Gandhian thought.

For each question I provided some prompting, but left the questions open-ended so that former students could determine whether the question fit their experience. If it did, they could draw upon that experience in their responses. As well, I kept the questions short so as not to demand too much time of my respondents, knowing full well that people are much less likely to bother with extended questionnaires. I kept the questions brief in the hope that my former students would be encouraged to respond. Realizing that it is an act of goodwill when anyone responds to an appeal such as mine – or as one respondent put it, "Still assigning homework after all these years?" – I wanted to honour their time.

Contacting former students was both easy and difficult. Over my years of teaching I have maintained contact with many students, more than a few of whom are now colleagues, with completed doctorates and university positions. These and other former students with whom I have kept in contact were easy to contact via email, and almost all of them readily responded to the questions. Social networking sites like Facebook made it easy to locate others, either through a name search or by tracking them through the web of friends of friends. Web searches located others, although here as on the Facebook pages, shared common names made it difficult at times to identify the right person. There were students I remembered whom I wanted to contact, but had no means with which to do so. At the time of this study, I had already retired from my university position, so I had no institutional support to help with the research or to help locate alumni.

Not being able to locate students was one problem; another was partial recall. I had shredded all my old class lists when I cleaned my files upon retirement, assuming that I would never again have need for them. When it came to this study I was wrong on that score, as I would have had a much wider net of former students to contact (although I do not regret for one second that shred-fest). As a result, an unintentional bias is built into this study. The responses do not come from a random selection of former students, but rather from former students with whom I am still in contact or from individuals whose names I remembered for one reason or another. Such students were more engaged with the material, or more motivated, or more talkative, hence more memorable. It is not that their involvement in class discussions revealed them to be more receptive to Gandhi's teachings – in fact, that was often not the case. Rather, their participation reflected interest in the material that, as their responses to my questions will demonstrate, remains strong. Put another way, their evaluations of Gandhi's activism provided them with useful analytic tools. Now, in later life and on their own career paths, many of these former students have on occasion considered the applications of Gandhi's teachings.

Respondents

Relying on memory and the sleuth work mentioned above, I attempted to contact via email twenty-eight former students. Of these, twenty-two responded, stating their willingness to help out with the case study. I received no response whatsoever from the other six. In the end, seventeen former students sent in write-ups, ranging in length from one to three pages. Workload, family concerns, and other reasons prevented the other five from providing detailed responses. Over two decades of teaching were represented in these responses. Among the respondents were people who had taken the Gandhi course in the late 1980s, the early 1990s, the mid- to late 1990s, and on into the first decade of the 2000s. My earliest years of teaching as well as my last years were represented.

The respondents are somewhat diverse. Several are of Indian origin, either born in Canada to immigrant parents or born abroad. Their backgrounds reflect the Indian diaspora; Indian communities from the Caribbean, Africa, the Middle East, and South Asia are represented. Other respondents come from a range of Euro-Canadian backgrounds. With one or two exceptions, the respondents hold postgraduate degrees; several have completed or almost completed doctorates. Their professions include publishing, journalism, library science, community development, policy analysis, university work as faculty and senior staff, teaching, and marketing. Some of the respondents are still in graduate school. The professional categories represented in this list reflect how the respondents were identified and contacted.

All of the respondents stated that they had retained much of the content of the course – a lot, in fact. One of the assigned readings in the course was Gandhi's autobiography, and it was not surprising that the former students had good recall of the details of his life, "his years in South Africa and his activism for indentured workers, his career as a lawyer, his violent treatment of his wife and his eventual movement away from such violent behaviours, as well as some of his stranger habits when he was older and living in the ashram." Former students remembered campaigns, earlier ones in India that turned violent, the carefully organized Dandi Salt March, "his going to meet Winston Churchill wearing his homespun cotton dhoti," and his taking his niece to his "bed, naked, as a test of his sexual desires."

But their recall did not stop with those recitations. Often the respondents highlighted something of Gandhi's life or teachings that they recalled, and then followed up with their own commentary, as in the case of the individual who mentioned Gandhi's testing his desires by sleeping naked with his niece. She doubted that she would ever forget that, but went on to discuss his teachings on how desire can be controlled. Observing that Gandhi's teachings had had a lasting impact on her, she stated that the course helped her "put a lot of things in perspective." She continues "to ponder the ideas of desires and [continues] to be frustrated by a consumeristic culture that feeds off of desires." Her response – combining recall of an event in Gandhi's life with critical commentary, then application – reflected a recurrent pattern in the responses. In what they wrote, former students returned again and again to a critical assessment of their observations.

The links between the political and personal dimensions of Gandhi's teachings likewise repeatedly appeared in the responses. One former student identified "satyagraha as both a political and personal movement" as the "first thing that comes to mind" when asked what she remembered. Another said much the same, citing recall of "satyagraha, and the importance of this idea for Gandhi's methods of non-violent resistance." Equally important for this respondent was "learning that Gandhi's vision of Indian Self Rule was really more than just liberation from the British, and that Gandhi kept pushing for that larger vision in his political struggles." These and other former students cited "the 'big' Gandhian [ideas] … *ahimsa*/non-violence and satyagraha–non-violent resistance." Their recall maintained a critical edge, as seen in the following observations:

> I recall [Gandhi's] emphasis on self-sacrifice, and that changing his opponent's mind meant appealing to his or her humanity. The satyagrahi nonviolently suffers oppression, deprivation, violence and imprisonment with the ultimate goal of changing the oppressor's mind through his or her own sense of justice or compassion for the one who is suffering. I remember thinking that this system can be very powerful, as long as the oppressor has the capacity for giving in to his or her humanity. There are

many situations in which bureaucracy, for example, or group-think can desensitize the oppressor to the suffering of the oppressed. In situations like that, I believe satyagraha will fail.

For another former student, the course mattered because of the deeper understanding of violence/non-violence that the study of Gandhi's "experiments with truth" offered. This former student set his explanation in the context of his own life. He had often faced violence or bullying, both physical and psychological, earlier in life due to his mixed racial background. Of "East Indian origin (father's side) from the Caribbean, from the same type of Indian diaspora" as Gandhi's compatriots in South Africa, this student grew up in a locality where his "family were the only people of colour." For him, "no matter how many times [he] faced bullies, or prejudiced people, as a youth [his] emotional response was always to fight back aggressively, because [he] felt he had no other means." Through the study of Gandhi's life, however, he began to see non-violence "more spiritually" as "a means of effecting change … By not doing, not responding how others would want one to respond (violence in response to violence), [one] may affect in them a change, [a chance] to view the conflict differently."

This individual has gone on to apply and experiment with Gandhian techniques of conflict transformation, with mixed results, learning more each step of the way. As he put it, "I spent the next (at least) 15 years trying to figure out how to make satyagraha work in my life and what it meant." Among his insights was recognition of the importance of communication: "Change cannot be affected without communication," and often, the fear of engaging with another, "the fear of conflict through engagement of my opponent" prevents communication, which in turn inhibits any meaningful non-violent resolutions.

Effects

The Value of Critical Thinking

In addressing the question of what they recalled from the course, a good number of the former students highlighted the critical thinking skills they had gained. As one former student put it: "The main thing I took away from the course is the ability to think critically about what otherwise has been presented in media and popular culture as a very two dimensional understanding of what Gandhi stood for … [The] course challenged this representation." Now a university professor himself, he went on to add that the course also gave him a deeper appreciation of "Gandhi's intelligence." He observed that Gandhi's "utilization of print media and other modern forms of communication" demonstrated "that behind the serene monastic image" he had associated with Gandhi (an image that he felt Gandhi "spent considerable time producing and managing") "was a systematic and brilliant mind." Likewise, another former student wrote of being struck by how politically astute he was.

Another former student wrote about "analyzing [Gandhi's] autobiography critically" and becoming aware "that it was not a simple, straightforward retelling of his life." She spoke with appreciation of learning to do a "good, critical reading of a text." These observations about what was gained from taking a Gandhi course speak to the larger goals of a liberal arts education. Here, the analytic tools so prized by liberal arts educators were working at several levels. First, the students had moved past being passive recipients of the material at hand – in this case, passive recipients of popular understandings of Gandhi and his teachings. To accept views and claims uncritically was no longer possible after class discussions that situated, contextualized, and interrogated information and writings.

Often, the most effective challenges to complacency came from the students themselves through their participation in the give and take of class discussions. Informing these discussions was a dialectic through which students learned to examine their own understandings by responding to the challenges and questions that others posed. An outcome was often not simply the defence of the earlier held view, but a refinement of it that took into consideration the validity of others' views. A further outcome – a second level – was an enriched understanding of what Gandhi did and what he stood for. More nuanced understandings resulted. As one former student put it, "after the course I felt I understood Gandhi's political philosophies much better, but I also understood him as a person, who was both a great soul and also a flawed human being, much better from our readings and discussions." Class participants came to a better understanding of the development of Gandhi's thought, and how over a career of personal and political activism spanning many decades, he devised and modified his strategies.

In doing that, students saw how Gandhi interrogated his own actions and understandings, in the process drawing upon both his successes and his failures, as well his understandings of the social and political arenas in which he was working. One former student noted that "aside from the actual teachings of ahimsa and satyagraha, I think the most important thing I took away from [the Gandhi] class was the idea of critical thinking in general." Her observation pertained not simply to thinking critically about Gandhi, but also to the fact that Gandhi himself provided an example of critical thought in praxis. In her words, "what struck me the most was that Gandhi did what he did because he had the training and wisdom to question authority and the status quo, in a way that was consistent with his ethics and beliefs." For her, the application of Gandhian thought involves not a mimicking of Gandhian ideas, but instead an ability to question. She wrote, "I feel so fortunate to have been exposed to thinkers like Gandhi and so many others throughout my liberal arts education – I'm not sure where I would be if I hadn't been [exposed to these thinkers]; certainly I wouldn't have some of the tools I have now in terms of critically interpreting the society/culture I live in." In fact, her advocacy of the value of this formation is so strong that she now works in the field of promoting liberal arts education.

Her comments along with the others above are as much a testimony to the worth of a liberal arts education in the current educational climate preoccupied with practical training, as they are a testimony to the utility of a Gandhi course. These comments highlight how liberal arts training – here, a study of Gandhi's life and thought – lends itself to a pedagogical process that enables students to take apart and reconstitute received wisdom.

Continued Questioning

Critical thinking is one aim of liberal arts education. Another is the encouraging of continued learning. The aim is not to give students the sense that they have mastered the material and hence need not think of it any more. Such an approach forestalls further questioning. Instead, the intent is to instill in students the desire to seek better understanding, and to continue to do so long after a class is over. One can compare this process to the planting of a seed that takes time to germinate.

Gandhi himself offers a model of this approach through his continued experiments with the power of non-violence and proactive love in the political and social arenas in colonial South Africa and India. Informing those experiments was a logic based on an unshakable faith in the human capacity for empathy. Its feasibility, however, was tempered by the realities of the Indian independence struggle, particularly the human capacity for violence, as seen for example in the horrific communal violence that followed Partition.

The question of the feasibility of Gandhi's concept of *satyagraha* was one that former students continued to ponder. Here is how one former student put it:

> I regard [Gandhi] and his teachings as historically relevant, and deeply philosophical/intellectual. One of the first words that came to mind was satyagraha, I think perhaps because it was a point of struggle throughout the course. His satyagraha campaigns which I believe he regarded as universally applicable were at times bewildering. I think that perhaps in the

context of my very modern and very western life, I could not connect very well with his ideas. I could never quite access and grasp them the way I wanted to. Perhaps my soul-force is not nearly developed enough.

What is striking in these remarks is the unwillingness to dismiss Gandhi's ideas, matched with frustration at not being able to grasp them in the way Gandhi did. The issue was not a lack of comprehension, for this former student was more than capable of that. Rather, the issue was one of resonance – or, put another way, of sharing Gandhi's outlook. The comment, "Perhaps my soul-force is not nearly developed enough," points to the conceptual gap separating them. In what is no small irony, this individual is perhaps questioning whether anyone, Gandhi included, has such perfected soul-force.

Others addressed the same issue:

> The other thing that has stuck with me [the first being Gandhi's notion of self-determination as expressed in *Hind Swaraj*], which I ponder over from time to time, was Gandhi's firm belief in the good in everyone, and that the method of satyagraha was intended to appeal to that good nature which is present in everyone. I often wonder how much it would take to truly reach that aspect of each person.

She goes on to state that although others may find this belief far too idealistic, too time-consuming, too costly, and not feasible in some conflict situations, she still takes to heart the conviction "that this goodness is indeed there, and should always be appealed to through non-violent forms of protest." Whether it is universally applicable, however, remains a question for her. By the same token, another person spoke of finding inspiration in Gandhi's outlook. "I think about [Gandhi] at lot when I wonder if anyone can really make a significant, positive difference. I also think about him when I question the strength and effectiveness of kindness and goodwill."

Another former student took a pragmatic approach to the question of applicability of *satyagraha*:

> I also recall the instance where one of Gandhi's satyagraha campaigns [at Chauri Chaura, 1922] became extremely violent, a turn of events that distressed him greatly. Following that, the very successful Dandi Salt March was very carefully organized. To me, it was an indication that satyagraha movements can work, but perhaps only [in] very specific circumstances, with participants who are well-schooled in the movement's premises.

Here the respondent is suggesting that success in a movement aimed at political and social transformation depends not only on commitment to the movement's means and methods, but also on discipline. Another former student considers the importance of a focused cause as a catalyst. Reflecting on Gandhi's Salt March, "how a small necessity for common life can be used to initiate a movement," and comparing it with the 2007 Saffron Revolution in Burma sparked by rising gas prices, she queries, "Does a movement need a direct threat to daily life to achieve such dramatic results?" For her, the question is not merely theoretical, as her current position as the program coordinator of a human rights organization for minority groups operating out of Thailand deals directly with the ways and means of strategizing effective change.

Leadership was another concern. The question of charisma continued to fascinate but also trouble one individual: "I wonder how one person had so much influence and power over a group of people dedicated to a movement that sought peace." Another thought logistically: "How can change be implemented without a leader of such calibre [as Gandhi]?" She added that it was not just his calibre, but also his willingness and readiness to assume the responsibility of leadership. Again the question is not merely theoretical. The former student mentioned above who is deeply involved in human rights work in Asia raised a similar question: "Will [social and political movements] work without a figurehead? ... Would other current struggles for self-determination benefit from a Gandhi-like leader?" In the context of her work with groups that had been marginalized by reasons of ethnicity, religion, economic disparity, and other vectors of minority status, this same individual raised other questions about Gandhi's theories of non-violence, about which more will be said below.

Impact

In various ways, my former students found lasting value in their exposure to Gandhi's life and teachings. One person went on to study concepts of non-violent resistance (in a contemporary Buddhist context) at the PhD level. One particularly ecologically-minded individual highlighted "the example Gandhi set of self-sufficiency, of making his own clothes," and his warnings about the entrapments of technology. Recognizing that other thinkers and activists have expressed similar views, she noted the parallels between Gandhi's critiques of the British textile industry's impact on India and contemporary critiques on the industrial food complex. For her, in some ways, Gandhi's advocacy of *swadeshi* (own production) was more encompassing, and she registered disappointment "that more aspects of our basic needs, such as clothing, have not become part of [the support local] movement in the same way that food has." Sharing Gandhi's view that the personal is political, she emphasized the importance of self-sufficiency as well as community formation.

Another former student of Indian descent "who has never lived in India" described how the course gave her a feeling of being connected to her roots. The ability to speak with conviction about Gandhi and his teachings had given her a sense of pride. Other former students mentioned travel and how the sight of monuments to Gandhi prompted reflection. One person spoke of finding Gandhi statues everywhere, and never giving "up on trying to figure out non-violence and what it meant," while aware of the irony that his travels had taken him to "so many places affected by violence, with conflict … central to the operation of so many cultures."

Yet another former student described going to India, a country that had caught his imagination thanks to the Gandhi and other undergraduate Religion and Culture courses. While there he sought to explore Gandhi's legacy in the nation he had helped shape. He visited Gandhi's ashram in Ahmadabad, queried Indians as to how they viewed Gandhi (with the question of apotheosis in the back of his mind), and sought out a lecture by one of the Mahatma's granddaughters. The memory of Gandhi was the trail he pursued. There was more, however, than just intellectual curiosity to his story. He and his wife went on to volunteer at Corrymeela, a peace and reconciliation retreat in Ballycastle, Northern Ireland. The mood at the centre expressed the trust in human potential that Gandhi shared; their work brought them in contact with others who "worked to activate social change through non-violence." Reflecting back on this period in their lives, this former student noted that he and his wife "were inspired to go there because of the kinds of things we valued, such as Gandhi's use of non-violent activism."

Application

Another former student likewise travelled to India, where she spent time with an organization based on Gandhi's principles of non-violent social transformation. Its goals included the empowerment of women through economic self-sufficiency and social change. There she saw Gandhian teachings at work, including *swadeshi*. She wrote how the women "spun their own fabric and dyed it using natural dyes." Since then her activism had taken her to more than a few places. She had gone on to volunteer in Israel/Palestine with Sabeel, a non-violent Christian Palestinian Liberation theological organization that condemns all use of violence. While there, she acted in solidarity with the Palestinian people, going through checkpoints with them, visiting refugee camps, helping farmers cultivate lands they could not reach, and "most importantly, [I listened] … [watching my] friends resist the Occupation without hatred and violence, but with a sense of hope." As well, she had visited the Christian Peacemaker Teams, "who literally 'get in the way' of violence in order to protect those who are vulnerable and in hopes of diffusing the tensions." Other activism had taken her to Cairo and to Toronto in preparation for the G20 Summit in 2009. For her, non-violent resistance remained a key focus. She wrote that "when thinking about the ways that [she] can engage critically in social justice issues within Canada and around the globe," she continued to ponder certain of Gandhi's teachings about *satyagraha* and *ahimsa*.

With regard to her work and to that of the couple mentioned above who volunteered in Northern Ireland, one cannot argue for direct linkage – that the study of Gandhi directly led to their work in the field of conflict resolution. Nonetheless, their appreciation of Gandhian teachings played a role in their social involvement. Arguably, their interest in Gandhi's theories of non-violence was already in place, factoring into their choice to take a course focused on Gandhi's life and thought in the first place. What the course – coupled with their real-life experiences – offered was a better means of appraising Gandhi's theories and their workability. As the person involved in the planning sessions for the G20 protests observed, in light of the physical assaults her friends suffered during the protests, many were now questioning the efficacy of non-violence. Some were arguing for other tactics. At the time of her writing, she honestly did not know where she stood on this issue.

The career of another former student has followed a similar trajectory: she is the program coordinator for a human rights NGO. I have already introduced some of her thoughts on work for social change. Initiatives on behalf of the Canadian government led to her current work through an internship with the Canadian International Development Agency (CIDA). Although CIDA no longer funds the project, its earlier support opened the way for her work in this field. The organization she now works for promotes and protects the rights of minority communities by empowering human rights activists in minority communities in Africa, Asia, and non-EU Europe. She does not participate directly in the communities' struggles for self-determination and human rights; instead, she offers those communities training in how to amplify their efforts.

Her work often leads her to consider Gandhi's non-violent resistance. As she explains, Gandhi's influence looms large; because the organization focuses on human rights, its work takes for granted a non-violent approach, especially in terms of the methods chosen by activists. Even so, questions remain. In her words,

> I consider myself a pretty strong believer in non-violence, primarily as a result of learning about Gandhi and his methods toward achieving Indian

independence. But once I started working with people who are ostensibly working on the promotion and protection of human rights in their
country, and as I realized that many secretly or subtly advocate the use
of violence in some circumstances or as a "compliment" to human rights
work, it really made me question the assumption of non-violence that I
was coming from.

In the field, whether in "Sri Lanka, Nepal, Burma, Aceh, Papua, Mindanao,"
or other conflict zones, she encounters workers whose stance on non-
violence varies from complete support to complete disregard, with many
advocating whatever means are warranted in the circumstances. She rarely
meets activists who are completely committed to non-violence "the likes
of which Gandhi would approve," and she questions "whether the full support of non-violence like we saw in Gandhi really exists in these modern
movements for self-determination and the achievement of human rights
for minority communities." More importantly, she wonders "if the use of
non-violence could really have a significant impact in these situations."

Her work brings into sharp focus what happens when theory meets
the ground. As she observes, Gandhi's teachings defy indiscriminate repro-
duction. In some situations the simple application of what seems to be a
Gandhian approach may prove untenable. Gandhi would be the first to
point that out, as his was a situational logic. For him, context and circum-
stance always mattered. As this former student and now human rights activist points out, those who would utilize Gandhian theories of non-violent
social change require a deep understanding of the realities on the ground.

Notwithstanding the challenges her work poses, she has not lost faith
in Gandhi's teachings: "It is the contrasts between the movement of which
he was a part, modern movements for self-determination and the current
methods used toward achieving human rights in Asian countries, that keeps
me reflecting on Gandhi's teachings and practices, and inspires me to keep
them alive in my work." She also wonders whether more exposure to Gandhi's theories in praxis would matter. She finds that human rights workers
tacitly acknowledge the notion of non-violence. Comprehension, however,
is a different matter altogether. She asked: "How much does the theory and
methodology of non-violence actually reach these human rights defend-
ers?" She wonders whether non-violent activism would be more successful
if it was better informed by a sharper interrogation of Gandhi's teachings.
She does not advocate wholesale application, but she does call for a careful
study of Gandhi's campaigns – his theories in action – with a view to weigh-
ing how his thought can be applied to current situations of human rights
deprivations. Like other former students cited earlier, she remains engaged

with Gandhi's views of conflict transformation through rapprochement. But also like them, she does not view his teachings as simply reproducible; what matters instead are the creative outcomes that can result when his ideas are carefully critiqued.

These individuals seek real outcomes from Gandhi's teachings. So does another former student, who works with at-risk children aged five to fourteen. She states that she draws on and applies "Gandhi's teachings on a daily basis in [her] personal and work life." Her work "involves conflict resolution and teaching those with very little skills and ability to resolve problems effectively, without resorting to violent means." She explains that on many occasions she has introduced Gandhi's ideas, his life, and his teachings:

> I teach diversity to children. I have introduced Gandhi's ideas, his life and teachings, on numerous occasions. They don't understand him or relate to him as much as they adore the Buddha and his teachings, but they do appreciate his ability to resolve conflict without violence. For more of these kids, they have learned that violence is one of the only viable solutions to problems. Also, many children are initially closed off to the idea of learning about different cultures and religions. My response is to introduce Gandhi's idea that learning about different cultures and religions only strengthens one's own beliefs and faith. This idea seems to make sense to most of them and it helped open them up to learning about difference while simultaneously strengthening the idea that it is ok to believe and have faith in spite of what others believe or think. It is a very powerful lesson.

She observes that "the children with whom I work seem to understand and learn from his teachings and they are fascinated by his life story and practices." She finds that Gandhi's teachings affirm difference at several levels. When she relays aspects of Gandhi's life to her students, his ideas prompt them to think of ways other than violence to broker conflict. Also, his demonstrated interest in religions other than his own can help these children mitigate the fear and intolerance that are often root sources of conflict.

Personal Applications of *Satyagraha*

Many who studied Gandhi's teachings with me had found a way to incorporate them into their work; many also had found a place for those teachings in their personal lives. On this latter account as well, my former students likewise had much to say. Many identified the importance of implementing non-violence and conflict transformation in their own lives. Several spoke of wanting to impart to their children a morality that echoed Gandhi's, a "standing up for the oppressed, fighting for equality, and non-violence."

Gandhi was an exemplar of these teachings, but they are not his alone, as one person pointed out when he observed that his "Protestant mother had drilled these same values into [my] head since [I] was a child." Still, he noted, "the lessons of Gandhi's life are something that have been internalized for [me] and have become part of the value system [I try] to pass on to [my] own children."

Another person spoke of drawing upon Gandhi's views of conflict transformation within his household:

> The course on Gandhi shaped me and has had a significant impact on where I stand in life, now. In my personal relationship, my wife and I declared our household a non-aggressive household. Learning something from what Gandhi taught, and modifying it to the needs of a household, we use our words to resolve problems and not behaviours. We recognize that there is a difference between being assertive and presenting a case for what we strongly believe and taking action to support our beliefs, as opposed to using aggression to push our will over anyone who disagrees with us.

He recounted that he and his wife "ha[d] passed this system of conflict resolution and problem solving on to [their] children." Those children were still young, yet he saw them applying what they had learned. He found it edifying "to see them use these tools to the best of their abilities, even if they have varying degrees of success." He went on to remark:

> If we can teach our children to solve their problems non-violently, to engage with conflict, but not fear it, and to communicate how they would like things to change and what they are trying to do with their actions toward creating that change, then we hope that other children may learn a different way of problem solving than through aggressive means, which is still so evident on the playground and social circles in classes. We ask ourselves, and our children, how is it you would like to be? What would you like to see change in the world? We have Gandhi's famous saying, "Be the change you want to see in the world" prominently displayed in our home and seriously try to live by those words.

These comments testify to the couple's careful cultivation of a way of living that draws inspiration from Gandhi. They are aware of their choices, and they want to pass their understandings of the potential of self-awareness on to their children.

Another former student wrote that although she was unaware of ever having consciously drawn on Gandhian techniques, she had found an assimilation of Gandhian ideas of *anekantvada* (a teaching originally from the Jain tradition about the reconciliation of multiple points of view):

I *do* attempt to put myself in the "other's" position more often – and I think that learning about Gandhi really helped this to blossom within me. In conflict, I attempt to fully understand what my motivations may be for wanting a certain outcome and, in turn, attempt to fully understand what the other person's/group's/etc. motivations may be for wanting a certain outcome, or for acting in a certain manner.

It saddened her that this approach "is not something that is employed on a larger scale – the first move is always toward condemnation rather than understanding (or so it seems)." She identified a crucial element in Gandhi's teachings of *satyagraha*: "The reason Gandhi's method of conflict transformation was so revolutionary is that immediate understanding was implicit in the method – how else could you accept an action of violence toward your person without retaliation?" Noting that other factors, both spiritual and moral, can contribute to the withholding of retaliation, she maintained that even these factors should eventually prompt a more measured exploration of the causes of conflict. As she put it, "they all lead one to question: why? Why would this person act this way toward me? Answering that question can only lead to some form of understanding." That in turn begins the process of conflict transformation. As another person, a writer, put it: "To yield? Imagine it." Elsewhere he opined that the lesson Gandhi offered was "proof that utterly counter-intuitive ideas can work."

Another former student drew attention to this same process of considering others' positions. She observed that she was not a confrontational person by nature. When, however, she found herself in a conflict situation, she thought "it best to remain calm and polite and to give both sides the opportunity to express themselves and find common ground." Like the other person who noted that she did not consider her actions to be consciously Gandhian, this individual found that when she worked to find common ground, she did not think of herself "as enacting Gandhian principles," but she supposed "it is the kind of thing that a true satyagrahi learns to do."

Continued Inspiration

A meditation on Gandhi sent in by a writer who took the course in the post-9/11 world took up a similar theme of recognizing shared humanity. I've already quoted some of his words:

Gandhi's action and deep studies on Truth displayed that we can, by submission, sacrifice, and devotion to Truth be victorious over, as Hunter Thompson writes, "the forces of old and evil." That we can do it with dignity. That, if we hold ourselves to our highest standard, we triumph. That kindness exists in times of suffering, loss, in hardship. That through it all, our humanity binds us into more than the essential logical binary of an unstoppable force against an immovable object. Us versus Them.

To yield? Imagine it. To let the other side wash over and reveal there was no actual difference, no need to be separate in the first place. Our singular humanity. Our final slip of the binary noose …

Gandhi drowned the "I" in an overwhelming sea of empathy. He knew that, at our best, we bypass that switch in the brain and become something bigger than any of us could be; I become us. We become everything and feel the suffering of the many as our own.

So for some students, Gandhi's inspiration continued. But that was not the case for all of them. One person wrote that she rarely thought about Gandhi except when a reference to him came up. In her words, "my thought is influenced by the current socio-economic situation and often more modern thinkers." Although committed to positive change, she noted that she "cannot think of a time that [I had] drawn upon or applied any of Gandhi's teachings in particular." Indeed, she would "be hard-pressed to provide a detailed description of his thought and beliefs." Others, while remaining interested in Gandhian thought, said much the same – that Gandhi's teachings had little resonance for them. When his thought and style of activism came up in conversation, the knowledge they had gained from the Gandhi course proved useful, but otherwise, it had no direct relevance to them. Still, one person who was quite candid regarding the absence of "substantial or lasting impact" had considered from time to time "how the troubles of the Western world could use some Gandhian influence in terms of developing consciousness, compassion, and emphasis on cultivating morality for the common good." And another former student, a journalist-activist of Sri Lankan descent, envisioned how a Gandhian approach to conflict could help mitigate the violence in her country of origin. Pressed, however, on the question of whether she had ever drawn on Gandhi's teachings in her work, her answer was "no." But she was now thinking that she would like to give them a try.

Conclusions

So what do these responses tell us? First off, I would hazard that liberal arts courses that teach critical thinking skills do matter in the larger scheme of things. Former students were both cognizant of and appreciative of the skills they had acquired in the Gandhi course. Even at a distance of more than a few years (and in some instances more than two decades), they retained the ability to think critically about Gandhi's teachings. Also striking (for me at least) was the amount of information they had retained about Gandhi and his teachings. In their responses, many offered concise summaries of the material that we had covered in the course.

Related to that observation is another that speaks to Gandhi's legacy. More than a few former students mentioned that they continued to reflect on Gandhi's views of non-violence, his techniques of conflict transformation, and his larger pronouncements on human potential for positive change. Even those former students who admitted that they had never drawn upon any of Gandhi's strategies for personal or interpersonal change stated that they still contemplated his ideas. The skeptical among them admitted they did not share Gandhi's appraisal of the human capacity for goodness, or they tempered that appraisal with equal recognition of the human capacity for ill will. But somewhere Gandhi's ideas had struck a chord – otherwise, they would not still be pondering them from time to time. Only one of the former students I managed to contact stated flatly that she neither recalled nor cared about Gandhi's teachings.

Yet several former students described how they had tried to integrate into their lives – and those of their children – Gandhian ideals of consensual conflict transformation. For them, their study of Gandhi and his teachings was more than an intellectual exercise. They sought to cultivate the ability to reconcile differences by means commensurate with Gandhi's teachings. Their thoughtfulness perhaps echoes a typically Canadian approach to conflict, one that tempers aggressive impulses with attempts to understand first the source of conflict, followed by attempts to mitigate its expression. Some pointed out that their style of interpersonal interaction had not resulted from their study of Gandhi; rather, Gandhi's thought had reinforced some of their own conclusions regarding the nature of conflict. They were quick to identify the resonance between areas of Gandhi's thought and their own. It seems from their comments that Gandhi's teachings had found a place in their awareness of their own interactions. Clearly, these individuals were not slavish followers of Gandhi's teaching – devotees, as it were. Rather, their systems of thought had developed in ways that integrated their reflections on Gandhi's ideas. This suggests that their study of Gandhi did have some impact on their personal formation.

With regard to larger political and social arenas, the results from this small case study are telling. Two individuals identified correlations between the work they were now doing and Gandhi's advocacy for social change. They described how in reflecting on their current work, they turned for inspiration to Gandhi's various experiments in social and political reform. This did not mean adapting Gandhian strategies wholesale. Rather, their ongoing consideration of Gandhian non-violent resistance served as an analytic tool for critiquing their own work.

Also telling – although the sample on which this case study is based is too small to gauge its actual significance – is that those former students who engaged Gandhi's thought in human rights work did so beyond Canada's borders. With one exception – the G20 protests in Toronto in 2009 – their efforts at effecting meaningful change in people's lives at the political level took place outside North America. Given the limited sample, no conclusions should be drawn from this. Even so, it is tempting to suggest at least one implication: that activism on a global scale should take place elsewhere and not here. This may offer as much a commentary on understandings of Canada as it does on Gandhi's teachings. At the same time, one person working with at-risk children in Canada was emphatic about the importance of Gandhi's teachings in her work. In her diversity workshops with children, she found that Gandhi served as a useful model in affirming difference. In a country made up of people from many diverse backgrounds, religions, and ethnicities, those lessons are invaluable.

To return to the design of this case study, the questions I put to former students sought to determine whether they had applied or selectively appropriated any elements of Gandhi's teachings, whether they had used or implemented Gandhian techniques or attitudes, and whether they had integrated any elements of Gandhian thought into their lives. Surprisingly – or perhaps not surprisingly – in the responses returned to me, I found evidence of all three impulses, albeit to varying degrees. In teaching a Gandhi course, it was never my aim to transform students into practising Gandhians. My aim was to get them thinking about Gandhi and to enable them to ask good, hard questions about his teachings. That they were able to do this, and in the course of being "inspired and brought down to earth at the same time," suggests to me that these Canadian students found something valuable in the exercise.

Note

1 Rushdie, "Mohandas Gandhi."

ॐ

The Gandhian-Inspired *Mahila Shanti Sena* Movement in India and Its Canadian Connection

Anne M. Pearson

This chapter examines the creation and development of the *Mahila Shanti Sena* (MSS), or women's peace brigade, founded in Bihar, India, in 2002, exploring in particular the significant Canadian connection to this Gandhian-inspired movement. The MSS is a loosely organized movement, based in northeastern India, aimed at fostering women's leadership in the creation of a culture of peace and prosperity at local and especially village levels. Women help other women find solutions to problems they face, including domestic violence, alcohol abuse, poverty, and lack of access to education and employment. The MSS provides training in collective action leadership, women's legal rights, and conflict resolution, while promoting the Gandhian tradition of engaging in constructive village service. The MSS is not identified with any particular religion, political party, or social group. It does evoke and utilize principles that Gandhi had identified as crucial to India's development, including non-violence, equality of women and men, education as a prerequisite for self-determination, self-reliance, consultative decision-making, service, and the spirit of sacrifice for the common good.

The Formation of the *Mahila Shanti Sena*

In encouraging women to become actively engaged in the nationalist movement, Gandhi described them as having special capacities for self-sacrifice and for leadership in peacebuilding. He said that the world had been too long dominated by "masculine" aggressive qualities and that it was time that the "feminine" qualities came to the fore. He described non-violence as "woman's inborn virtue," and he suggested that men need to generate womanly qualities in themselves to become non-violent, as he himself had done. Women, he thought, were accustomed to making sacrifices for the family, and they could now extend that spirit of sacrifice to the country. He invited all women to enlist in his non-violent army. Thousands of Indian women from all walks of life did respond to his call in the 1930s and 1940s to become actively involved in India's struggle for independence. Yet after independence, the momentum behind the encouragement of women's leadership in political and social arenas dwindled, and the linkage between women's advancement, the country's development, and the achievement of a culture of peace was obscured.[1]

Furthermore, Gandhi's call for bottom-up, locally directed, and inclusive social, political, and economic development was largely ignored by India's political leadership. While Article Forty of India's constitution provided that "the state shall take steps to organize village *panchayats* [councils] and endow them with such powers and authority as may be necessary to enable them to function as units of self-government,"[2] it had not been meaningfully implemented. The lack of implementation led to growing demands for a stronger constitutional mandate for local governance. These demands were met by the Seventy-Third and Seventy-Fourth Amendments to the Constitution of India in December 1992, which, among other provisions, required the reservation of one-third of the total number of *panchayat* seats for women.[3] With the enactment of these amendments, new hopes were raised for women's influence in local governance. In the northeastern state of Bihar, a state with one of India's highest illiteracy rates and population densities, the April 2001 elections resulted in 45,000 women being elected to *panchayats*. Most of these women found themselves elected to public office for the first time, and many of them found themselves ill equipped for the challenge due to illiteracy and inexperience with village councils and public decision-making.

Acharya Ramamurti, renowned Gandhian and long-time director of the Bihar-based organization *Shrambharati Khadigram*,[4] realized after these elections that the unprecedented numbers of women now sitting on these councils represented an extraordinary opportunity for women to regain the lost momentum of the heady years leading to India's independence. As council members, women could begin to influence policy priorities at the local level in ways that truly met the needs of women, children, families, and communities. Then in his nineties, Ramamurti began to work on a plan to invite some of the elected women, among other women, to a week-long training camp to assist them in becoming better equipped for their new roles, and in facilitating change in their communities. Referring to Gandhi's idea of establishing a *shanti sena* ("peace brigade"), he decided to call the trained women the *Mahila Shanti Sena*, or "women's peace corps."[5] "The village community needs an army of peace-workers, who will not fight among themselves but are willing to solve problems and resolve conflicts and disputes peacefully," Ramamurti said. "In this task of neighbourhood-building, women are likely to be better than men. That is the rationale of Mahila Shanti Sena ... Can we not use her [woman's] creative talents to make society more humane and enlightened?"[6] What Ramamurti had in mind also was Gandhi's statement that "if nonviolence is the law of our being, the future is with women."

The first MSS training took place in 2002, followed by a meeting of Gandhian activists and academics, who gathered in the village of Vaishali, Bihar, to consider the implications of *panchayatiraj*, the need to promote participatory democracy and peacebuilding and women's role therein. Vaishali was chosen as an auspicious location for this event due to its historical association with the Buddha and also Mahavira. Furthermore, the ancient republic of Vaishali had been the first kingdom in India to experiment with democracy, and it is near the area where Gandhi launched his *satyagraha* against British control over indigo cultivation. Indeed, during this campaign, Gandhi also first introduced women-led education initiatives.[7]

Professor Rama Singh of McMaster University (Hamilton, Ontario, Canada), who had met Ramamurti in 1998, organized a delegation from the McMaster Centre for Peace Studies and the Edmonton-based Mahatma Gandhi Canadian Foundation for World Peace. Thus it was that I had the privilege of attending the founding of the MSS in February 2002, just as a fresh outbreak of Hindu–Muslim communal violence erupted in Gujarat. At this gathering, the first cohort of one hundred or so *shanti sainiks* ("peace workers"), rural and largely low-caste women who came from nearby districts, shared with us personal stories of hardship as well as songs they had created during their week of training. Included in such stories were statements like this one: "I was just nine when I got married – I did not even know the meaning of marriage – no daughters should be forced to be married so young. My daughter will be married according to *her* wishes. Education is crucial." Another said: "If women become the leaders, there will be a change in women's conditions [such as] an increase in education. Many women die in childbirth – there would be a reduction in such crimes." One woman noted that for women to become leaders, they would need to start at home with themselves, and "we have to peacefully oppose men and others in our homes who try to suppress us. We need the support of other women. We have to work together to be successful. To get the society that we want will take many painful steps. Even members of your own families will oppose you. But we need to persevere. Can we all accept the challenge of this suffering to bring about change?" And finally, one woman concluded that "in this gathering, with this orange scarf [worn by all the *Shanti Sena* women], I feel very proud and fortunate. After learning about peace here, I want to go to every village [and tell what happened]. I should follow my duty and light the whole nation. I beg all of you that you can see a better future for women."

From words like these, communicated in a heartfelt and powerful manner by women who had direct experience of the effects of poverty, who suffered systemic and social violence, who lacked education, and who often lacked encouragement, it was clear that they knew what the priorities should be. It was a matter of working together to find solutions – not from the government, not from some outside agencies, but from among themselves. That is what the MSS is all about.

Development of the MSS

Much has transpired in the ensuing years – too much to adequately convey in this brief chapter. Suffice to say that hundreds of women in seven states (Bihar, Uttar Pradesh [UP], Assam, Manipur, Arunachal Pradesh, Tripura, and Odisha) have taken the vow to be *Mahila Shanti Sainiks* following training, while tens of thousands have participated in peace marches, assemblies, and one-day workshops.[8] Partnerships have formed between local MSS groups and NGOs, from the UN Children's Fund (UNICEF) in Bihar, to the *Tamulpur Anchalik Gramdan Sangh* in Guwahati, Assam, to *Unnayun* in Odisha, among others. Relationships with Indian universities and with Gandhian organizations have been established. Despite minimal funds (and the deaths of Acharya Ramamurti and his right-hand man in the North-East, Gandhian elder Ravindra Upadhyaya, in 2010), numerous stories of success have been reported. The MSS has focused on peacebuilding, conflict resolution, and problem-solving skills to an unusual degree among comparable grassroots development organizations. Violence and the threat of violence remain constant hindrances to the security and sustainable development of many local communities in India. Women are often targeted by violence (or certain forms of violence). That they are being given some simple tools to prevent and reduce conflict, and to address direct violence, and that they are being supported by the strength of numbers, are extraordinary features of the MSS, bearing witness to its name. Inspired by the vision of the MSS and emboldened to take action, women *shanti sainiks* have worked collectively in villages to close toddy shops where the easy availability of alcohol was allowing the squandering of scarce resources by male family members. Cases of rape and domestic abuse situations – often ignored by local police – have been addressed, as have been disputes between neighbours. Literacy training, self-help groups, and small businesses have been established, each success creating a momentum for change and instilling greater confidence and respect among the women protagonists.

The March 2012 issue of the MSS newsletter offers several reports of *shanti sainik* actions described by the women themselves at a meeting in Bubhaneshwar, Odisha, including the following. According to Mamata Misra, "a peaceful protest by 150 MSS women in front of the Block Development Office resulted in allocation of much needed funds for a road in the village, which now reminds everyone of the power of unity and purpose."[9] Misra adds that

> Damayanti from Sambalpur spoke … about her group's initial struggles, the opposition women faced from men of the village and police. Then came an opportunity to prove oneself by solving a big problem affecting the whole village. Her village had a dispute with a neighboring village. Her villagers had a fish farm where they had worked very hard. But just before harvest time, some people from a neighboring village started claiming the fish farm and the fish as theirs. The men of the two villages started fighting … [but] the men from the neighboring village had more power and filed court cases against them. At this point, the women resolved to do something about the injustice. They came in great numbers riding tractors, bicycles, and on foot seeking justice in the case and offering their testimony about the truth of the matter. They won not only the fish for the village but also the respect of others in their ability.[10]

At such gatherings of women *shanti sainiks*, stories of challenges and successes encourage women to continue to struggle for justice and social change. Unfortunately, because of inadequate funding and the lack of a central organization, such regional gatherings cannot be held as often as would be beneficial to maintain the movement's momentum. Furthermore, MSS's decentralization, along with its need to partner with like-minded NGOs (organizations that normally have their own particular mandates and are beholden to their funders), has caused the MSS to lose some of its focus on implementing Ramamurti's Gandhian-inspired vision. Thus, for example, a rapid action force capable of intervening in local developing conflicts has yet to be created.

The Canadian Connection to the MSS Beyond Its Founding

To raise awareness of the MSS in India, to enable fundraising, and to share learning from India that might be applicable in the Canadian context, MSS International was established as a Canadian-incorporated NGO in 2008. Rama Singh, its founder, continues to travel to India regularly and has helped organize various conferences related to the MSS where members of the MSS, Gandhian scholars, members of other NGOs who have partnered with or otherwise supported the MSS, and university faculty can meet and share information about the goals, strategies, and successes of the *Mahila Shanti Sena*. McMaster University's Centre for Peace Studies has been a sponsor of some of these meetings. Singh has also established an e-newsletter that keeps readers informed of the progress of the MSS. McMaster Emeritus Professor Gopal Mohanty has played an important role in fanning the flames of the MSS in his home state of Odisha; he too travels to India regularly.

Canadian Student Interns with the MSS

Significantly also, McMaster's Centre for Peace Studies successfully applied for funding from the Canadian International Development Agency (CIDA), managed by a grant program through the Association of Universities and Community Colleges (AUCC) over several years, to send one or two undergraduate students to India for up to three months to learn about the MSS. As of December of 2012, thirteen students have participated, and each has returned to Canada greatly affected by their experiences. They have also received credit for their trips, primarily through writing papers and theses within the requirements of specific departments or programs. I have supervised a number of these papers, which have used the MSS as a case study to investigate the role of civil society in strengthening democracy, the promotion of education for girls, gender and health issues, Gandhian agriculture and poverty reduction, and the building of effective forms of local governance. Students had access to interpreters and were able to conduct interviews with dozens of women involved with the MSS. Some of these papers were then sent back to India in the hope that their analyses would be helpful to the MSS.

One young woman, Ashley, the first of two students to visit India and the MSS on an AUCC-CIDA internship, reflected on her experience as follows: "Acharayaji and Ravindrabhai planted the MSS seed. Since then, the women have truly rolled with it. I remember walking somewhere with Ravindrabhai – the man with a story worthy of a Rushdie novel – and he said, 'Ashley, you know, the very act of us walking here – in conversation, a man and a woman – is changing things. It's changing minds; and that's enough." She continues: "I have gotten to know the 'development' industry rather well since my time with the MSS, and it's entirely lost sight of the importance of changing minds through direct and simple action, peaceful and hyper-local. The MSS has not yet lost that." She went on to say that the women and men of the MSS

> have shaped my life in ways small and large, concrete and diffuse. I went back to India in late 2011 and as I landed in the fancy New Delhi airport thought that while many foreigners would use this as a reason to say – "well, hello India! Let's see what you've got in store for this century!" – I just thought about Bihar, UP and Assam and the vast income inequalities. And I thought about how grateful I was to have "been under the hood," to an extent, of small parts of India … A revolution – I learned from the MSS – was built with slow, intentional and community-based efforts, and was as much about the mind as it was about the community.

Another student, Miekela, related to me that

> after taking many theoretically heavy courses in political science, traveling to India to participate in a program with the MSS was my first big practical field experience. The personal interviews that we conducted … were truly a life changing experience, on a very simple level, actually. It demonstrated to me how much you can learn about people simply by asking. The women that were a part of this movement were looking for changes and the way they understood change was very much about sharing their experiences (with one another, but also with us) … When one of the only tools you have is your story, words become much more powerful.

When I asked Miekela, a law student, about her experience with the MSS, she expressed interest in the intersection of feminist theory, social movements, and law. She credits her experience with the MSS as "hugely significant" for her postgraduate research and career choice.

Yet another student, Nicole, commented:

> As a westerner in … rural India … I was often expected to hold higher knowledge. Women were constantly asking what they should do to improve their situations, or how they should act in particular circumstances. I never approached this internship with the intent of teaching anything, and I wish the women I spent time with knew how much they have taught me, and how much insight and knowledge have been taken back with me to Hamilton. Reflecting upon my experiences now, I believe that women here can learn so much from the MSS movement. Within Hamilton, it is so easy to accept the life we have here, without thinking

critically or challenging the structures that we live in. We often fail to consider how powerful we are, and what changes can be achieved with a unified front. My biggest lesson from India has been in the importance of community; the understanding that no individual or family can achieve success, unless the community as a whole is thriving together.

Finally, a more recent intern, Chelsea, remarked:

Being both a philosophy student and a justice-oriented activist is like playing a logic game: it takes a lot of hard work to reconcile armchair radicalism and direct action. And so, the enlightenment of discovering Gandhi was much like the satisfaction that comes with successfully solving for *x* ... Beginning with my involvement with the Gandhi Peace Festival and extending into the internship offered through McMaster's Centre for Peace Studies, I have had the opportunity to observe – and, in some cases, to test – Gandhi's philosophies of *ahimsa*, *satyagraha*, and *swaraj*. His emphasis on the role of women in building peace, embodied by the women of *Mahila Shanti Sena*, has transformed my relationship with social justice. Connecting with women in India gave me some much-needed perspective on what my role is in challenging global mechanisms of oppression and structural violence. Listening to what their needs are, and their suggestions about what I can do to improve the quality of their children's lives, inspired me to fuse my academic endeavours with my personal commitment to activism ... As a direct result of my internship experiences, I am working towards dedicating my skill set to enhancing a global culture of peace from the grassroots.

Chelsea has a special interest in studying the violent repercussions of industrialized agriculture.

Universities in Canada have a long history of providing opportunities for their undergraduate students to study abroad. University partnerships with organizations like the World University Service of Canada (WUSC) also have a history of providing students with opportunities to engage in what today is often called "service learning." The more recently inaugurated CIDA-AUCC grants were explicitly intended to enable undergraduate students to familiarize themselves with the Canadian government's current (and often annually changing) development assistance priorities, such as poverty reduction, education, and the advancement of women. While the government seems to expect students to be of assistance to the particular population targeted in the grant application, it is far more the case that the Canadian students are the primary beneficiaries of the encounter. In addition, universities are increasingly interested in supporting experiential learning opportunities for their students. No doubt, most students who have the chance to travel, live, and study abroad, especially in so-called developing nations, are enriched by the experience. The students who participated in the CIDA–AUCC internships run through McMaster's Centre for Peace Studies have been especially fortunate insofar as they have been able to meet two of India's outstanding elderly "Gandhians" and to meet and learn from men and women who are striving to enact local, grassroots, practical solutions to the myriad systemic and particularistic challenges they confront every day.

Conclusion

With the 2011 installation of a bust of Gandhi at McMaster, the annual fall Gandhi Peace Festival at City Hall in Hamilton (a festival that celebrated its twentieth anniversary in 2012 with the installation of a full-size statue of Gandhi on the grounds of Hamilton City Hall), the Annual Gandhi Lectureship on non-violence (given in 2003 by Acharya Ramamurti himself), a regular semester course taught on Gandhi, and the relationship with the Gandhian-inspired MSS in India through student internships especially, Gandhi seems to be alive and well in Hamilton. The ongoing efforts of particular individuals from McMaster University and the Hamilton Indo-Canadian community to promote knowledge about Gandhi and the relevance of his teachings for us today in Canada, as well as in India, cannot be underestimated. There have long been pockets of Indians who blame Gandhi for India's partition, among other things. And in India and on the Internet, Gandhi has lately been targeted, especially online, as a racist, sexist autocrat. Such invective can influence Canadians who know little about Gandhi's life and who have scant first-hand knowledge of his voluminous writings. If Gandhi's legacy is to be made meaningful in Canada, we need to counteract uninformed vilification of him and translate his most universally enduring principles into action for positive social change leading to a culture of peace and non-violence.

Notes

1 An earlier version of this section of the paper was previously published as "The Mahila Shanti Sena: New Women's Peace Movement in India," *Peace Magazine* 20, no. 1 (January–March 2004): 15–19.

2 Quoted in Jain, *Panchayat Raj*, 4–5. Jain provides an excellent overview of the history of the Panchayat Raj Institutions (PRIs) up to 1996, and offers a preliminary analysis of its effects on women and local governance in India. Jain notes that in the mid-1980s women represented just 4.4 percent of the membership of national and state assemblies. By 1994, already 330,000 more women had entered politics as a result of PRI. As of 2004, it is over one million. See also Jha, ed., *Women in Panchayati Raj Institutions*.

3 The main features of the act are (a) a three-tier system of Panchayati Raj for all states having populations of over two million; (b) Panchayat elections held every five years; (c) reservation of one-third of seats for Scheduled castes, Scheduled tribes, and women; (d) appointment of State Finance Commissions to make recommendations as regards the financial powers of Panchayats; and (e) the constitution of District Planning Committees to prepare development plans for the district as a whole. The "Panchayati Raj Institutions have been endowed with such powers and authority as may be necessary to function as institutions of self-government and contain provisions for devolution of powers and responsibilities upon Panchayats at the appropriate level with reference to (a) the preparation of plans for economic development and social justice; and (b) the implementation of such schemes for economic development and social justice as may be entrusted to them." Quoted from "Panchayati Raj."

4 Since its founding in the district of Jamui, Bihar, in 1952 by a close associate of Gandhi, Dhirendra Mazumdar, the organization *Shrambharati Khadigram*, led for fifty years by former professor turned Gandhian activist, Acharya Ramamurti, operated on the principle that people must by themselves find solutions to their problems if those solutions are to be meaningful and effective. Shrambharati was established to facilitate local problem solving, employment, and rural development by offering training workshops in such areas as health, housing, food and agriculture, small engine repair, and literacy education. After some twenty-five years, the organization began to focus also on the development needs of women and children, particularly in the poorest rural localities of Bihar and neighbouring Uttar Pradesh. Shrambharati's abiding vision was that of building a self-reliant, violence-free social order in India. Since Ramamurti's death, Shrambharati's viability has been in question, since the property on which it has operated may be repossessed by the Indian federal or Bihar state governments.

5 On Gandhi's ideas regarding peace brigades, see for instance "Our Failure," in *Harijan*, 26 March 1938, *eCWMG* 73, 24–25; and "Qualifications of a Peace Brigade," in *Harijan*, 18 June 1938, *eCWMG* 73, 243–45. Gandhi envisioned establishing a non-violent army that could replace the police (or work alongside them) and that would seek "occasions for bringing warring communities together, carrying on peace propaganda, engaging in activities that would bring and keep them in touch with every single person" in their locality; they would be "messengers of peace" whose qualifications and training would be similar to those of a *satyagrahi*.

6 Ramamurti, quoted in "Mahila Shanti Sena."

7 See Gandhi, *An Autobiography*, 349–53 (Chapters 17 and 18). In addition to basic education, the little village schools that were initially established in Champaran taught hygiene, diet, and related topics that were of great concern to Gandhi. He was particularly interested in reaching the village women, so he brought a number of "ladies" from his ashram in Gujarat, including Kasturbai, to come and help, for he believed it was through women that other women were best reached – a view similarly held by Acharya Ramamurti.

8 MSS training schedules are designed to cause minimal disruption to women's routines in their homes, work, and families and so to maximize attendance. The topics included in the training address a spectrum of women's issues and concerns, from the pernicious effects of early marriage, dowry, alcohol, and debt on women's lives, to the need and means for the education of girls, to conflict resolution techniques. Raising consciousness about issues, sharing problems, and discussing strategies for their resolution all help create a sense of commonality, of confidence and of shared responsibility to move forward and be agents of change. Those involved in the MSS are overwhelmingly volunteers, com-

mitted to the means and aims of the MSS, and determined to bring about healthy change in their communities. Participation in the MSS has cut across caste/*jati*, class, and religious lines. Any woman over eighteen years of age can become an MSS member. While a large percentage of the participants have been low-income and often illiterate labourers, others have come from a cross-section of socio-economic and educational backgrounds. Its organization is largely decentralized, non-hierarchical, and based on a consultative and collaborative decision-making process.

9 See Misra, "Listening to Women," 14.

10 Ibid. See similarly Dhar, "MSS' Commitment and Women's Resolve."

"Gandhi" in Canada in the Latter Part of the Twentieth Century

Paul Younger

Mohandas K. Gandhi never visited Canada in his lifetime. He did, however, know a lot about Indians who lived outside of India in his own day and would no doubt have taken a keen interest in the Indian community developing in Canada in the later decades of the twentieth century. In any case a Gandhian "presence" was an important part of the way that Indians and other Canadians understood India during those decades, and this chapter represents an effort to reimagine some of the different roles that "presence" played.

On 2 October 1969, Nancy Cassells and I co-hosted a conference at McMaster University generously funded by the Canada Council. The conference was intended as a celebration of one hundred years after the birth of Mahatma Gandhi. McMaster University was quietly cooperative, and the Canada Council was enthusiastic. What was a surprise was that the newly arrived members of what would be a substantial Indo-Canadian community were ecstatic and came from considerable distances. At much the same time I began to teach a course called "The Life and Thought of Mohandas K. Gandhi"; I would teach it every other year until 2007. This paper represents an effort to reconstruct some of the discussions that took place at that initial conference and during the next four decades in that class.

South Asian Immigration into Canada

In 1957 John Diefenbaker became Prime Minister of Canada. He was born of immigrant Ukrainian parents, and he proudly introduced a Bill of Rights in 1960 and then had the immigration law changed in 1962 so that all quotas based on race and national origin were abolished. With those restrictions removed, the push to recruit medical doctors and university professors of all kinds quickly focused on well-trained people of South Asian and East Asian backgrounds. By 1967 a points system had been introduced to govern immigration, and because knowledge of English was central to this system, a much wider pool of South Asians qualified.

At the centre of this early immigration of South Asians were the Sikhs, who had long been interested in coming to Canada. By 1905, more than 5,000 Punjabis had already found work in the lumber camps of British Columbia. At the time, the local British citizens had resorted to a head tax to keep control of the Chinese labourers working on the railway, and they responded with similar hostility to this new influx of Asian labour. In 1907 a general anti-Asian riot broke out in Vancouver, and British Columbian society became bitterly divided along racial lines.

In both the United States and Canada at the time, some South Asian migrants on the west coast were linked with the *Ghadr* movement, which promoted armed rebellion against the British Empire. The British introduced spies into the South Asian community, and BC officials attempted to block further immigration by insisting on a "continuous journey" ticket from one's country of origin, knowing full well that no such tickets were available from India. When the community attempted to challenge the continuous-journey rule by bringing a shipload of new immigrants on the *Komagata Maru* in 1914, the ship was stopped in the harbour and eventually turned away. After this incident, the Sikh community's numbers slowly declined.

In the United States, most Sikh men took common law Mexican wives and melted into the society. In Canada, the *gurdwara* in Vancouver served as a community rallying point, and its members decided to maintain a distinctly Sikh community and to keep their distinguishing marks – a turban and beard. Only after Indian independence in 1947 did Canada introduce a small quota for Indian immigration, and that allowed Sikh numbers to start to grow once again. By 1967, large numbers of Hindu and Muslim immigrants were arriving from South Asia; but many Sikhs were arriving along with them, and other South Asian immigrants soon learned that the Sikh community in Canada had deep roots and was already well organized.

In 1974 Canada wrote a whole new immigration law that provided for generous treatment of political refugees. This allowed three new streams of South Asian society to become part of the Canadian story. As early as the 1960s a number of Indians fleeing the dictatorial regime of Forbes Burnham in Guyana had been arriving in Canada on the points system, and because they had a good knowledge of English they settled in quickly, thus preparing the way for even larger numbers in the 1970s. Then in 1972, all Gujaratis were ordered out of Uganda by Idi Amin. The Canadian immigration law of 1974 was designed to assist them, and many headed for Canada; this soon drew other Gujaratis to Canada from Britain and India. By the 1980s, Canadian refugee policy was extending help to Sri Lanka's Tamils, who were being forced to flee their country as their government limited their rights and then set out to crush the Tiger rebellion that arose there.

We will discuss below how these South Asian immigrants struggled to find the right sense of identity for themselves. But there were two aspects of the early immigration itself that introduced Gandhi's name into the story at that early stage. One aspect of the start of South Asian immigration into Canada that one might overlook is the way it was linked with the post-colonial atmosphere of the time. When one recalls the aggressive racism on the west coast in the first decades of the century, one realizes that until 1962 Canada was a quasi-colonial society. Racist immigration quotas were part of that long-standing colonial attitude, and one has to pause in order to remember that the post-colonial attitude that informed the government's actions in 1962, 1967, and 1974 moved Canada in a very new direction. Each of these changes in immigration policy was framed in terms of an overall post-colonial policy granting all communities true equality. If anything, the post-colonial enthusiasm of 1960s Canada tended to go beyond equality and shine a spotlight on the newly arriving communities and the cultural heritages they were bringing with them. These new cultural traditions were more than welcomed; indeed, it was widely hoped that they would give Canada a new "multicultural" identity.

In the context of this post-colonial euphoria, it was common for people of all backgrounds to bring up the name "Gandhi" and recall that it was he who had led the long fight against colonialism. Although he had not lived to see much of the post-colonial joy with which diverse peoples in all parts of the world were able to form fresh new societies, much of the new optimism was credited to his belief that the end of colonialism would be a good thing. While Canada was geographically removed from the key events associated with the end of colonialism, its decision to throw open its doors to Asian immigrants brought it dramatically into the vortex of post-colonial excitement that was engulfing the world in the 1960s. The name "Gandhi" was an interesting part of that excitement.

A second aspect of the South Asian immigration into Canada that became evident at the time was that there were many subcultures within the South Asian community. When Prime Minister Pierre Trudeau and other Canadians encouraged immigrants to "keep your culture," it was not altogether clear to immigrants with an Indian background which aspects of their complex cultural heritage this comment referred to. Indian immigrants were excited to find fellow Indians from so many different backgrounds in Canada, and they were almost as interested to find that there were also sub-cultures within Canadian society. Trudeau's writings on "federalism" were thought of as explaining how this respect for pluralism should work within the framework of national unity, but his way of describing the federal system seemed complicated. While he encouraged a pluralist style of society, his arguments were deeply embedded in the specific issues of Quebec history. In that context he most often seemed to be arguing against the narrow forms of ethnicity that limited individual rights, and as prime minister he fought hard against those who hinted at the need to create a separate political entity in Quebec.

The new South Asian immigrants had their own reasons to be anxious about federally defined subcultures. On the Indian subcontinent too there had long been discussions of cultural plurality. There the focus had been on whether religions, regions, or castes should define nationality, and at the time of independence a painful partition of India had occurred. In Canada, Canadian *and* Indian issues of subcultural identity continued to be discussed, and in addition, new questions were raised for South Asians because of the large numbers who had for generations enjoyed a Caribbean or East African identity.

Immigrants from the Caribbean and East Africa were especially aware that it was Gandhi who had fought for local cultural identity in South Africa; others, however, knew that he had differed with Nehru on these matters and could be counted on to stand up for the smaller party in such disputes. In the debates between himself and Nehru, Gandhi had always been opposed to Nehru's centralizing arguments. Nehru, he felt, had inherited the centralizing institutional structures of the British, and, as independence approached, he had wanted to go further and minimize the role of India's languages and subcultural identities. Among the South Asians who immigrated to the United States in the 1960s, Nehru's approach seemed correct, and they tried to suppress their subcultures for the sake of remaining a unified community as they blended into American culture. In Canada, by contrast, Gandhi's willingness to honour the subcultural richness of India seemed a better way to go. The Sikhs, Guyanese, and East Africans had all arrived in Canada with distinct cultural identities, and a generation later, that would be even truer of the Sri Lankan Tamils, who came to constitute the largest single group of South Asians in Canada. In the Canadian setting, the struggle to preserve a subcultural identity and to resist hegemonic cultural homogeneity seemed to fit the situation, and all parties were pleased to find that the name "Gandhi" could be used to champion the cause of those who wanted to resist centralizing tendencies.

Searching for an Identity

South Asian families in the first wave of immigration to Canada were pleasantly surprised to find work and to feel comfortable in the local communities in which they settled. For a time, worship at home was all they planned to do by way of bringing their heritage with them, and it was often the respectful curiosity of neighbours that helped put in place public celebrations of Diwali, Baisaki, and Eid. By the 1970s, provincial officials were thinking through some of the implications of the much talked about multiculturalism and suggesting to leaders in the Sikh, Muslim and Hindu communities that if they wanted to celebrate marriages in their own way, they would have to form religious communities. The process was simple: they needed to supply a short list of persons who wanted to worship together, and then they would be free to call themselves a *gurdwara*, mosque, or temple and would have tax-free status, as well as the ability to appoint clergy and to define their worship traditions as they chose. This very democratic way of establishing religious traditions was new to the immigrants, and it quickly gave them both a decentralized set of community structures and the sense of a place within the larger Canadian social structure.

Canada was re-examining its own identity in the 1960s. In some brilliant lectures in the 1950s, Trudeau had defined the larger Canadian social structure as a *federal* one. He pictured the cultural parts as separate and distinct, but linked together into one society through regional and national political institutions. South Asians understood this formula as respectful of their religious heritages, and they responded positively when Trudeau insisted that a Charter of Rights and Freedoms be added to the repatriated constitution in 1982 in order to provide clear guidelines for the courts with regard to religious rights.

In 1965, George Grant wrote a nationalist manifesto for Canada titled *Lament for a Nation*. In that widely discussed book he tried to show how the philosophical underpinnings of cultural plurality in Canada made it a very different kind of nation than the United States next door. Grant framed his argument carefully for the political elite of Canada, and he did not mention Gandhi in his book, but he had a personal fascination with Gandhi. He was curious as to how Gandhi used traditional religion and philosophy in his political endeavours and how he understood the cultural plurality of India. Scholars have since followed up on clues that Grant left in this regard and have been able to show quite clearly the philosophical similarities that exist between the "critical traditionalism" (Ashis Nandy) for which Gandhi argued as India sorted out its cultural options, and the position that Grant laid out in defence of Canadian nationalism in 1965.[1] Grant, of course, could not know in 1965 that the name "Gandhi" would play an important symbolic role as Indo-Canadians sought to establish their identity within the pluralist society of Canada later in the century. Indirectly, however, he may be seen to have influenced that choice of a central symbol when he insisted that the Department of Religious Studies at McMaster University, which he headed up at that time, make one of its major emphases the study of Indian philosophy.

For the South Asians in Canada in the 1970s, much of the philosophical discussion that engaged people like Grant and Trudeau was difficult to join. The political ramifications as they were reflected in Canada's stance against the Vietnam War were clear, and most South Asians were mildly anti-American and proudly Canadian. They were a bit surprised to have discovered in Canada a homeland that (in Grant's adaptation of Plato's phrase) believed that community started with "a love of one's own," and that they were being encouraged to keep their cultural heritage. They were excited to find so many South Asians in Canada, and they found that they agreed with Gandhi's oft quoted observation that two Indians meeting in a neutral situation would be much more interested in each other than two Englishmen in the same situation. An energetic quest for an Indo-Canadian identity began almost before the first South Asian immigrants left the airport.

South Asian immigrants to Canada in the 1960s were ambivalent about Gandhi. On the one hand, most of them were teenagers when he was assassinated in 1948, and in some ways that event had elevated him to sainthood. On the other hand, most of the immigrants came from the urban, English-medium education system, and they had not quite understood his way of harnessing the energy of the village masses. They were not sure how literally he meant his opposition to modern industrialized society to be taken, and they were well aware that as engineers and doctors they were pushing in a very different direction. They knew that he had had bitter ideological rivals in India, but they felt that the causes of the *Dalits* and the *Hindutvas* were not relevant to Canada and would only prove divisive in this setting. The "Gandhi" path, whatever that was, seemed unifying and perhaps the best way to go. What proved decisive, however, in this search for an Indo-Canadian symbol was the way that the Canadian neighbours reacted so positively to the name "Gandhi." The name "Gandhi" was something one's neighbours could safely mention in the first conversation. Even if they could seldom go on and say much more about "Gandhi" than that he seemed Christ-like, or perhaps an amusing hippie, they felt that they had paid their cultural compliment and appropriately welcomed their new neighbour. If the immigrant had been lukewarm about the "Gandhi" symbol before, the enthusiasm of the neighbour settled the question. From then on the question became, How do we go about building our Indo-Canadian identity around this central symbol?

By the time the second generation of Indo-Canadians headed to university, the symbol "Gandhi" had long defined their identity. The issue they now faced was the new one of figuring out how to make sense of this symbol. Their parents had already begun that process when they arranged to have statues of Gandhi erected in public spaces in almost every major city in the country. In two or three places they had even gone a step further and established a festival or lecture series that offered the public a sense of how that symbol addressed Canadian issues. For the students of the second generation, who had grown up with that symbol already in place and their own identity somehow tied to it, the challenge was a bit different. Did they really want to rediscover the historical figure behind that symbol? Did they want the heritage associated with that name to become an ongoing part of their new Canadian identity? What if the historical figure of Gandhi and the symbolic "Gandhi" with whom they had grown up were sharply different? Would the name "Gandhi" help them link their two very different meaning systems of "traditional India" and "contemporary Canada"? Or would a gulf open wide if they tried to have the historical Gandhi address the questions of contemporary Canada? Biblical scholars who have thought about this kind of problem for a long time speak of studying the "hermeneutical arc" that ties the historical Jesus to the "Christ" figure of the contemporary church, but the university students setting out to study "Gandhi" in the latter part of the twentieth century had no such scholarly pattern already in place to guide them. The truth was that they had little idea what they were getting into when they registered for a course on Gandhi.

As it turned out, students found that the hermeneutical arc associated with studying "Gandhi" was not as formidable as the one that Christians had to construct to make their message credible. South Asian students realized that their parents' generation had needed some kind of symbolic link with their homeland, so they approached the course hopefully, aware that at the very least they would be making their parents happy. Nevertheless, they still worried that they might be turned off by something that felt very distant from their post-colonial world. Arriving in class, they quickly realized that the non–South Asians in the class had a very different set of expectations. They had grown up realizing from their high school textbooks that Canada was until recently a very colonial place. They did not personally feel that way, so they approached a course on Gandhi eager to show how anti-colonial they were. Were these two perspectives about to come into conflict? Or would they complement each other?

When the South Asians realized that the non–South Asians were thrilled with Gandhi's insights into their post-colonial concerns with war and feminism, they began to wonder if he might be more relevant to their life in Canada than they had earlier thought. When the non–South Asians realized how much insight the South Asians could draw out of Gandhi's references to ideas from the *Bhagavad Gita*, they too began to look behind the post-colonial secularism in which they had been raised and examine "Gandhi" as more than an anti-colonial figure. As the discussion proceeded, the differences between the South Asians and the non–South Asians almost disappeared and they established discussions among themselves to which the voice of "Gandhi" was invited to contribute. Even though the nature of those discussions changed significantly over the four decades in which I was involved with the course, it seemed to me that the views of the "Gandhi" that we could bring to those discussions continued to be relevant and that he had addressed questions about human behaviour that students were still concerned with in a very distant time and place.

"Gandhian" Discussions of Canadian Society

The "American" War (the 1960s)

When South Asian immigrants began pouring into Canada in the 1960s, the public discussion was preoccupied with the Vietnam War. Starting in 1965, thousands of draft dodgers and deserters began crossing into Canada from the United States, and university campuses were characterized both by colourfully dressed hippies (who mocked authority in any form) and by others committed variously to protesting against tradition, violence, and traditional power structures. These communities focused their serious critiques on the "American empire" and its bombing of villages in Vietnam. In March 1965, Prime Minister Pearson let Canada's official opposition to the war be known when he called for a pause in the bombing in a speech in Philadelphia and was roundly criticized for his stand the next day by US President Lyndon Johnson. George Grant suddenly became the favoured speaker for antiwar rallies across the country as he tried to lay out the connection between the West's commitment to technological progress and the evolution of the American-style empire and its use of war as a matter of policy. Canada stated its opposition to the war more officially when in 1967 it placed an embargo on the sale of Canadian resources for the war effort, and in 1969 when Canadian immigration officials were instructed that they could no longer ask about the draft status of US immigrants. Nevertheless, the Canadian attitude towards war and the technological energy that fuelled it was still far from clear.

When the class on the life and thought of M.K. Gandhi was first taught at McMaster University, the Vietnam War was the central focus. Antiwar hippies were a majority in the class, and my paper at the 1969 conference supported by the Canada Council was "Gandhi as a Hippie." It featured a photograph of Gandhi in his loincloth walking up the vast stairway of the British Parliament buildings in order to mock the colonial empire of the 1930s. The substantial argument in those early versions of the course centred on Gandhi's brilliant nationalist manifesto of 1909 titled *Hind Swaraj*. Even at that early date, Gandhi recognized that militarism and colonialism were ephemeral phenomena stemming from a civilizational misdirection that had placed machinery and the accumulation of material things at the centre of national purpose. He condemned that preoccupation as a blind "whirlpool" or "vortex" of the "Machine Age," and he argued that the pursuit of *swaraj* or true spiritual freedom characterized the human spirit and would eventually assert itself again. His immediate concern at the time was that Indians such as Savarkar and others with whom he had been arguing in London just before he left to return to South Africa might themselves jump into the "vortex" with their new love for violence, and he wanted to make clear that Indian tyrants were no better than British ones.

Grant in *Lament for a Nation* had set out much the same kind of argument, and many in the class were familiar with his work. As the class saw it, Gandhi was strong on the spiritual side, and Grant was strong in his analysis of technology. In comparing the two arguments, Grant's followers tended to feel that Gandhi had not demonstrated sufficiently the deeper links between technology and empire in Western civilization. On the other hand, the hippies argued that Grant's hope to find a Platonic streak still surviving somewhere in the Christian tradition was little more than wishful thinking, and that in truth his message, laid out also in his 1969 book *Technology and Empire*, was that our destiny was to succumb to the inevitability of technological empire.

Gandhi's argument in 1909 was only programmatic and intended to link the debate about the use of violence within the Indian community with the civilizational struggle that had originally established the now decaying colonial regimes, whose ends were starting to come into view. Gandhi had quickly added depth to his civilizational analysis by getting permission to publish Leo Tolstoy's brilliant *Letter to a Hindoo*, which had been written to a radical (pro-violence) young Bengali named Taraknath Das, who was running a school in Vancouver at the time. Although he had long been recognized as one of the great writers of his time and had more recently been writing as someone deeply immersed in Christian thought, Tolstoy had answered Das's arguments in favour of violence by constructing scripture-like paraphrases of segments in Krishna's argument in the *Bhagavad Gita* that recognized the spiritual basis of all true action. Gandhi would later go on and show how the non-violent actor's action had to be "grounded in truth," or *satyagraha*. What he was calling for was not a pacifist's simple refusal to fight but a lifelong pursuit of self-cultivation or *svadharma*. For the hippies in the class, that was enough, and they were prepared to assert that "Gandhi" had established a spiritual basis for non-violence. The draft dodgers in the class, and among the tutors, were somewhat less comfortable relying on the spiritual foundation of non-violence and tended to argue that Canada needed to prove that non-participation in the war was good national policy.

For Gandhi in South Africa, the preliminary view set out in *Hind Swaraj* was sufficient for his role in 1909, and he developed his Tolstoy Farm as a refuge where people could reflect on the spiritual energy needed to be a *satyagrahi*. When he returned to India in 1914, he found that there were many complex socio-political issues involved in the approaching post-colonial world for which he would have to develop appropriate strategies, and his spiritual foundation was often put to a severe test in those settings. For the hippies, who were the majority in the class at the time, the spiritual foundation was the key thing, and they were thrilled to have well-grounded support for their antiwar effort and even for their disdain for the machine age. For the Indo-Canadians in the class, this implicit radicalism was all a bit much, but they found the respect that the name "Gandhi" brought to their cultural heritage attractive, and they were relieved that they could associate themselves with a name that both their parents and their class-mates admired.

Women Are the Model (the 1970s)

It is difficult to remember how few women there were in university classes in Canada in the early 1960s, because by the end of the decade they were often in the majority. Soon after, they began to define classroom discussions. Among Indo-Canadians the transformation was even more notable. Among recent South Asian immigrant families, the prevailing expectation was for each family to produce at least one male doctor or engineer, and/or find a marriage partner for their daughter with those credentials. Those expectations, though, were quickly thrown aside in the Canadian setting. Beginning in the 1970s, the most prominent subgroup in the class was Indo-Canadian women pursuing a biology degree, with a view to earning a medical degree. Many had been pressured into the sciences and were eager to take arts electives; some even gathered the courage to switch to the arts as their university experience unfolded. Sikh and Sri Lankan Tamil families continued for some time to hesitate about exposing their daughters to what they considered the alien culture of the university; however, most Indo-Canadian women were able to convince their families to blend their thinking on feminist issues with that of the community around them.

Gandhi's life story came as a total surprise to all the women in the class. The playful comfort he felt when socializing with the British landladies who looked after him as a lonely student in Britain set the tone for the respect he would show throughout his life for the strength of character that he found most women possessed. In reconstructing his earlier memories, he explained this strength of character by recalling the many vows his mother had kept and the religious routines that characterized her life. He felt confused in some ways by the sexual maturity his wife already possessed when they married as teenagers, but he recognized the inner strength she later demonstrated, and he tried to recognize the leadership that she and other women brought to their political activities. By the end of his life he was surrounded with caring, courageous women, who seemed to have come to the cause almost equally from cultural backgrounds in India and the West.

During the 1970s, one of the most active student centres on campus was the Rape Crisis Centre. The women leading that centre at the time had on their own learned about a conversation Gandhi had had with a woman coping with having been raped. He had suggested to her that instead of threatening the intended offender, she might have tried to raise his level of consciousness by asking about his family. The leaders of the Rape Crisis Centre had been testing the practical potential of this unusual approach in their training programs. They came to feel that they needed a deeper sense of how Gandhi understood human nature, so they joined the class. Over the next few years it sometimes seemed as if the course on Gandhi had become a course on women's studies as students expanded the range of questions and explored the biological grounding of violence, the traditional roles of women in various societies, and the erosion of women's roles in technological society.

Indo-Canadian women in the class sometimes found it odd that "Gandhi" was being used to address women's issues. They had grown up trying to moderate "Indian" families' efforts to "protect" their daughters from the imagined sexual freedom and immodest behaviour of Western girls, and their assumption had largely been that they would have to look to Western models to gain insight into women's potential. They were now to learn that Gandhi's thinking on the matter had started long before. As early as 1909, his disdain for the ephemeral colonial power made it possible for him to recognize that the "Orientalist" argument the British had constructed – an argument contrasting the "noble," "masculine" colonial conquerors with the "effeminate" peoples they had come to rule – was an example of the misguided use of gender categories to describe a power struggle. Instead of accepting that imagery and trying to adopt some minor forms of violence and masculinity, as many colonially educated Indians did, Gandhi turned the argument on its head and tried to learn from the women around him about the traditional style of female courage – a style that no colonial argument could touch. Suzanne Rudolph's keynote lecture at the 1969 conference at McMaster University was an early version of her brilliant chapter in *The Modernity of Tradition* on how Gandhi's charisma depended on his ability to appropriate tradition in this way as he fought a modern struggle for political control. What the women in the class came to realize was that in Gandhi's view, the issue was not what degree of freedom women could gain in contexts governed by "male" figures, whether in the form of colonial rulers, parents, or business managers. He set completely aside that form of civilizational model and looked instead at contexts around the world where women had been looked to as the models of what was civilized.

The "Gandhi" the class began to look to in these discussions of women's issues was not the saintly figure who had inspired opposition to the American war, but a more down-to-earth figure whose traditionalism entailed an effective turning away from all sorts of blind alleys in Western civilization. What was not clear at the time was whether there was a civilizational discussion under way in the West that the ideas of "Gandhi" might conceivably weigh in on. In 1982, Richard Attenborough's film *Gandhi* gave the impression that the Christ-like "Gandhi" did indeed have all the answers – most especially perhaps for the Western women in the story. IBM, the techno-wizard company of the day, then threw in its opinion with huge billboards of a near naked "Gandhi" and the "think differently" motto that amounted to a mockery of all forms of serious discussion (a theme later taken up by the Apple computer company). For the feminists in the class, at least, this was a serious new starting point, and they went off to find out where else a civilizational critique could be discussed. For the Indo-Canadian women and others, "Gandhi" was an inspiration for whom they had new respect, but they had their own lives to live and were not sure where his inspiration would fit in.

Post-Colonial Pluralism (the 1980s)

By the 1980s, communities labelled visible minorities by Statistics Canada were appearing everywhere on the streets of Canada's largest cities. On the campus of McMaster University they looked like a majority, and student newspaper editorials and many course outlines were wrestling with the meaning of multiculturalism. The Quebec Referendum of 1980 had unnerved the country, and the introspection it generated raised new doubts about the daring leadership that Trudeau and others had shown in moving so decisively toward the unknown future of multicultural pluralism. An opportunistic writer like Neil Bissoondath knew how to feed the self-doubts of the Canadian intellectual community when he chose the controversial title *Selling Illusions: The Cult of Multiculturalism in Canada* (1994) for his rather bland critique of the policy. The national policy itself was never really in question after the 1971 legislation on bilingual and bicultural rights included multicultural clarifications in a number of places, but the strong statement of minority rights in the 1982 Canadian Charter of Rights and Freedoms that was added to the Constitution brought the courts into the discussion, and the 1988 legislation on multiculturalism provided some funds for the preservation of minority cultural activities. In the 1980s, people realized that what mattered was whether Canadian society would really become multicultural, and the first task was determining what form that multiculturalism would take.

In the 1980s, for the first time, the majority of students in the course "The Life and Thought of M.K. Gandhi" were of Indo-Canadian heritage. That majority was not overwhelming, however, and the discussions continued to be multifaceted. Of somewhat greater sociological significance was that Indo-Canadians had begun to identify themselves in terms of their cultural subgroups. Sikhs and Tamils especially began to identify themselves clearly and even at times tended to sit in different parts of the classroom. Sikhs were especially uneasy at this time. A kind of Sikh chaplain sometimes attended the class, and many of the male students wore special turbans associated with the cause of *Khalistani* independence. But at the same time, some Sikh women in the class talked about how oppressive they found the fierce new ethnicity in their community, especially the insistence that they marry uneducated men from the Punjab. Sri Lankan Tamil men were sometimes willing to explain to the class the roles they had played in the Tiger-led separatist war in Sri Lanka, but they had to be very careful about what they said because whether they were involved in that cause or not, the Canadian authorities assumed that they were at the heart of some of the gang culture in Toronto. In the Tamil case, the women in the class had largely won their battle at home and were eager to show the class how prepared they were to make the most of their assimilation into Canadian culture. Students with East African or Caribbean backgrounds seemed less eager than Sikhs and Tamils to insist on their subcultural identity, and because the societies in which their parents had been raised were already pluralist in some ways, they portrayed themselves as in a good position to address the questions posed by a pluralist society in Canada. When Air India Flight 182 was bombed on 23 June 1985 and supporters of an independent Khalistan were named the likely suspects, the roles of South Asian minorities in the Canadian mosaic became scrambled in a variety of ways. Some Hindus thought it was time to support the Sikh leaders' calls for a separate identity, but most Canadians still thought of South Asians as a group. Trudeau's strong emphasis on minority rights was reflected in the way the press coverage of the bombing referred only loosely to the Canadian citizens who had been killed, and Sikhs and other South Asians quickly distanced themselves from this "criminal behaviour." Within months, the first Sikhs had been elected to the British Columbia legislature and to the federal Parliament.

The debate over minority rights and cultural pluralism had largely stalled in Canada after the euphoria of the 1960s. The framework of those rights had been firmly established in the Constitution, but Trudeau's narrow focus on constitutional rights and Grant's distraction by the even narrower fight against reproductive technologies had left the public discussion of culture rudderless. Within the South Asian community, the constitutional framework seemed for the time being to be leading to a satisfactory set of social arrangements. The employment rate for South Asians coming out of university was measurably higher than for other Canadians, and with the encouragement of provincial governments, *gurdwaras*, temples, and mosques were springing up everywhere. Most Canadians either ignored these developments or felt that they were consistent with the commitments made a generation earlier, but South Asians wanted more reassurance that their cultures would be blended into the societal whole if they continued in this pattern.

Gandhi's way of combining his legal training and vast knowledge of world affairs with his trust in tradition produced many almost comic juxtapositions of seemingly unrelated issues. Ashis Nandy's brilliant retrospective essays on some of these issues are helpful in bringing out how thoughtful Gandhi's stances on specific issues were and how effective he had been in rallying the support of the masses and in addressing, very early on, issues that would later prove to be major cultural tangles in post-colonial South Asia.[2] The South Asians in the class who had started to recognize in the 1980s how diverse South Asian culture was were now surprised to learn that Gandhi had been wrestling with such issues in South Africa at the beginning of the century. Gandhi's insistence that the working-class Tamil majority among the Indians in South Africa be given a role in the community leadership had been a surprise to the Gujarati Muslim businessmen who had brought him to South Africa and were providing him with a living. Ashis Nandy describes the policy that Gandhi adopted in this setting as "putting the periphery into the center." In the context of South Africa, that meant that the poor Tamil plantation workers were moved to the centre of the Indian political movement where the businessmen expected to be; in the context of Canada, it meant that Sikhs, Tamils, Guyanese, Ismaili Muslims, and many others could legitimately feel that their subcultures might be seen as at the heart of an expanding South Asian community.

Gandhi honoured all of the subcultures of India and delighted in showing off his knowledge of Tamil, and as a traditionalist he argued that each region should have its own official language. But he was what Nandy calls a "critical traditionalist" in that he demanded that the tradition being honoured in this way address the contemporary situation. For the South Asians in the class, this meant they could proudly say that they supported the new *gurdwaras*, temples, and mosques and the traditions they preserved, and at the same time they could say they were proud of the many South Asian faces that were now visible in business advertisements and in the media. In the Canadian setting this kind of critical traditionalism had become a consensus position among South Asians by the 1980s, and people were prepared to force the recognition of the South Asian place in Canadian society by erecting statues of Gandhi in every corner of the country.

Religion and the Human Psyche (the 1990s)

Although the course on Gandhi at McMaster was taught in the Department of Religious Studies, the discussion in the course was most often about politics or social theory, and Religious Studies majors sometimes did not stay. The early hippie interest in the course had something to do with their fascination with Eastern spirituality, but the more serious among them soon were using "Gandhi" to critique the Vietnam War and the associated obsessions with technology and progress. By the last decade of the century, however, new strains of spirituality had begun to creep into the discussion as a new generation tried to figure out how humans were tied to their environment and what were the common foundations in the religious life of different societies.

For the Indo-Canadians in the class, these new questions had a welcome neutrality about them. Their parents had been desperately worried they might face the old colonial questions about "idol worship," and they had been relieved to find that Canadians were quietly helpful in encouraging them to establish their own places of worship. The second generation had long thoughtlessly taken the routines of temple life for granted, and they were developing into indifferent practitioners of Hindu ritual. They were as curious as anyone else in the class to delve into the new questions being asked about religion.

At first, "Gandhi" did not seem to be the logical place to look to for answers to these new questions. His statues were a source of pride to the students' parents, but they did not directly address questions of religion, and they seemed to serve more as symbols of South Asian ethnicity than as invitations to religious inquiry. Temples sometimes allowed dance classes, yoga classes, and lectures by *swamis* to be held on their premises, but classes that experimented with blending styles from a number of cultural settings and lectures on interfaith topics were usually held elsewhere. With Indo-Canadian spirituality safely routinized, it was usually the non-Indo-Canadian students who in the 1990s came to the "Gandhi" class with new questions about spirituality in general and religion and the environment in particular.

By the 1990s, student questions about the environment had begun to evolve from the simpler political questions about how to oppose coal-fired electrical plants towards the "deep environmental" (see Norwegian scholar Arne Naess) question of how to re-establish the bond between humans and their environment.[3] Gandhi had set a good example on the simpler environmental issues when he insisted on a clean *ashram* environment and bluntly declared his disgust at the pollution associated with factories and the dehumanizing dimensions of urban life. But the students wanted to know more about his idiosyncratic lifestyle and his determination to live in farm and *ashram* settings and to blend in with the natural world around him. In particular, they noted that he had an obsessive interest in diet and sexuality and that even his dress and his body image made a strong statement about how he defined the human psyche and how he understood a human's place in the natural order.

As the discussion of the psyche and the environment began, the students found for the first time that they had to figure out how Gandhi's own views were related to those of his tradition. Clearly, Gandhi had strong personal views on diet and sexuality, and he sometimes enjoyed shocking his audience by the way he asserted them. On the other hand, he always explained his views in language that was profoundly traditional. Unlike modern gurus, who quickly prescribe patterns in diet and sexuality for their disciples, Gandhi felt strongly that discipleship was inappropriate and that each individual needed to experiment and establish his or her own ties with the surrounding world. What he did accept from tradition was the pattern of thinking that equipped the mind, in much the same way that the patterns of diet and sexuality helped the body and the emotions find their way. Although (as far as I know) Gandhi never stepped back and laid out the seven levels of psychic experience as found in traditional Indian discussions, he used that pattern repeatedly. Whether the discussion was on diet, reincarnation, or the final realization of *Brahman,* the traditional view of the human psyche was always in view and what the class spoke of as spirituality was being discussed.

Earlier discussions of Indian spirituality in the West had tended to start with Vedanta and the end of the process – the point where a human reaches the divine. Yet Indian philosophical texts, even when concerned with the end, usually review all the levels of human experience. Most of those texts assume that the body (*rupa*), the feelings (*vedana*), and the mind (*manas*) have been mastered, that a person's *svadharma* or life path has been developed in accordance with one's personal characteristics (*samskaras*) or karma, and that the theological issue is how universal consciousness (*buddhi*) and personal resolve (*ahamkara*) transform the psyche into the divine perspective or *atman.* Gandhi was certainly aware of this complete system of thought, and especially of the interest that people in the West had taken in Vedanta and Yoga and the last stages in the process. But in his own life, he had chosen to look at the system from the other end and concentrate on the first stages. He thought that by developing disciplined forms of diet, sexuality, and conversation, a person became established in his environment and became capable of true action or *svadharma.* By writing about his own struggles to master the discipline associated with the life of the body, the emotions, and the mind, he provided a picture of a human being dependent on and profoundly linked with the natural order of things. His central message was that only as one is established in that discipline does one become capable of *svadharma* or self-generated action in the world.

A few of the students in the class had read Naess's "The Shallow and the Deep" and could see links between Gandhi's view of the self and Spinoza's self-realization theory on which Naess's environmental views were based. Recognizing the deep bond between human consciousness and the natural order of things is crucial, but for Gandhi this was not a mystical insight so much as a discipline that was difficult to master. For many students in the class, the question of how to gain self-understanding through discipline became the focus of a new form of self-analysis. Establishing an identifiable diet was a new idea for many, but once discipline was initiated at that level, it quickly affected the other levels. Soon the question on everybody's mind was How does this work? How does the discipline of the body, the feelings, and the mind affect the course of the *svadharma*? Here Gandhi retreated into the traditional language of *nis kama karma* or discovering the ability to act without attachment, and that made it hard for the class. Gandhi had often argued that if the discipline had been thorough, the non-violent action would have succeeded. It was as if there was a direct link between the exercise of discipline and the rest of the spiritual endeavour. Or, to put it differently, the link between the human psyche and its environment (physical and spiritual) was defined by the opening exercises of discipline. This claim was hard for the class to accept without challenge. Some non–South Asians thought that this model of human behaviour was a bit idealistic and insisted on a spiritualistic interpretation of everyday behaviour. South Asians, by contrast, found it familiar and realized that in many ways it was the way that their grandparents had thought about their human experience. For both groups it was a challenge. It did seem to be a way of life that was at some distance from their life in North America, but it did not answer their questions about their responsibility to their environment. If they cared about peace and non-violence, as they thought they did, would it really be necessary to develop a whole path of personal spirituality or *svadharmic* action to support that belief? And was it necessary to start on that path with discipline in the mundane areas of diet and sexuality? How would that help with non-violence? Many in the class were not sure they were with "Gandhi" on this.

Just as this discussion was beginning to make students feel uneasy, a Muslim student who had been relatively quiet asked if he could describe an incident that had happened to him over the weekend. He had been standing in the lineup for a bar for over two hours when two other Muslims he did not know pushed into the line beside him. Surprising himself, he told them, "This is not fair to those behind us in the line." The bigger one replied, "What nonsense." Threateningly, he then said, "Do you want to step outside, bro?" His friend, however, was intrigued and asked the student what made him think that way. He tried to say something about Gandhi and thinking differently, but what he was surprised by and wanted to convey to the class was how absolutely fearless he felt. Then he went on and explained to the class how his action seemed quite outside himself. For the first time in his life he had taken an action that came from somewhere deep inside who he was. He then concluded with a laugh that the action must have been *nis kama karma* because he still had no personal investment in it and could not even believe that he was now describing it to the whole class.

The bundle of questions was finally out there. Is it really the discipline of diet, sexuality, and mind that establishes our bond with the natural order and that enables us to act without self-interest (*nis kama karma*)? And is that the necessary prelude to the higher experience of *buddhi* ("universal consciousness"), and *atman*, which makes it possible for us to live as *satyagrahis* (those who have grasped truth)? And, finally, is it really someone who has grasped truth who has the quiet courage to work for *sarvodaya* ("the uplift of all")? The class erupted into announcements of lifestyle changes for some and new research projects for others.

For those eager to do further research on the spirituality of action, I pointed them to the *Bhagavad Gita*. "Gandhi's" thoughts on spirituality consistently used the traditional vocabulary, but he carefully refused to allow himself to be treated like a spiritual teacher, and he kept his focus on enabling people to act politically. "Gandhi's" limitations as a spiritual teacher were clear, but his arguments led one naturally to the *Gita*. For the class, however, the introduction of the *Gita* raised a new question: Was this bundle of questions about the human psyche a "Hindu" bundle? Was the *Gita* a "Hindu" text? Up to this point in the course, we had not had occasion to discuss what it would mean to picture "Gandhi" as a Hindu. Students were aware of the close contacts the historical Gandhi had had with Christians, Sikhs, and Muslims and some of the playful comments he had made about belonging to each of those communal groups. Within the Canadian Indo-Canadian community, this ambiguity with regard to religious identity continued in a slightly different form. In this context it was important that the "Gandhi" of the statue represent all the South Asian communities of Canada, and because the religious communities of South Asia were more or less equally represented in this context, "Gandhi" had grown to represent them all. For the students in the class, the question was not so much "Is 'Gandhi' a Hindu?" but "Is the *Gita* necessarily a Hindu text?" As it turned out, some of the best papers on the *Gita*'s understanding of action were written by Muslim, Sikh, and Christian students. For them it was easier to ignore the religious dimensions of the story and concentrate on the logic of the argument. Their argument was that the historical Gandhi had read the text in precisely that way when he tried to identify the psychological foundations for political action. He had worked hard to find the philosophical underpinnings of political action, but he had also always insisted that he was not a religious teacher. The students tried to honour that distinction, but certainly for those who had experimented with new disciplines in diet and were pretty sure that they had discovered a *svadharma* that would influence the rest of their lives, the "Gandhi" they had met was some kind of guru or spiritual teacher.

Afterword

On 12 September 2001 the classroom intended for the "Gandhi" class was filled to overflowing, with students sitting in all the aisles. In the first row were seven female students dressed for the first time (as I was to learn later) in *hijabs*. The events of the day before had shaken the confidence of everyone, but none more so than the second-generation Muslim students who had grown up so quietly in the multicultural Canada of the day. The question from student after student who spoke up that evening was "Can 'Gandhi' provide a different direction for our world?" With Muslim students in the lead, the course on "Gandhi" began after 9/11 to become a discussion of how it would be possible to imagine a civilizational model rooted in nonviolence. I taught the course a few more times and began to wrestle with this question and then handed on that responsibility to Anne Pearson in 2007.

What the recall of this decades-long experience of teaching Gandhi in a Canadian classroom has done is somewhat of a surprise to me. Some students may remember me as a bit of a Gandhian, and I would be happy if they did, but what I find myself reflecting on is how much the teaching of this course taught me about the construction of imagined communities. From the beginning, this course seemed to be about building community. Initially I was most aware of the need to construct a sense of community within the class. There were about 150 students with perhaps a half dozen of Indian background, and with a couple of tutors who were opinionated draft dodgers from the United States, and a professor who had spent a number of years in India and was new to Canada. Figuring out how to organize a discussion that engaged everyone in that situation was not easy. Within a few years the enrolment pattern in the class had changed. The students of Indian background gradually became the majority, and we had mostly female tutors, some of whom were graduate students from India. Because of the interests of this new community, the course's questions turned more and more to how the Indian immigrant community of Canada was taking form and how the name "Gandhi" was coming to be the central symbol of that community. And, finally, as the student complement became primarily second-generation immigrants who wanted to wrestle with the central questions they were facing about the values they would pass on to their children, the focus of the course came to centre on those questions. I now see that these were three different levels at which the issue of imagined community was being engaged, and I am intrigued that a course on Gandhi taught in far-off Canada would have that kind of deep engagement with the life of those students.

In his enormously popular book titled *Imagined Communities: Reflections on the Origin and Spread of Nationalism* (1983), Benedict Anderson stuck largely to the political history of recent centuries, but he also opened up for many of his readers a curiosity about the power of the community-building process.[4] With the throwing aside of the colonial experience and the tidal wave of resettlement that took place in the later part of the twentieth century, the processes of community-building were exposed to view as never before. Because this process took place for the first time under the banner of freedom, the role of the imagination in giving it inspiration and direction was evident for the first time. When the course on Gandhi at McMaster University was introduced for the first time in the 1960s, it was not yet clear that a major Indo-Canadian community would be developing in Canada or that Canada would be open to reimagining its values and becoming a truly multicultural society. Reflecting back, I should have had some sense of how the name "Gandhi" might transform a social situation. Black women in Trenton, New Jersey, had introduced me to the "Gandhi" they were using to define the non-violent path they wanted blacks from Mississippi to use as they assimilated into the once all-white society of Trenton. When their chosen candidate was elected mayor, I knew that the imagination of the community was developing along the lines they were hoping it would, but I still did not know why the symbol of "Gandhi" worked so well.

Teaching a course on Gandhi for four decades has allowed me to see the emergence of a symbol first-hand. From beginning to end I talked about Achyut Patwardan and Jaya Prakash Narayana, who had worked closely with Gandhi and knew a lot about how he understood the workings of Indian society and how he interpreted the arguments of the *Bhagavadgita*. What I now see is how the imagination of the community I was working with took these ideas and transformed them into the building blocks of community life associated with the symbol "Gandhi." People sometimes have customs, languages, or religious practices that they have long shared with others, but in the development of an imagined community, be it a classroom, a city, or a nation, they have to figure out once again what symbolic focus their community needs. What the adoption of "Gandhi" as a symbol in both Trenton and Canada illustrates is that the process of imagining a community is wonderfully complex and that we need to observe with care if we are to recognize the range of the imagination.

Notes

1 See Schwartzentruber, "Gandhi's Whirlpool." See also the essays in Baruna, ed., *Gandhi and Grant*.
2 See Nandy, *At the Edge of Psychology*; and *Bonfire of Creeds*.
3 Naess, "The Shallow and the Deep."
4 Anderson, *Imagined Communities*.

Mahatma Gandhi and Winnipeg, Manitoba

Klaus Klostermaier

While Mahatma Gandhi and the Canadian city of Winnipeg might seem, at first blush, to have little or no relationship, a closer look reveals that admiration of the Mahatma matters in this city. On 15 October 2013, for example, Justice Murray Sinclair, Chief Judge of the Provincial Court of Manitoba and chair of the Truth and Reconciliation Commission, received the Mahatma Gandhi Peace Award from the hands of the president of the University of Winnipeg, Lloyd Axworthy. In his acceptance speech, Justice Sinclair called Mahatma Gandhi his hero and expressed his delight to be connected with him in his own peacemaking work. The annual award had been instituted in 2012 by the Mahatma Gandhi Centre of Canada.

On 15 August 2013, India's Independence Day, a short stretch of an inner-city road leading to the (as yet incomplete) Canadian Museum of Human Rights in Winnipeg was (re)named Mahatma Gandhi Way in the presence of delegations from provincial and municipal governments. The Mayor of Winnipeg, Sam Katz, declared:

> Mahatma Gandhi was a spiritual and political leader whose influence is still felt today. He was the personification of peace. To this day we still turn to his words for inspiration as well as for understanding. His teaching of non-violence and social change has given hope to millions of people facing oppression around the world. Gandhi selflessly dedicated his life to human rights and made many sacrifices to ensure and protect the freedom of others. It is only fitting *Mahatma Gandhi Way* leads to the

Canadian Museum of Human Rights, a national centre devoted to promoting respect for others and encouraging reflection and dialogue.[1]

The renaming of the street had been proposed by Dr. G. Dakshinamurti, president of the Mahatma Gandhi Centre of Canada, who had once met Gandhi as student leader while participating in the "Quit India" movement that Gandhi had started.

Just a few years earlier, on 27 August 2010, a statue of Mahatma Gandhi was unveiled in Winnipeg as a gift to the Canadian Museum of Human Rights by Her Excellency Mme. Shashi U. Tripathi, High Commissioner of India to Canada, on behalf of the Government of India's Council for Cultural Relations. The gift was made possible through the efforts of Dr. Naranjan S. Dhalla, founder of the India–Canada Culture and Heritage Association.

As a resident of Winnipeg, my personal involvement with Mahatma Gandhi extends back a long time. He had been one of my heroes since my teens, and I had devoted a long chapter to his ideas in my PhD dissertation at the Gregorian University in Rome (1961), dealing with modern Hinduism and the social reorganization of India.[2] On the occasion of Gandhi's hundredth birthday (1969), I had prepared an anthology of his writings with a biographical introduction for Hegner-Bücherei Cologne.[3] I am thrilled to see that even today, textbooks prepared for ethics classes in Germany are quoting from my translations of the Mahatma's words. I also included a chapter on Gandhi in my *Survey of Hinduism* (1989, 1994, 2007), which is widely used as a textbook in North American universities.[4] Last year I was asked to contribute a paper to a volume on world peace. I chose to write a chapter on "Mahatma Gandhi's *Ahimsa*: A World without Violence?"[5]

In a graduate seminar titled Masters of Spiritual Life that I conducted over many years at the University of Manitoba, I always included Mahatma Gandhi as one of the masters. I believed that over and above his engagement with Indian independence, he taught that politics as well as economics needed a spiritual foundation in order to benefit society. Adela Diubaldo Torchia, one of the participants, wrote a PhD dissertation on Gandhi's ideas, which was recently published under the title *Gandhi, Ecology, and World Religions* (2013).[6]

While it is certainly praiseworthy to highlight Gandhi's engagement for justice and peace, as was done by Winnipeg's mayor, it must be emphasized that Gandhi's socio-political and economic ideas cannot be understood without his spirituality. Gandhi's dream of a free India consisting of half a million self-sufficient villages may have been a utopian idea, and his expectation that India would become a beacon of non-violence for the whole world may have been overtaken by later Indian political realities, but his moral principles have proven timeless and are universally valid. Gandhi consciously connected with the great spiritual traditions of all of humankind – the *philosophia perennis* of the world. His *Ashram Bhajanavali* – a collection of texts used in the Sabarmati Ashram (the training centre for his most committed followers) for communal worship – contains Hindu *bhajans*, Christian hymns, Muslim prayers, and Buddhist meditations. Gandhi was a lifelong student of religious literature and practice.

Gandhi never visited Canada, but he probably would have found Canada in many ways a country to his liking. Many of the socio-political ills he spent his life fighting are absent in today's Canada. There is little or no visible religion-based violence or racial discrimination. There is an overall sense of community and co-operation in the population at large, and there is a social system that works for the benefit of all. Canadians from a great many ethnic backgrounds and social strata can live together in peace and enjoy a life that is free of many problems that beset their countries of origin.

Why, then, does Gandhi matter to Canada? I contend not simply that Gandhi has found admirers in the city of Winnipeg (and in other Canadian cities), but that all Canadians should take seriously his teachings.[7] In the remainder of this chapter, let me elaborate on some of his key teachings and their relevance.

Truth Is God

In several ways, Gandhi's principle of embracing Truth has implications for Canadians. Gandhi took pride in his reversal of the traditional saying "God is Truth" by proclaiming that "Truth is God." He called his autobiography *Experiments with Truth*, and it would not be wrong to refer to his entire life as "Dialogues with God." He coined the term *satyagraha* to designate his political activity: "truth-grasping," not violence or deception, would lead to genuine freedom. For his most devoted co-workers he founded the Sabarmati Ashram near Ahmedabad, Gujarat. He asked them to take five vows, specified in a little book titled *Ashram Observances in Action*.[8] And the first vow that his most intimate followers had to take was truthfulness. Truth, he said, was not just abstaining from telling some untruth to one's fellow-humans: "'Truth is God.' ... God alone is."[9] The notoriously elusive question "What is Truth?" he answered by pointing to the "small still voice" inside. In connection with "human rights" – a term that had not been coined during his own lifetime – he made a pertinent remark that deserves to be pondered: "It is because we have at the present moment everybody claiming the right of conscience without going through any discipline whatsoever that there is so much untruth being delivered to a bewildered world."[10]

In his autobiography, he explains:

> For me truth is the sovereign principle ... This truth is not only truthful-
> ness in word, but truthfulness in thought also, and not only the relative
> truth of our conception, but the Absolute Truth, the Eternal principle,
> that is God ... I worship God as Truth only. I have not yet found Him, but
> I am seeking after Him. I am prepared to sacrifice the things dearest to me
> in pursuit of this quest ... Often in my progress I have had faint glimpses
> of the Absolute Truth, God, and daily the conviction is growing upon me
> that He alone is real and all else is unreal.[11]

Such a commitment to Truth has implications for Canadian politics. While politics is often perceived as a game of deception in which the most astute win out, in the long run Gandhi's principle of truthfulness may be the only guarantee of good national and international relations. In a country like Canada, with a population from so many different ethnic and religious backgrounds, truth in the sense in which Gandhi conceived it must be the brace that holds us together. Gandhi's engagement on behalf of the socially and economically weakest stratum of Indian society – the people whom he called "Hari-jan," God's folk – has its parallel in Canada's endeavours to do justice to its Native people. For good reason, the Canadian government has established a Truth and Reconciliation Commission, and it is a fitting coincidence that the man who chairs it considers Mahatma Gandhi his hero.

Reflecting his commitment to Truth, Gandhi called his life-program *satyagraha*, "truth grasping," and he considered *ahimsa*, "non-violence," to be its core:

> I know only one way – the way of ahimsa. The way of *himsa* goes against
> my grain. I do not want to cultivate the power to inculcate *himsa* ... The
> faith sustains me that He is the Help of the helpless, that He comes to one's
> succour only when one throws himself on His mercy. It is because of this
> faith that I cherish the hope that God will show me one day a path which
> I may confidently commend to the people.[12]

Gandhi considered *ahimsa* the basis of all existing societies: if people were not fundamentally non-violent in their daily lives, humankind would have been eliminated long ago. Gandhi did not accept the Darwinian notion of "nature red in tooth and claw"; rather, he saw violence as a deviation from human nature. Significantly, he translated his belief in *ahimsa* into political action: when faced with unjust racist legislation in South Africa, he did not call on his fellow-countrymen to revolt but arranged peaceful mass demonstrations. His tactics worked and prevented bloodshed and inter-racial hatred.

For Gandhi, *ahimsa* had far-reaching personal implications: in order to practise non-violence, one had to be free from greed, ambition, and the desire to dominate others. *Ahimsa* was a tool not only to win political victories but also to improve social relations on a daily basis. And not to forget: "Ahimsa is not the goal: Truth is the goal. But we have no means of realizing truth in human relationships except through the practice of ahimsa. A steadfast pursuit of ahimsa is inevitably bound to truth – not so violence. That is why I swear by ahimsa. Truth came naturally to me. Ahimsa I acquired after a struggle."[13]

Gandhi connected everyday working for a living with *ahimsa*. He saw in bread-labour a divine obligation and a source of joy. He believed that "God created man to work for his food, and [God] said that those who ate without work were thieves."[14] In the particular circumstances in India in which he worked, he connected spinning with *ahimsa*. On his travels through India he noticed that the small subsistence farmers had neither work nor income during the hot summer months. They idled their time away. To provide an occupation and modest gain, Gandhi revived the old cottage industry of spinning and weaving, which had been abandoned after the introduction of cheap imported industrial cloth. His co-workers discovered some old spinning wheels, improved their mechanism, and manufactured new ones. Gandhi himself devoted every day to spinning and made his co-workers take a vow to do it. He elevated the spinning wheel to a national symbol and saw in it the embodiment of *ahimsa*.

This loyalty to *ahimsa* is also relevant for Canada and its orientation to the larger world. Canada has been known as a peaceful country and has been recognized for its peacekeeping missions in many dangerous parts of the world. Significantly, Gandhi would have approved of this: "My non-violence does not admit of running away from danger and leaving dear ones unprotected. Between violence and cowardly flight, I can only prefer violence to cowardice. I can no more preach non-violence to a coward that I can tempt a blind man to enjoy healthy scenes. Non-violence is the summit of bravery."[15]

Gandhi as Ecologist

Gandhi hated big cities and disliked industrial developments. In spite of the dirt and stench he found in many Indian villages on his journeys, he extolled village life as the only really worthwhile life. He dreamed of an India consisting of self-sufficient villages, where everything needed was locally produced. By teaching cleanliness and moderation, he reformed village life in many parts of the country. He foresaw that the introduction of technology and the industrialization of India would destroy much of what he valued. One of its results was the uncontrolled growth of enormous slums on the outskirts of big cities and the migration of millions away from the villages. In spite of the great mutual respect that Gandhi and Jawaharlal Nehru, India's first prime minister after independence, had for each other, they did not see eye to eye on the matter of India's economic future. Nehru was fascinated by modern technology – he called the factories and the electricity-generating complexes the "temples of the New India" – whereas Gandhi would have preferred to pull them down and invest in the development of villages. He wrote:

> Machinery is like a snake-hole which may contain from one to a hundred snakes. Where there is machinery there are large cities; and where there are large cities, there are tram-cars and railways; and there only does one see electric light … Honest physicians will tell you that, where means of artificial locomotion have increased, the health of the people has suffered. I remember that, when in a European town there was scarcity of money, the receipts of the tram-way company, of the lawyers and of the doctors, went down, and the people were less unhealthy. I cannot recall a single good point in connection with machinery.[16]

In the 1950s, Gandhi's views looked hopelessly old-fashioned, yet today we recognize that there was deep wisdom in them. Gandhi was an ecologist before the word ecology became fashionable. He had great respect for nature, and he feared that human interference would do irreparable harm. He was right, as we know today: unless we redirect our technologies to support instead of exploit nature, we will have to bear the consequences in terms of the destruction of nature and harm to humans. Gandhi correctly saw the link between industrial expansion and the exploitation of natural resources. In his *Constructive Program* of 1945 – his most ambitious attempt at national economics – he tried to translate *ahimsa* into postwar Indian reorganization. He expressed his dislike for big cities often enough, so his preference for village life came as no surprise. The free India he was dreaming of consisted of half a million self-sufficient villages. This was his notion of an earthly Kingdom of God. Yet however much he glorified preindustrial rural culture, Gandhi was enough of a realist to accept the inevitability of modern technology and the concentration of humanity in big cities. He had first-hand experience of rural squalor and village squabbling, and he did not reject the financial support of industrialists and big-city tycoons. The number of humans on earth has at least tripled since Gandhi's times, and technology – setting aside its harmful consequences – has made life better for a great percentage of people.

And this observation brings us to consider the relevance of Gandhi's ecological sensitivity to Canada. Life in a country like Canada with its present population would be inconceivable without electricity, automobiles, railways, and many other technological developments. If Gandhi visited Canada today, he probably would not advocate a return to village life, the destruction of factories, and the elimination of motorized vehicles, but he would keep insisting on *satyagraha*, truth-grasping, and *ahimsa*, non-violence. He might express his admiration for communities like the Amish, who refuse to employ motor cars and who live without television, but he probably would not call on the rest of Canadians to follow their example. Just as it would be pointless in today's India to expect the masses living in the big cities to return to village life, so it would be counterproductive to denounce technology wholesale and dismantle all industry. What Gandhi would probably demand is fairness and justice, efforts to minimize harm to nature, and the development of soft technologies. His often quoted observation that nature offers enough to satisfy the needs of all, but not their greed, is true also in today's economy: it is the insatiable greed of some bankers, industrialists, and Internet sharks that distorts the balance between legitimate needs and available resources.

In 1973, E.F. Schumacher, a reputable British economist, wrote a book titled *Small Is Beautiful: Economics as If People Mattered* that tried to apply Gandhian ideas to contemporary economics. That book's subtitle is at the heart of all of Gandhi's thinking and should be the criterion for all progressive planning in Canada: the interests of people, not of states or industrial conglomerates, belong front and centre. Also in Canada – largely because of its proximity to the United States and the influence of American-based firms – the risk is real that a brand of economics will be pursued in which people do not matter. Interest groups hide behind anonymous firms, and lobbyists influence political decisions, thus circumventing open democratic processes. A Gandhian *satyagraha* would both uncover and prevent such abuses.

Gandhi's Continued Relevance for India and Canada

Most of what Mahatma Gandhi did and said was in the context of India's struggle for independence in the first half of the twentieth century. India did gain freedom, although as two nations, not one. India did make great economic progress, albeit not on the basis of Gandhian economics but on modern Western terms. Many of the problems that Gandhi foresaw did materialize: vast stretches of nature were sacrificed to industrial development, inequality between the rich and the poor increased, and technology took over much of the life-world of most people.

How then is Gandhi still relevant for India and Canada? Gandhi inspires peace activists and ecologists, he is quoted by people who work for the mutual understanding of people of different religions, and he is the patron saint of social workers who advocate for the rights of the dispossessed. While always on the side of the poor, Gandhi cannot be appropriated by any political party or by any partisan interest. And for Indians and Canadians alike, one key part of his relevance we find expressed in his *Talisman*, a statement of *ahimsa*: he recommended that politicians visualize the face of the poorest and weakest human being they had seen in their life and then ask themselves whether the intended action was of any use to that person.[17]

Conclusion

There is a lot of Gandhian writing in the literary market. It is important to keep Gandhi's autobiography available, for it is a timeless classic in its own right. Perhaps it is time to put together a selection of Gandhi's utterances of relevance to Canadians today, considering the popularity he still enjoys. Our young people especially need to learn why their elders keep erecting Gandhi statues and renaming city streets after him. Gandhi's life touched so many people and his thoughts cover so many issues that today's Canadians will find inspiring. Gandhi's conviction that *ahimsa* was in the end a more powerful tool to change the world than reliance on military force and violent revolution, has inspired peace activists all over the world. It has persuaded among others Karen Ridd, the daughter of Carl Ridd, a former professor of Religious Studies at the University of Winnipeg, to engage herself on behalf of political prisoners in Central America and to gain their freedom.[18] Gandhi's memory and spirit are alive in Winnipeg, Manitoba. May they live and flourish across Canada.

Notes

1 Bender, "Winnipeg Names Street." The event drew some comments from the public. While most of these were positive, some criticized the choice of a "foreign" celebrity over against Canadian promoters of human rights.
2 Klostermaier, *Der moderne Hinduismus*. A revised version was published in 2012.
3 Klostermaier, *Mahatma Gandhi*.
4 Klostermaier, *A Survey of Hinduism*.
5 Forthcoming.
6 Torchia, *Gandhi, Ecology, and World Religions*.
7 It makes sense to preserve the memory of great human beings, whose lives have been an inspiration to their contemporaries and whose example could inspire us today. More specifically, Gandhi's words do not carry the taint of religious sectarianism or of political opportunism. His admission of failures and errors makes his successes and triumphs all the more credible. His language is simple and his thinking is profound. Reading his *Auto-*

biography or perusing the many topical anthologies published by the Navajivan Trust is still a spiritual refreshment and a moral encouragement.

8 Gandhi, *Ashram Observances in Action*.

9 Gandhi, "Speech at Meeting in Lausanne," 8 December 1931, *eCWMG* 54, 269.

10 Ibid., 270.

11 Gandhi, *An Autobiography*, xi.

12 Gandhi, "'What Are We to Do?'" in *Young India*, 11 October 1928, *eCWMG* 43, 83.

13 Gandhi, "Talk with a Friend," in *Harijan*, 23 June 1946, *eCWMG* 91, 53.

14 Gandhi, "The Great Sentinel," in *Young India*, 13 October 1921, *eCWMG* 24, 414.

15 Gandhi, "Hindu–Muslim Tension: Its Cause and Cure," in *Young India*, 28 May 1924, *eCWMG* 28, 49.

16 Gandhi, in Parel, ed., *Hind Swaraj and Other Writings*, 110.

17 A facsimile of the *Talisman* can be found between pages 88 and 89 of Tendulkar, *Mahatma*, vol. 8.

18 Mentioned in Nagler, *The Search for a Nonviolent Future*, 26–29.

ॐ

Who Speaks for the Conscience of Canada? Twenty Years of Hamilton's Gandhi Peace Festival: Local Lessons, Global Relevance

Rama S. Singh

From coast to coast to coast, hello Canada! This is Gandhi Peace Festival, from Hamilton, the home of Gandhi Peace Festival and the peace capital of Canada! Mr. Gandhi has arrived, in spirit as well as in four hundred and fifty pounds of pure gold – I mean, bronze. I am of course talking about the Gandhi Statue which is standing next to us right in front of the City Hall. The statue is a gift from the Government of India and the Indo-Canadian community of Hamilton. We have with us distinguished national and international guests, many people from across Canada as well as from south of the border, and we have the most loving people of all, I mean the Hamiltonians, to welcome you. So I offer you a very warm welcome and say, let's get the ball rolling and celebrate the Twentieth Anniversary of the Gandhi Peace Festival in Hamilton.

These were my opening remarks at the Hamilton Gandhi Peace Festival on Saturday, 29 September 2012. It was a beautiful day, and the gathering was one of the most colourful that we have had at City Hall. Busloads of senior citizens from Toronto, in full Indian regalia with Indian dress and tricolour Gandhi caps and flags, came to welcome the father (bapu), M.K. Gandhi, to Canada. It was an emotional scene, and many cried. The Gandhi Peace Festival is unique, perhaps the only event of its kind anywhere. Since its inception, in 1993, it has come a long way. Started by the India–Canada Society and co-sponsored by the Centre for Peace Studies at McMaster University and the City of Hamilton, the peace festival has become a cultural landmark in Hamilton.

The festival as we know it started in 1993 in the form of a celebration of India; this turned into an annual festival starting with the 125th anniversary of Gandhi's birthday in 1994. From the very beginning, the Gandhi Peace Festival strived to be inclusive, and as time went by it began to engage with the wider community and to expand its area of operations. It is an illustration of Gandhian-inspired activism at a popular level in Canada.

To appreciate the presence of Gandhi and promotion of Gandhian ideals in a modern, Canadian setting, I will address the following questions: What is the Gandhi Peace Festival? Why was it initiated? What has it achieved, and what have we learned? Finally and significantly, what do we need in Canada, practically speaking, to achieve our long-term goals?

The Nature of the Gandhi Peace Festival: An Experiment in Peace Building

Started by the India–Canada Society of Hamilton and co-sponsored by the Centre for Peace Studies, McMaster University, and the City of Hamilton, the Gandhi Peace Festival has grown in its structure and now enjoys the support of a large and diverse group of peace and human rights organizations from Hamilton and the surrounding region. Over the years, in an effort to make it more inclusive, a Gandhi Peace Festival Advisory Council has evolved. The council now oversees the festival, but the India–Canada Society still plays the major role. Financially, the festival is supported by the India–Canada Society, the City of Hamilton, and members of the Indo-Canadian community. The Gandhi Peace Festival started with the following objectives:

1. To promote non-violence, peace and justice;
2. To provide an avenue for various peace and human rights organizations within the local community to become collectively visible, and exchange dialogues and resources;
3. To build on local interest and dialogue in peace and human rights issues which develop around the world.

Each year the festival selects a theme that reflects a national or international topic of concern. In 2012 the theme was "The Gandhian Path to Peace: Truth, Nonviolence, Service." Each year, a distinguished lecturer is invited to speak on the chosen theme at City Hall. In 2012, the festival key-note speaker was the Consul-General of South Africa. Among the regular invited guests are various city officials, the McMaster University president, the Consul-General of India, local MPPs and MPs, and guests from abroad.

The festival consists of a formal welcome by Hamilton's mayor, cultural programs, a peace walk in downtown Hamilton, free Indian vegetarian food, and live music. Each year, the festival also seeks to invite entertainers from different communities. Starting with less than fifty participants, the festival has grown, and it now attracts about five hundred people from the wider community. We have done everything we can to make the festival inclusive. Admission is free and is open to all. The number of young people attending the festival has grown, and students from McMaster University and Mohawk College have played major roles.

But the Gandhi Peace Festival is more than a public gathering and affir-mation of Gandhi's principles of non-violence. Central to the festival are a series of educational activities that foster reflection on the nature, prob-lems, and meanings of peace and non-violence. First and foremost among these events is the annual Gandhi Lecture on Nonviolence. The first of these public lectures was given by Dr. Karan Singh, statesman and scholar from India. The Gandhi Lecture has brought to McMaster University some of the most interesting scholars and activists from around the world, includ-ing Gene Sharp (United States), Adam Curle (United Kingdom), Douglas Roche (Canada), Medha Patkar (India), Fatima Meer (South Africa), Low-itja O'Donoghue (Australia), Acharya Ramamurti (India), Sulak Sivaraksa (Thailand), Satish Kumar (UK), Narayan Desai (India), Rajmohan Gandhi (United States), Richard Falk (United States), Chris Hedges (United States), and Ela Bhatt (India).

Related to this lecture are other peace-building activities. One of these is the "Writing for Peace" contest, initiated in 2004 and open to local high school students. Students write an essay on the theme of the peace festival that year, and prizes (cash and a certificate) are awarded to the winners. Two students each from grades nine/ten and eleven/twelve are selected each year. In 2010, this program was changed to "Peace Awards for Youths," with the recipients chosen for their peace and volunteer work in the community.

Another activity is McMaster Peace Week (Mac Peace), an annual week established in 2004 to promote the Gandhi Peace Festival on the McMas-ter University campus. A students' committee, under the guidance of the Centre for Peace Studies, has been registered under the McMaster Students Union. Mac Peace consists of a week-long program focusing on peace- and human-rights-related issues presented in the form of workshops, lectures, round tables, movie nights, lunchtime music concerts, and so forth. The

McMaster Student Union (MSU) and the Ontario Public Interest Research Group (OPIRG) are major supporters.

Another activity, this one intended specifically to celebrate the life and work of Dr. Martin Luther King, Jr., is a Gandhi–King Dinner Event. The first was organized in October 2008; the second in March 2012. The first was graced by the presence of Reverend Samuel Kyles, who had stood on the balcony in Memphis with Dr. King on the fateful day he was murdered. The second focused on reducing hate crime, and hosted Daryl Davis, an American jazz and blues musician and social activist. He talked about "transforming hate" and showed how he had been able to engage a number of Ku Klux Klan (KKK) members and been able to persuade them to give up their hoods and gowns. It was a remarkable achievement in the transformation of hate into friendship.

In the future, we plan to expand on these activities by launching a regular Gandhi–King Community Forum and inviting speakers to talk about local and national issues of community importance. The purpose will be to engage local social activists and scholars on a year-round basis and build a solid mosaic of community support.

The Origins of the Gandhi Peace Festival

At the risk of dwelling on my own past, it was my own experiences, my own evolving sense of how to look at the world, that convinced me that here in my home of Canada (as much as anywhere else in the world), we need to embrace Gandhian principles as a guide to life. Gandhi asks us: "Be the change you wish to see in the world." If one said that this is easier said than done, one would be right. But, perceptive man that he was, Gandhi knew that the solution to all problems begins with the self. His solution consists of three steps: self-observation (*atm nirichhan*), self-examination (*atm parichhan*), and self-correction (*atm sodhan*). This essentially means that we need to start observing our own life, honestly and critically examining what is right and what is wrong, and correcting what needs to be corrected or changed in order to bring our life into line with how we wish to live or how we would like others to live.

By the time I finished grade eight, the farthest distance I had travelled was 9 kilometres; that was the distance to my secondary school. By the time I graduated from high school, the farthest I had travelled was 12 kilometres, the distance to my high school. By the time I graduated from university, I had travelled a whopping distance of 300 kilometres to Kanpur. When I received my immigration papers for Canada, I felt that I was on the top of the world. I was going to fly halfway around the world! The village boy thought he had it made. You will agree that for a boy from a village where no one had finished grade twelve before him and no one could read telegrams in English, this was not a bad achievement.

I felt that I was on the top of the world, that is, until one day I read that the earth was like a grain of sand in the universe. For all the stars we can see, the universe is pretty much empty, and there are very few grains of sand, few bodies of any kind, in this vast empty space. I was shocked. I had never felt so small in my life; my ego had been pricked, so to speak; the needle had hit the balloon! This observation that my life in the universe was relatively insignificant convinced me to stand back from my very small concerns, from my development on a material level, and think more about the value of the world community of which I was a part. With what awareness of Gandhi that I had, I began looking more at myself and choosing to value the security and well-being of others. My new realization of the universe's size changed my outlook on life, my outlook on everything. It changed my course in life. I had not gone mad; rather, I had begun to put things in perspective.

A second experience that pushed me to develop the Gandhi Peace Festival is my education. I am an evolutionary biologist by training, and I earn my living teaching and researching biology. For nearly forty years I have taught a course called "Human Diversity and Human Nature." The name of the course may have changed, but the major topics have pretty much remained the same. They include these: class; caste and race; intelligence quotient (IQ) and intelligence; race and immigration; science and gender; human behaviour; complex disease; the roles of nature and nurture; and altruism. I have learned much from teaching this course, especially that evolutionary biology can be distilled into three words: diversity, change, and control of destiny. Life depends on diversity, change is part of life, and humans control their destiny. We are not chained by our genes. We do not notice, but we have changed the world in unimaginable ways.

Look around yourself; there is very little that is "natural." Your house, your workplace, buildings, schools, roads, gardens, swimming pools, even parks, are all human-made. Humans love to modify their surroundings. We have developed amazing abilities and have transcended our biological limits. We do things we are not designed to do: we have no wings, but we can fly; we are land creatures, but we can dive deep into the ocean; we can climb high mountains. We explore beyond our planets; we go to the Moon and Mars. And what is the lesson from all this? It is that nature has endowed us with basic potential, but we can find ways to go beyond that and around biological limits or natural constraints and to control our own destiny. The

Gandhi Peace Festival, I reasoned, would be essentially an experiment in learning how to control our own destiny in the most constructive possible way: by promoting non-violence as a way of seeing the world.

What Have We Achieved and What Have We Learned?

Organizers of the Gandhi Peace Festival believe that over the past twenty years, we have managed to develop a stronger culture of peace and non-violence in its different forms. The Gandhi Peace Festival is widely known in Canada, and we have begun to network with various groups across Canada. Presently we are working with the Mahatma Gandhi Canadian Foundation for World Peace (Edmonton) and a number of social and religious organizations from Toronto area. We also hear about Gandhi peace festivals in other parts of the world. We can measure the growth of such culture, such consciousness-raising, in various ways. For one, the attendance at the peace festival has grown and has become more diverse. It started with a somewhat ethnic flavour, but now over 60 percent of the attendees are non-ethnic, and most of them are young, mostly students. We have made repeated attempts to include people from the First Nations, and we have had spectacular success in honouring Native traditions. For another, because of the Gandhi Peace Festival and other peace-related activities, the stature of Hamilton as a city engaged in peace work has grown. We keep getting messages to this effect from around the world. We also feel that we have succeeded in trans forming the city into a place that realizes that peace is more than protest and that efforts to bring it about are not limited to young radicals. Peace issues are *life* issues; they relate to food, shelter, health, and the environment. This is why the city, the university, the Hamilton Community Foundation, the YMCA and YWCA, Rotary Clubs, religious institutions, and service and support groups have all slowly joined in the peace festival directly or indirectly. Noteworthy with regard to Hamilton's development as a peace-oriented city is that local peace groups have become better organized. Examples of active groups, besides the Gandhi Peace Advisory Council, include Culture of Peace Hamilton, the Department of Peace Group, Voice of Women, Amnesty International, the Hamilton Centre for Civic Inclusion, Physicians for Global Survival, Fix Our World, and many others. We are branding Hamilton as the city of peace and the peace capital of Canada!

While the peace festival and related activities have provided an avenue for engaging community and promoting community dialogue about the role and importance of peace, we have a long way to go. For all the talk about community harmony, away from workplaces there remains benign neglect as well as community division and isolation. Temples, *gurdwaras*, mosques, synagogues, churches, and other places of worship end up behaving like embassies and operate with their own cultural rules that promote homogeneity within and heterogeneity between groups. One goal of the peace festival has been to break down religious, ethnic, and cultural barriers and to appeal for a unified community and families.

From my vantage point within the Gandhi Peace Festival, I think that we in the community have learned, over the years, some essential lessons about peace and peacebuilding, lessons that can help us in the Gandhi Peace Festival become better ambassadors of peace. First, "peace" does not mean the same thing to all people. The meaning of peace varies from place to place, even from person to person. It can denote inner calm and contentment – a feeling, that is, like the simple peace in your quiet backyard, peace through meditation, and peace from the hustle and bustle of everyday life. It can also denote a state of freedom from pain and anxiety, freedom in the form of a full stomach, a roof over one's head, decent health, and freedom from fear of persecution, torture, and death. This inescapable diversity of meanings, from the ephemeral to the eternal, has arguably weakened the meaning of peace in everyday conversation. But second and related, we have come to understand that the later and more basic sense of peace – peace as a freedom from want, fear, and deprivation, is essential, valid, and increasingly necessary in the world. The times have changed. Over the course of the past half century, extending from the hippie movement and the Vietnam War to Greenpeace to deep ecology to climate change to the financial meltdown and the Occupy Movement, peace has come to mean more than just the inner serenity that people crave; it is now a matter of life and death. Peace now means the elimination of poverty and hunger; of industrial pollution in an age of dwindling resources; of rampant corruption; of the growing divide between the rich and the poor; and of growing religious disharmony and intolerance, both local and global. The Gandhi Peace Festival must define and then promote peace as the elimination of an immoral and overindulgent individualism and lack of sensitivity to those on the social margins.

As we have better understood what constitutes peace, the peace for which we must lobby and which we must affirm ("what is peace"), we have also learned something about how to foster it. For one thing, the single most important step in achieving any success in peacebuilding is to bring people together. As they live their lives, the masses will be busy with work and family and with putting food on the table. We should not expect them to regularly engage in community issues related to peace. Peacebuilding is an art of people who can spare a moment. In every community there are people who enjoy the respect of their community and who thankfully are able to spare time and/or resources for community causes. The world has become a better place because of such people, who despite being busy making a living, find ways to help the community grow and our humanity grow. We need such people, and we need to bring them to the community forum. For another, peacebuilding is a process with clear outcomes, and it requires solving problems. It requires us to focus on the things that prevent peace. Furthermore, peace is not possible without sacrifices, and it requires that peacebuilders be connected to the people, the community. Finally, Gandhi's advice "Listen to your conscience" must be the start of any individual initiative taken in the name of peace and social work. All of us tend to yearn to do big things, to move the mountain so to speak; but it is the little things we can do that will make a difference, at least locally.

Who Speaks for the Conscience of Canada?

From the standpoint of the Gandhi Peace Festival Organization, Gandhi's principles are making increasing sense. As the world experiences turmoil ranging from terrorism to economic exploitation, from environmental catastrophes to political and moral defeatism, as well as discord between people and governments, even while more and more resources are wasted on militaries and war machinery, Gandhi's emphasis on *ahimsa* (non-violence) as a guiding life principle and as a mode of social change (*satyagraha*) is making more sense. As unchecked greed destroys the environment, and as the divide between the rich and the poor keeps widening, Gandhi's message of *sarvodaya* (universal uplift) is making more sense. And as our population moves from traditional ways of making a living and as demands grow on governments and educational institutions, while the population also grows and urbanization swallows up more and more agricultural land, Gandhi's principle of *swaraj*, of a life grounded in ethics and sensitive to the limitations of technology in fostering inner peace, is making more sense.

Individually, each of us speaks for our own conscience, but who speaks for the conscience of Canada? Who speaks for the conscience of the nation? This is not a rhetorical question; it is a serious question about pride in ourselves and in nation-building. *Speaking up for one's community, or one's country*, is the first step in taking responsibility for constructive peacebuilding. More individuals taking a stand, a public stand, for the peace we require, is the need of the hour.

It is becoming clearer and clearer that our government does not speak for the conscience of the people. All governments, elected or not, are based on ideological partisan politics and are interested first in protecting their own interests and the interests of their close supporters. They also pay close attention to short-term interests to secure their own re-election, with the result that any long-term national agenda suffers or at least gets postponed. The invention of parliamentary democracy, even if based on adversarial interests, amounted to a revolution in human civilization. All over the world, however, it is becoming clear that many governments are ignoring the wishes of the people and are paying more attention to their own self-interests. This is true generally of *all* parties, be they left, right, or centre. That is why committed social activists tend not to seek elected positions and instead work for people from outside the government. They survive and enjoy respect because they speak for *all* people. All nations have seen such social activists, but one might suggest that the breed is dying out. Gandhi never held any office, but he spoke for the conscience of millions. Where are the Gandhis of today? Where are the Gandhians of Canada? The Gandhi Peace Festival is one attempt to raise the conscience of Canadians and to expose the serious drawbacks of divisive politics. More such attempts by social activists are necessary. Our parliamentary institutions are living in the past; they are outdated, and they need overhauling. Politicians try to divide and rule and to stick labels on people of different political persuasions as if people are of different breeds with different needs. The voices of ordinary people, speaking for, reflecting on, and debating the dimensions of peace that we know to be essential, are necessary for advancing the cause of peace in all of its dimensions.

Epilogue: A Gandhi Memorial in Hamilton

In 2010, thanks to the efforts of the City of Hamilton, a full-size statue of Gandhi was installed at the City Hall to mark the twentieth anniversary of the Gandhi Peace Festival. It was a gift from the Indian Council of Cultural Relations (ICCR) and was obtained through the efforts of the municipal government and the local Indo-Canadian community. It will stand as a reminder of our commitment that the people of this city will stand together and speak on behalf the poor, the oppressed, and the exploited. We owe it to ourselves, to our community, and to our humanity.

The plaque at the Gandhi statue reads as follows:

Mahatma Gandhi (1869–1948)

This statue of Mohandas Karamchand Gandhi, received as a gift from the Government of India and obtained through the efforts of the City of Hamilton and the local Indo-Canadian community, recognizes the twenty-year contribution made by the Gandhi Peace Festival to the cultural life of the city and the promotion of peace, nonviolence and social justice.

Born and educated in India and with a law degree from London, England, Gandhi moved to South Africa in 1893. There he experienced firsthand the indignity of racism against blacks and Indians. With truth and non-violence as his uncompromising moral principles, Gandhi launched his civil disobedience movement and experimented with the use of satyagraha (Soul Force) as a constructive weapon against oppression. Gandhi returned to India in 1915 and championed the non-violent struggle for Indian independence.

His open, utterly simple life and his perseverance on behalf of the poor masses everywhere caught the attention of the world. He preached the universal Law of Love and lived a life of service. He was affectionately called Bapu (Father); he held no office but spoke for the conscience of millions; he was revered and addressed as Mahatma (Great Soul). When asked about his message, he said:

"My life is my message"

The City of Hamilton   2 October 2012

Appendix

Materials for an Appreciation
of Gandhi in Canada Today

Materials listed below in Sections I–III, but not used in the chapters, do not appear in the bibliography.

I. Some Key Writings by and about Mahatma Gandhi

Bondurant, Joan. *Conquest of Violence: The Gandhian Philosophy of Conflict*. Princeton: Princeton University Press, 1958.

Bose, Nirmal Kumar. *Selections from Gandhi*. 2nd ed. Ahmedabad: Navajivan Publishing House, 1957.

Brown, Judith. *Gandhi: Prisoner of Hope*. Delhi: Oxford University Press, 1992.

Gandhi, Mahatma. *The Essential Writings*. Edited with an Introduction and Notes by Judith M. Brown. Oxford World's Classics. Oxford: Oxford University Press, 2008.

Gandhi, M.K. *An Autobiography, or The Story of My Experiments with Truth*. Translated from the Gujarati by Mahadev Desai. Ahmedabad: Navajivan Publishing House, 1927.

———. *Hind Swaraj and Other Writings*. Edited by Anthony J. Parel. Cambridge Texts in Modern Politics. Cambridge: Cambridge University Press, 1997.

———. *Sarvodaya (The Welfare of All)*. Edited by Bharatan Kumarappa. Ahmedabad: Navajivan Publishing House, 1954.

———. *Satyagraha in South Africa*. Translated from the Gujarati by Valji Govindji Desai. 2nd ed. Ahmedabad: Navajivan Publishing House, 1950.

II. Select Associations in Canada Working to Implement Gandhian Ideas

This list consists mainly of associations with a broadly Gandhian outlook, and a selection of related associations focused on peace activism and study.

Education for Peace Canada, Vancouver. http://efpinternational.org/efp-canada

Ekta Canada, a partner of *Ekta Parishad*. http://ektacanada.weebly.com

The Gandhi Peace Project, Centre for Peace Studies, McMaster University, Hamilton. http://www.humanities.mcmaster.ca/~gandhi/festival/index.html

Gandhi Society of Calgary, Calgary. http://www.gandhisociety.org

Mahatma Gandhi Canadian Foundation for World Peace, Edmonton. http://www .gandhifoundation.ca

Mahatma Gandhi Centre of Canada Inc., Winnipeg. http://www.gandhicentre.ca/index .php

Mahatma Gandhi Peace Council of Ottawa. Ottawa. http://www.gandhiji.ca

Natraj Youth Cultural Organization, Toronto. http://nycocanada.com/index.html

Nonviolent Peaceforce – Canada, Toronto. http://www.nonviolentpeaceforce.org/non violent-peaceforce-canada

Peace Brigades International: Canada, Ottawa. http://www.pbicanada.org/index.php/en

The Real Gandhi Farm, Queens County, Nova Scotia. http://www.angelfire.com/clone2/ gandhifarm (This farm appears to have been sold in recent years.)

Salt. http://store.saltmatters.com

III. Some Publications Relevant for Study and Application of Gandhian Ideas in Canada

Certain of these books focus on studying Gandhi-inspired activism; others offer more practical advice in applying Gandhi's teachings. This list is not exhaustive; it is intended to point interested readers to further resources.

Aikens, Anne Marie. *Racism: Deal with It Before It Gets under Your Skin*. Toronto: Lorimer, 2005.

Bay, Christian, and Charles C. Walker. *Civil Disobedience: Theory and Practice*. Montreal: Black Rose Books, 1975.

Brower, Michael, and Warren Leon. *The Consumer's Guide to Effective Environmental Choices: Practical Advice from the Union of Concerned Scientists*. New York: Three Rivers Press, 2009.

Cortright, David. *Gandhi and Beyond: Non-Violence for a New Political Age*. 2nd ed. London and New York: Routledge, 2009.

Cronish, Nellie, Barbara Selley, and Suzanne Havala. *The Complete Idiot's Guide to Being Vegetarian in Canada*. Toronto: Prentice-Hall of Canada, 2000.

Danesh, H.B., Sara Clarke-Habibi, and Stacey Makortoff. *Education for Peace Student Manual*. Book 1. Education for Peace Integrative Curriculum Series, vol. 10. Vancouver: International Education for Peace Institute, 2007.

de Pape, Brigitte, and Erika Shaker. *Power of Youth: Youth and Community-Led Activism in Canada*. Our Schools Our Selves, vol. 21, no. 3. Ottawa: Canadian Centre for Policy Alternatives, 2012.

Ellwood, Wayne. *The No-Nonsense Guide to Degrowth and Sustainability*. London: New Internationalist, 2013.

Finkel, L. Ann. *Gandhi: The Truth Can Fight*. Powell River: Ti-Jean Press, 1997.

Fleras, Augie. *Unequal Relations: An Introduction to Race and Ethnic Dynamics in Canada*. 6th ed. Toronto: Pearson Prentice Hall, 2010.

Forward, Martin. *Inter-Religious Dialogue: A Short Introduction*. Oxford: Oneworld, 2001.

Francione, Gary L. *Animals as Persons: Essays on the Abolition of Animal Exploitation*. New York: Columbia University Press, 2009.

Franklin, Ursula, and Sarah Jane Freeman. *Ursula Franklin Speaks: Thoughts and Afterthoughts*. Montreal and Kingston: McGill–Queen's University Press, 2014.

Gandhi, Arun, ed. *World without Violence: Can Gandhi's Vision Become Reality?* New Delhi: Wiley Eastern for the M.K. Gandhi Institute for Nonviolence, 1995.

Hardiman, David. *Gandhi in His Time and Ours*. New York: Columbia University Press, 2003.

Holmes, Robert L. *Non-Violence in Theory and in Practice*. Belmont: Wadsworth, 1990.

Juergensmeyer, Mark. *Gandhi's Way: A Handbook of Conflict Resolution*. Berkeley: University of California Press, 2002.

Menzies, Heather. *Reclaiming the Commons for the Common Good: A Memoir & Manifesto*. Gabriola Island: New Society Publishers, 2014.

O'Brien, Anne Sibley, and Perry Edmond O'Brien. *After Gandhi: One Hundred Years of Nonviolent Resistance*. Watertown: Charlesbridge, 2009.

Quinn, Michael S., Wayne A. Freimund, and Len Broberg, eds. *Parks, Peace, and Partnership: Global Initiatives in Transboundary Conservation*, Energy, Ecology, and the Environment 4. Calgary: University of Calgary Press, 2012.

Sandberg, L. Anders, and Sverker Solin. *Sustainability, The Challenge: People, Power and the Environment*. Montreal: Black Rose Books, 1998.

Scalmer, Sean. *Gandhi in the West: The Mahatma and the Rise of Radical Protest*. Cambridge: Cambridge University Press, 2011.

Shepard, Mark. *The Community of the Ark: A Visit with Lanza del Vasto, His Fellow Disciples of Mahatma Gandhi, and Their Utopian Community in France*. 20th Anniversary Edition. San Pedro: Simple Productions, 2011.

Sunstein, Cass R., and Martha C. Nussbaum, eds. *Animal Rights: Current Debates and New Directions*. Oxford and New York: Oxford University Press, 2004.

Vasil, Adria. *Ecoholic: Your Guide to the Most Environmentally Friendly Information, Products and Services in Canada*. Toronto: Vintage Canada, 2007.

Wadden, Marie. *Where the Pavement Ends: Canada's Aboriginal Recovery Movement and the Urgent Need for Reconciliation*. Toronto: Douglas and McIntyre, 2009.

Warner, Tom. *Never Going Back: A History of Queer Activism in Canada*. Toronto: University of Toronto Press, 2002.

Wastebusters, Ltd. *The Green Office Manual: A Guide to Responsible Practice*. London and Sterling: Earthscan, 2000.

Weber, Thomas. *Gandhi, Gandhism, and the Gandhians*. Foreword by Rajmohan Gandhi. New Delhi: Roli, 2006.

Wine, Jeri Dawn, and Janice L. Ristock, eds. *Women and Social Change: Feminist Activism in Canada*. Toronto: Lorimer, 1991.

Bibliography

Aho, James. *Religious Mythology and the Art of War: Comparative Religious Symbolism of Military Violence*. Westport: Greenwood Press, 1981.

Anderson, Benedict. *Imagined Communities: Reflections on the Origin and Spread of Nationalism*. New York: Verso Books, 1983.

Andrews, C.F. *Mahatma Gandhi's Ideas: Including Selections from His Writings*. New Delhi: Anmol, 1987.

Ansbro, John J. *Martin Luther King, Jr.: Nonviolent Strategies and Tactics for Social Change*. Maryknoll: Orbis Books, 1985.

Attenborough, Richard. *The Words of Gandhi*. 2nd ed. New York: Newmarket Press, 1996.

Azad, Maulana. *India Wins Freedom*. London: Longmans, Green, 1960.

Baird, Robert D. "The Convergence of Distinct Worlds: Nehru and Gandhi." In *Indian Critiques of Gandhi*, 19–39. Edited by Harold Coward. Albany: SUNY Press, 2003.

Bakker, Hans. *Gandhi and the Gita*. Toronto: Canadian Scholars' Press, 1993.

———. *Towards a Just Civilization: A Gandhian Perspective on Human Rights and Development*. Toronto: Canadian Scholars' Press, 1988.

Banerjee, Sikata. *Make Me a Man!: Masculinity, Hinduism, and Nationalism in India*. Albany: SUNY Press, 2005.

Baruna, Arati, ed. *Gandhi and Grant: Their Philosophical Affinities*. Delhi: Academic Excellence, 2010.

Battiste, Marie. "Enabling the Autumn Seed: Toward a Decolonized Approach to Aboriginal Knowledge, Language and Education." In *Schooling in Transition: Readings in Canadian History of Education*, 277–86. Edited by Sara Z. Burke and Patrice Milewski. Toronto: University of Toronto Press, 2012.

Baum, Gregory. *Nationalism, Religion, and Ethics*. Montreal and Kingston: McGill–Queen's University Press, 2001.

Behiels, Michael D. "The Expansion of a Nation: 1867–1990." In *Canada: Its Regions and People*, 445–524. Edited by Michael D. Behiels and K.S. Mathew. New Delhi: Munshiram Manoharlal, 1998.

Behiels, Michael D. and K.S. Mathew. "Introduction." In *Canada: Its Regions and People*, vii–xii. Edited by Michael D. Behiels and K.S. Mathew. New Delhi: Munshiram Manoharlal, 1998.

Bender, Jim. "Winnipeg Names Street after Mahatma Gandhi." *Winnipeg Sun*, 15 August 2013. http://www.winnipegsun.com/2013/08/15/winnipeg-names-street -after-mahatma-gandhi.

The Bhagavad Gita. Translated by Ramanand Prasad. Fremont: American Gita Society, 1988.

Bhana, Surendra, and Goolam H. Vahed. *The Making of a Political Reformer: Gandhi in South Africa 1893–1914*. New Delhi: Manohar, 2005.

Bissoondath, Neil. *Selling Illusions: The Cult of Multiculturalism in Canada*. Toronto: Penguin Books, 1994.

Bright, J.S. *Frontier and Its Gandhi*. Lahore: Allied Indian Publishers, 1944.

Brown, Judith M. *Gandhi and Civil Disobedience: The Mahatma in Indian Politics, 1928–1934*. Cambridge: Cambridge University Press, 1977.

——. *Gandhi: Prisoner of Hope*. Delhi: Oxford University Press, 1992.

——. *Gandhi's Rise to Power: Indian Politics 1915–1922*. Cambridge: Cambridge University Press, 1972.

——. *Global South Asians: Introducing the Modern Diaspora*. Delhi: Cambridge University Press, 2007.

Brown, Judith M., and Anthony J. Parel, eds. *The Cambridge Companion to Gandhi*. Cambridge: Cambridge University Press, 2011.

Burnet, Jean. "Immigration and Ethnic Relations since 1867." In *Canada: Its Regions and People*, 353–90. Edited by Michael D. Behiels and K.S. Mathew. New Delhi: Munshiram Manoharlal, 1998.

Canadian Bar Association. http://www.cba.org/public.

Chakravarti, P.C. *The Art of War in Ancient India*. Delhi: Oriental Publishers, 1972.

Christian, William. "George Grant and Mahatma Gandhi on Pacifism and Technology." In *Gandhi and Grant: Their Philosophical Affinities*, 16–29. Edited by Arati Baruna. Delhi: Academic Excellence, 2010.

Christian Century 60, no. 11 (1902), 333.

Coward, Harold. "Gandhi, Ambedkar, and Untouchability." In *Indian Critiques of Gandhi*, 41–66. Edited by Harold Coward. Albany: SUNY Press, 2003.

——, ed. *Hindu–Christian Dialogue: Perspectives and Encounters*. Maryknoll: Orbis Books, 1989.

——, ed. *Indian Critiques of Gandhi*. Albany: SUNY Press, 2003.

——, ed. *Modern Indian Responses to Religious Pluralism*. Albany: SUNY Press, 1987.

Coward, Harold, and Gordon Smith, eds. *Religion and Peacebuilding*. Albany: SUNY Press, 2004.

"CWMG Controversy." http://www.gandhiserve.org/e/cwmg/cwmg_controversy.htm.

Dabholkar, Devadatta. "Mahatma Gandhi: A Living Embodiment of Hindu-Christian Dialogue." *Journal of Hindu-Christian Studies* 5 (1992): 23–25.

Danielson, Leilah. *American Gandhi: A. J. Muste and the History of Radicalism in the Twentieth Century*. Philadelphia: University of Pennsylvania Press, 2014.

Das, Durga. *From Curzon to Nehru and Afterwards*. London: Collins, 1969.

Dei, George J. Sefa, and Stanley Doyle-Wood. "*Is We Who Haffi Ride Di Staam*: Critical Knowledge/Multiple Knowings – Possibilities, Challenges, and Resistance in Curriculum/Cultural Contexts." In *Integrating Aboriginal Perspectives into the School Curriculum: Purposes, Possibilities, and Challenges*, 151–80. Edited by Yatta Kanu. Toronto: University of Toronto Press, 2006.

Desai, Mahadev. *The Gospel of Selfless Action or The Gita According to Gandhi*. Translation from the Gujarati, with an additional introduction and commentary. Ahmedabad: Navajivan Publishing House, 1946.

Deshingkar, Giri. "Strategic Thinking in Ancient India and China: Kautilya and Sunzi across the Himalayan Gap." In *An Indian Quest for Understanding China*, 357–64. Edited by Tan Chung. New Delhi: Gyan Publishing House, 1998.

Desjardins, Michel. Review of *Religion and Peacebuilding*, edited by Harold Coward and Gordon Smith. *Studies in Religion/Sciences Religieuses* 33, nos. 3–4 (2004): 449–51.

Dhar, Hiranmay. "MSS' Commitment and Women's Resolve: A Report on Odisha State Level MSS Convention." *MSS Newsletter* 4, no. 1 (March 2012): 15–16.

Dikshitar, V.R. Ramachandra. *War in Ancient India*. 2nd ed. Delhi: Motilal Banarsidass, 1987.

Fernhout, Rein. "Combatting the Enemy: The Use of Scripture in Gandhi and Godse." In *Human Rights and Religious Values: An Uneasy Relationship?*, 120–32. Edited by Abdullahi A. Na'im et al. New York: Rodopi, 1995.

Galtung, Johan. "Violence, Peace, and Peace Research." *Journal of Peace Research* 6, no. 3 (1969): 167–91.

Gandhi, M.K. *Ashram Observances in Action*. Translated from the Gujarati by Mahadev Desai. Ahmedabad: Navajivan Publishing House, 1955.

———. *An Autobiography, or The Story of My Experiments with Truth*. Translated from the Gujarati by Mahadev Desai. Ahmedabad: Navajivan Publishing House, 1927.

———. *An Autobiography or The Story of My Experiments with Truth*. Translated from the Gujarati by Mahadev Desai, with a new introduction by Sunil Khilnani. London: Penguin Books, 2001.

———. "Between Cowardice and Violence." *mkgandhi.org*. http://www.mkgandhi.org/nonviolence/phil8.htm.

———. "Bullying." In *The Encyclopaedia of Gandhian Thoughts*, 34. Compiled by Anand T. Hingorani and Ganga Anand Hingorani. New Delhi: All India Congress Committee [I], 1985.

———. *Hind Swaraj and Other Writings*. Edited by Anthony J. Parel. Cambridge Texts in Modern Politics. Cambridge: Cambridge University Press, 1997.

———. *Hindu Dharma*. Edited by Bharatan Kumarappa. Ahmedabad: Navajivan Publishing House, 1950.

———. *The Hindu–Muslim Unity*. Pocket Gandhi Series, no. 10. Edited by Anand T. Hingorani. Bombay: Bharatiya Vidya Bhavan, 1965.

———. *Non-Violence in Peace and War*, vol. 1. Ahmedabad: Navajivan Publishing House, 1948.

———. *Speeches and Writings of M.K. Gandhi*. Edited by C.F. Andrews. 3rd ed. Madras: G.A. Natesan & Co., 1922.

Gandhi, Rajmohan. "Hinduism and Peacebuilding." In *Religion and Peacebuilding*, 45–68. Edited by Harold Coward and Gordon Smith. Albany: SUNY Press, 2004.

——. *Mohandas: A True Story of a Man, His People, and an Empire.* Delhi: Penguin Books India, 2006.

——. *Revenge and Reconciliation: Understanding South Asian History.* Delhi: Penguin Books India, 1999.

"Gandhi on Nonviolence" (1920). http://sfr-21.org/gandhi-nonviolence.html.

Gielen, Joris. "Mahātmā Gandhi's View on Euthanasia and Assisted Suicide." *Journal of Medical Ethics* 38, no. 7 (July 2012): 431–34. http://www.ncbi.nlm.nih.gov/pubmed/22375080.

Gorringe, Timothy. "Gandhi and the Christian Community." In *Indian Critiques of Gandhi*, 153–70. Edited by Harold Coward. Albany: SUNY Press, 2003.

Grant, George P. *Lament for a Nation.* Toronto: Anansi, 1965.

——. *Technology and Empire.* Toronto: Anansi, 1969.

Hardiman, David. *Gandhi in His Time and Ours: The Global Legacy of His Ideas.* New York: Columbia University Press, 2003.

Hawley, Michael. "Getting Past Orientalism: Gandhi, Multiculturalism, and Identity." *Religious Studies and Theology* 27, no. 2 (2008): 195–212.

——. "M.K. Gandhi and the Sikhs: Violence, Identity and Competing Modernities." In *Re-imagining South Asian Religion: Essays in Honour of Professors Harold G. Coward and Ronald W. Neufeldt*, 271–92. Edited by Pashaura Singh and Michael Hawley. Numen Book Series, vol. 141. Leiden: Brill, 2013.

——. "The Making of the Mahatma: Radhakrishnan's Critique of Gandhi." *Studies in Religion / Sciences Religieuses* 32, nos. 1–2 (2003): 135–48.

The Holy Bible. Revised Standard Version. Grand Rapids: Zondervan, 1989.

Hulan, Renée. *Canadian Historical Writing: Reading the Remains.* New York: Palgrave Macmillan, 2014.

Hunt, James D. *An American Looks at Gandhi: Essays in Satyagraha, Civil Rights, and Peace.* New Delhi: Promilla & Co., in Association with Bibliophile South Asia, 2005.

Husain, S. Abid. *Gandhiji and Communal Unity.* Bombay: Orient Longmans, 1969, 54. Quoted in Sheila McDonough, *Gandhi's Responses to Islam.* New Delhi: D.K. Printworld, 1994, 17.

Jaffrelot, Christophe. "Delhi, 30 Janvier 1948: Assassinat de Gandhi." *L'Histoire* no. 216 (December 1997): 64–69.

Jahanbegloo, Ramin. *The Gandhian Moment.* Cambridge: Harvard University Press, 2013.

——. *Introduction to Nonviolence.* New York: Palgrave Macmillan, 2014.

Jain, Devaki. *Panchayat Raj: Women Changing Governance.* UN Development Programme Gender and Development Monograph Series 5. New York: United Nations Development Programme, 1996 (September). http://www.devakijain.com/pdf/jain_panchayatraj.pdf.

Jha, Ashok Kumar, ed. *Women in Panchayati Raj Institutions.* New Delhi: Anmol, 2004.

Johnston, Hugh. *The Voyage of the Komagata Maru: The Sikh Challenge to Canada's Colour Bar.* Delhi: Oxford University Press, 1979.

Jordens, J.T.F. "Gandhi and the Bhagavadgita." In *Modern Indian Interpreters of the Bhagavadgita*, 88–109. Edited by Robert Minor. Albany: SUNY Press, 1986.

――――. "Gandhi and Religious Pluralism." In *Modern Indian Responses*, 3–18. Edited by Harold Coward. Albany: SUNY Press, 1987.

Juergensmeyer, Mark. *Encyclopedia of Religion*. 2nd ed. S.v. "Gandhi, Mohandas."

Kabir, Humayun, ed. *Maulana Azad: A Homage*. New Delhi: Government of India, Publications Division, 1958, 34. Quoted in Ian Henderson Douglas, *Abul Kalam Azad: An Intellectual and Religious Biography*, ed. Gail Minault and Christian W. Troll. Delhi: Oxford University Press, 1988, 276.

Karandikar, M. A. *Islam in India's Transition to Modernity*. New Delhi: Orient Longman, 1968.

Khan, Rasheedudin. "Portrait of a Great Patriot: Maulana Abul Kalam Azad (1888–1958)." In *Abul Kalam Azad*, 203–14. Political Thinkers of Modern India, vol. 17. Edited by Verinder Grover. New Delhi: Deep & Deep, 1992.

Kibriya, Mazhar. *Gandhi and the Indian Freedom Struggle*. New Delhi: APH Publishing, 1999.

Kirpal, Jeffrey J., and Rachel Fell McDermott. *Encountering Kālī: In the Margins, at the Center, in the West*. Berkeley: University of California Press, 2003.

Klostermaier, Klaus. "Hindu–Christian Dialogue: Its Religious and Cultural Implications." *Studies in Religion/Sciences Religieuses* 1, no. 2 (1971): 83–97.

――――. *Mahatma Gandhi: Freiheit ohne Gewalt*. Köln: Hegner, 1968.

――――. *Der moderne Hinduismus und die soziale Neuordnung Indiens*. PhD diss., Pontifical Gregorian University, 1961.

――――. *Der moderne Hinduismus und die soziale Neuordnung Indiens: Hinduismus und soziale Reformen in Indien*. Saarbrücken: AV Akademikerverlag, 2012.

――――. *A Survey of Hinduism*. 3rd ed. Albany: SUNY Press, 2007.

Koppedrayer, Kay. "Gandhi's *Autobiography* as Commentary on the *Bhagavad Gītā*." *International Journal of Hindu Studies* 6, no. 1 (2002): 47–73.

――――. Review of *Indian Critiques of Gandhi*, edited by Harold Coward. *Studies in Religion/Sciences Religieuses* 33, no. 2 (2004): 243–45.

――――. "A Week in the Life of Mahatma Gandhi." *World History Bulletin* 23, no. 2 (2008): 25–39.

Leys, Wayne R.A., and P.S.S. Rama Rao. *Gandhi and America's Educational Future: An Inquiry at Southern Illinois University*. Carbondale: Southern Illinois University Press, 1969.

Markovits, Claude. *The Un-Gandhian Gandhi: The Life and Afterlife of the Mahatma*. Delhi: Permanent Black, 2004.

McDonough, Sheila. *Gandhi's Responses to Islam*. New Delhi: D.K. Printworld, 1994.

Mehta, M., to Dr. Gordon Murray, 23 March 1956. Editor's collection.

Misra, Mamata. "Listening to Women Empowered by the MSS Movement." *MSS Newsletter* 4, no. 1 (March 2012): 13–15.

Miller, Rolland. "Indian Muslim Critiques of Gandhi." In *Indian Critiques of Gandhi*, 193–216. Edited by Harold Coward. Albany: SUNY Press, 2003.

Naess, Arne. "The Shallow and the Deep, Long-Range Ecology Movement: A Summary." *Inquiry* 16, nos. 1–4 (1973): 95–100.

Nagler, Michael N. *The Search for a Nonviolent Future: A Promise of Peace for Ourselves, Our Families, and Our World.* 2nd ed. Novato: New World Library, 2004.

Nair, Pyarelal. *Mahatma Gandhi: The Last Phase,* vol. 2. Ahmedabad: Navajivan, 1956.

Nanda, B.R. *Gandhi and His Critics.* Delhi: Oxford University Press, 1985.

———, ed. *Mahatma Gandhi: 125 Years. Remembering Gandhi, Understanding Gandhi, Relevance of Gandhi.* New Delhi: Indian Council for Cultural Relations and New Age International Publishers/Wiley Eastern, 1995.

Nandy, Ashis. *At the Edge of Psychology: Essays in Psychology and Culture.* Delhi: Oxford University Press, 1980.

———. *Bonfire of Creeds.* Delhi: Oxford University Press, 2007.

Neufeldt, Ronald. "The Hindu Mahasabha and Gandhi." In *Indian Critiques of Gandhi,* 131–51. Edited by Harold Coward. Albany: SUNY Press, 2003.

Newhouse, David, Cora Voyageur, and Dan Beavon. "Introduction." In *Hidden in Plain Sight: Contributions of Aboriginal Peoples to Canadian Identity and Culture,* 5, 13. Edited by Newhouse, Voyageur, and Beavon. Toronto: University of Toronto Press, 2005. Quoted in Renée Hulan, *Canadian Historical Writing: Reading the Remains.* New York: Palgrave Macmillan, 2014, 112.

"Panchayati Raj." *drdadhubri.org.* http://drdadhubri.org/programs/panchayat.asp.

Pandiri, Ananda M., compiler. *A Comprehensive, Annotated Bibliography on Mahatma Gandhi.* 2 vols. Ahmedabad: Navajivan, 2002, 2007.

Parekh, Bhikhu. *Gandhi: A Very Short Introduction.* Indian ed. Delhi: Oxford University Press, 2005.

Parel, Anthony J. "Introduction." In Gandhi, M.K. *Hind Swaraj and Other Writings,* xviii–xxix. Edited by Anthony J. Parel. Cambridge Texts in Modern Politics. Cambridge: Cambridge University Press, 1997.

———. "Principal Events in the Life of Mohandas Karamchand Gandhi." In Gandhi, M.K. *Hind Swaraj and Other Writings,* lxv–lxvii. Cambridge: Cambridge University Press, 1997.

Payne, Robert. *The Life and Death of Mahatma Gandhi.* New Delhi: Rupa, 1997.

Pearson, Anne. "The Mahila Shanti Sena: New Women's Peace Movement in India." *Peace Magazine* 20, no. 1 (January–March 2004): 15–19.

Pirzada, Syed Sharifuddin, ed. *Quaid's Correspondence.* Lahore: Services Book Club, 1987.

Premasiri, P.D. "The Place of Righteous War in Buddhism." *Journal of Buddhist Ethics* 10 (2003): 1–8.

Qureshi, Naeem M. *Pan-Islam in British Indian Politics: A Study of the Khilafat Movement, 1918–1924.* Leiden: Brill, 1999.

Ramagundam, Rahul. *Gandhi's Khadi: A History of Contention and Conciliation.* New Delhi: Orient Longman, 2008.

Ramamurti, Acharya. Quoted in "Mahila Shanti Sena (MSS) (Women's Peace Brigade)." *MSS Newsletter* 4, no. 1 (March 2012): 2.

Rauoof, A.A. *Meet Mr. Jinnah.* Lahore: Ashraf, 1944.

"The Real Gandhi Farm." http://www.angelfire.com/clone2/gandhifarm.

Robinson, Catherine A. *Interpretations of the Bhagavad-Gītā and Images of the Hindu Tradition: The Song of the Lord.* London and New York: Routledge, 2006.

Rudolph, Susanne Hoeber. *Gandhi: The Traditional Roots of Charisma.* Chicago: University of Chicago Press, 1983.

Ruffo, Armand Garnet. "Why Native Literature?" In *Native North America: Critical and Cultural Perspectives,* 110. Edited by Renée Hulan. Montreal: ECW Press, 1999. Quoted in Hulan, *Canadian Historical Writing: Reading the Remains.* New York: Palgrave Macmillan, 2014, 111–12.

Rukmani, T.S. "Tagore and Gandhi." In *Indian Critiques of Gandhi,* 107–28. Edited by Harold Coward. Albany: SUNY Press, 2003.

Rushdie, Salman. "Mohandas Gandhi." *Time Magazine.* 13 April 1998. http://www.time .com/time/magazine/article/0,9171,988159,00.html#ixzz2BMfwDQw6.

Salmond, Noel. "Both Iconoclast and Idolator: Gandhi on Worship of Images." *Studies in Religion/Sciences Religieuses* 31, nos. 3–4 (2002): 373–90.

Savarkar, Vinayak Damodar. *Hindutva: Who Is a Hindu?* Bombay: Veer Savarkar Prakashan, 1999.

Scalmer, Sean. *Gandhi in the West: The Mahatma and the Rise of Radical Protest.* Cambridge: Cambridge University Press, 2011.

Schwartzentruber, Paul. "Gandhi's Whirlpool: Swimming against Destiny in India and Canada, a Reflection on the Question of George Grant," 1–26. *Scribd.* http://www .scribd.com/doc/59194089.

Scott, David. "Response to Devadatta Dabholkar." *Journal of Hindu–Christian Studies,* 5 (1992): 25–28.

Seshachari, Candadai. *Gandhi and the American Scene: An Intellectual History and Inquiry.* Bombay: Nachiketa Publications, 1969.

Shah, Sayed Wiqar Ali. *Ethnicity, Islam, and Nationalism: Muslim Politics in the North-West Frontier Province 1937–1947.* Karachi: Oxford University Press, 2000.

Sharma, Arvind. "Accounting for Gandhi's Allegorical Interpretation of the Bhagavadgītā." *Studies in Religion/Sciences Religieuses* 32, no. 4 (2003): 499–509.

———. "Fearlessness (*Abhaya*) as a Fundamental Category in Gandhian Thought and Practice." *South Asia* 10, no.1 (1987): 35–52.

———. *A New Curve in the Ganges: Mahatma Gandhi's Interpretation of Hinduism.* New Delhi: D.K. Printworld, 2005.

———, ed. *Neo-Hindu Views of Christianity.* Leiden: Brill, 1988.

Shepard, Mark. *Mahatma Gandhi and His Myths: Civil Disobedience, Nonviolence, and Satyagraha in the Real World.* Los Angeles: Shepard Publications, 2002.

Sherwani, L.A., ed. *Pakistan Resolution to Pakistan, 1940–1947: A Selection of Documents Presenting the Case for Pakistan.* Karachi: National Publishing House, 1969.

Singh, Nikky-Guninder Kaur. "The Mahatma and the Sikhs." In *Indian Critiques of Gandhi,* 171–91. Edited by Harold Coward. Albany: SUNY Press, 2003.

Sinha, Mrinalini. *Colonial Masculinity: The "Manly Englishman" and the "Effeminate Bengali."* Manchester: Manchester University Press, 1995.

Sofri, Gianni. *Gandhi and India.* New York: Interlink Publishing, 1999.

"Spring Convocation 2010: Monday, 7 June, Wilfrid Laurier University." wlu.ca. http://www.wlu.ca/documents/41615/Spring_Convocation_Program.pdf.

Streets, Heather. *Martial Races: The Military, Race, and Masculinity in British Imperial Culture, 1857–1914.* Manchester: Manchester University Press, 2011.

Tendulkar, D.G. *Abdul Ghaffar Khan: Faith Is a Battle.* Bombay: Gandhi Peace Foundation, 1967.

———. *Mahatma: Life of Mohandas Karamchand Gandhi.* Illustrations collected and arranged by Vithalbhai K. Jhaveri, vol. 2. Bombay: Vithalbhai K. Jhaveri and D.G. Tendulkar, 1951.

———. *Mahatma: Life of Mohandas Karamchand Gandhi.* 2nd. ed., vol. 6. New Delhi: Government of India, Ministry of Information and Broadcasting, 1962.

———. *Mahatma: Life of Mohandas Karamchand Gandhi.* Illustrations collected and arranged by Vithalbhai K. Jhaveri, vol. 7. Bombay: Vithalbhai K. Jhaveri and D.G. Tendulkar, 1953.

———. *Mahatma: Life of Mohandas Karamchand Gandhi.* Illustrations collected and arranged by Vithalbhai K. Jhaveri, vol. 8. Bombay: Vithalbhai K. Jhaveri and D.G. Tendulkar, 1954.

Torchia, Adela Diubaldo. *Gandhi, Ecology, and World Religions.* Saarbrücken: Lambert Academic, 2013.

"University of Cambridge Centre of South Asian Studies Archive." http://www.sasian.cam.ac.uk/archive/papers/handlist/Handlist_H.htm.

Vorobej, Mark. "Structural Violence." *Peace Research: The Canadian Journal of Peace and Conflict Studies* 40, no. 2 (2008): 84–98.

Walli, Koshelya. *The Conception of Ahimsa in Indian Thought.* Varanasi: J.D. Bhattacharya, 1974.

Webster, John C.B. "Gandhi and the Christians: Dialogue in the Nationalist Era." In *Hindu–Christian Dialogue,* 80–99. Edited by Harold Coward. Maryknoll: Orbis Books, 1989.

Wilson, Boyd H. "Ultimacy as Unifier in Gandhi." In *Religion in Modern India,* 343–62. 2nd rev. ed. Edited by Robert D. Baird. Columbia: South Asia Publications, 1989.

Wright, Robert A. "The Glow in the Eastern Sky: The Impact of Mahatma Gandhi and Toyohiko Kagawa on the Canadian Protestant Churches in the Interwar Years." *Journal of the Canadian Church Historical Society* 32, no. 1 (April 1990): 3–23.

Young, Katherine K. "Hinduism and the Ethics of Mass Destruction." In *Ethics and Weapons of Mass Destruction: Religious and Secular Perspectives,* 277–307. Edited by Sohail H. Hashmi and Steven P. Lee. Cambridge: Cambridge University Press, 2004.

Younger, Paul. *From Ashoka to Rajiv: An Analysis of Indian Political Culture.* Bombay: Popular Prakashan, 1987.

———. "M.K. Gandhi: A Postcolonial Voice." In *Teaching Religion and Violence,* 268–94. Edited by Brian K. Pennington. Teaching Religious Studies. New York and Oxford: Oxford University Press, 2012.

Yusuf, K. M. "Maulana Abul Kalam Azad." In *Abul Kalam Azad,* 371–77. Political Thinkers of Modern India, vol. 17. Edited by Verinder Grover. New Delhi: Deep & Deep, 1992.

About the Contributors

Harold Coward is Professor of History and Founding Director of the Centre for Studies in Religion and Society at the University of Victoria. A Fellow of the Royal Society of Canada, he is the author or editor of numerous books, including *The Sphota Theory of Language* (1980), *The Philosophy of the Grammarians* (1990), *Scripture and the World Religions* (2000), *The Perfectibility of Human Nature in Eastern and Western Thought* (2008), and *Indian Critiques of Gandhi* (2003).

Alex Damm is Instructor in the Department of Religion and Culture at Wilfrid Laurier University. He is the author of *Ancient Rhetoric and the Synoptic Problem: Clarifying Markan Priority* (2013) and other essays on Christian origins. Damm is fascinated by the history of Christianity in both its European and South Asian contexts, and teaches a course on the life and thought of Gandhi.

Scott Daniel Dunbar, Lecturer at the Centre for Religious Studies at Monash University, Australia, is the author of the forthcoming book *Religious Conflict and Cooperation: An Introduction* (2017). He is co-editor of the *Journal of Religion and Popular Culture*, and has been appointed an Associate to Monash University's *UNESCO Chair in Interreligious and Intercultural Relations*. In addition to research and teaching on Gandhi, Dunbar has taught a range of other courses in religious studies.

Ramin Jahanbegloo is Professor and Vice-Dean of the School of Law and Director of Mahatma Gandhi Centre for Peace Studies at Jindal Global University in Delhi, India. He is the winner of the Peace Prize from the United Nations Association in Spain (2009) and the winner of the Josep Palau i Fabre International Essay Prize. Among his books are *The Gandhian Moment* (2013) and *Introduction to Nonviolence* (2013).

Klaus Klostermaier is University Distinguished Professor Emeritus in the Department of Religious Studies at the University of Manitoba. A Fellow of the Royal Society of Canada, Klostermaier has published numerous works in the fields of religious studies, especially Hindu studies, including *A Survey of Hinduism*, now in its third edition (2007), as well as *Mahatma Gandhi: Freiheit ohne Gewalt* (*Gandhi: Freedom without Violence*) (1968).

Kay Koppedrayer taught an undergraduate course on Gandhi from her first year as a faculty member of the Religion and Culture Department at Wilfrid Laurier University, Waterloo, Ontario, up to 2009, her last year of teaching. What she learned through her work with the course and from her students over those decades resulted in a series of journal articles and book chapters on Gandhi. Now retired, she continues to research and write.

Anne M. Pearson has taught numerous courses, including a course on Gandhi, at McMaster University, and her published essays and articles include an examination of women's religious lives and a study of the Hindu diaspora. A granddaughter of Canadian Prime Minister Lester B. Pearson, she works for the cause of peace in various contexts, including inter-religious dialogue and the *Mahila Shanti Sena* in India.

Rama S. Singh is Professor in the Department of Biology, McMaster University. His areas of research include population genetics, genomics, and evolution. He founded the Gandhi Peace Festival (Hamilton, 1993) and helped to initiate the Gandhi Lectures on Nonviolence at the Centre for Peace Studies, McMaster University (1996). He is co-founder of the *Mahila Shanti Sena* (2002) – a women's peace and development organization in India – and opened a girls' high school in his village (2004).

Paul Younger retired as Professor of Religious Studies at McMaster University after decades of teaching courses in Hindu studies, including a course on the life and thought of Gandhi. His published works include *The Indian Religious Tradition* (1970), *Introduction to Indian Religious Thought* (1972), *From Ashoka to Rajiv: An Analysis of Indian Political Culture* (1987), and *Playing Host to Deity: Festival Religion in the South Indian Tradition* (2002).

Index

Ambedkar, Bhimrao Ramji, 69–70, 73, 77
Anderson, Benedict, 140–41. *See also*
  Imagined Communities
Andrews, Charles Freer, 1, 68, 81
attitudes towards Gandhi in Canada:
  "ambivalence" in, 126; difficulty interpreting Gandhi, 127, 131, 132, 138;
  Gandhi as anti-colonial/post-colonial
  advocate and thinker, 123, 128; Gandhi as proponent of multiculturalism,
  124–25; Gandhi as representative of
  community/community concerns,
  140–41; George Grant's, 125–26;
  popularity of Gandhi across communities, 126–27, 138–39; relevance
  of Gandhi, 121–41, 128–29, 131–32,
  134–35, 135, 137–39, 139–40, 140–
  41, 143–44, 145–50, 154, 160–61.
  See also Canada; Gandhi; knowledge
  of Gandhi in Canada; relevance of
  Gandhi in Canada
Azad, Maulana Abul Kalam, 47, 50,
  53–55, 61

Baird, Robert, 72
Bakker, Hans, 9n7
Baum, Gregory, 73
Bhagavad Gita, 34–35, 42n5, 56, 76,
  77–78, 80
Brahmins, Chitpavan, 43n17
British Empire, 15, 16, 17–18; Canada
  and, 15, 16, 17–18
Brown, Judith, 25n45

Canada, 20, 41, 47, 59–61, 63–64, 76,
  79–80, 81, 89–108, 109, 111, 114–
  17, 160–61; as British dominion,
  12–13, 16–18, 19–20, 24n42, 24n44,
  24n45, 25n46, 122, 123; as colony:
  12, 20; culture and history, 3, 12–
  13, 19–20, 25n49, 121–25, 125–26,
  128–29, 132–33; India and, 16–18,
  20, 24n37, 63–64; multiculturalism
  and, 12, 123–27, 132–35, 136, 145;
  ordinary people as agents of social
  change in, 160–61; politics in, 146,
  160–61; post-colonial thinking in,
  123, 125, 132–35, 140–41; South
  Asians in/South Asian immigration
  to, 13–16, 18, 20, 22n16, 22n22,
  22n28, 24n36, 121–28, 140; support
  for Gandhi, 3, 63–64, 109–19, 123,
  124–25, 126, 127, 130, 131–32,
  134–35, 138–39, 139–40, 140–41,
  150, 153–54, 160–61. *See also* attitudes towards Gandhi in Canada;
  Gandhi; knowledge of Gandhi in
  Canada; relevance of Gandhi in
  Canada
Canadian Gandhi Foundation for World
  Peace (Edmonton), 158
Carleton University, 82–83
caste, 69–70, 71, 73
Centre for Peace Studies (McMaster
  University), 82, 111, 154, 155
Christianity, 27n65, 65–68; and Gandhi,
  65–68, 81

to understanding of Vietnam War, 128–30. *See also* attitudes towards Gandhi in Canada; Gandhi; knowledge of Gandhi in Canada
Ridd, Karen, 150
Rukmani, T. S., 70–71, 83

Salmond, Noel, 71, 82
sarvodaya, 6, 11, 160
satyagraha (including conflict resolution), 6, 11, 29, 30, 36, 38, 42, 50, 73, 78–80, 94–95, 97–99, 100–101, 103, 104, 105–6, 107, 109, 110, 111–13, 138, 145, 146, 162; cowardice, bravery, and 29, 36, 38, 40, 42, 42n3; relevance to Canada, 149, 160. *See also* Gandhi; non-violence/violence; peacebuilding
Savarkar, V. D., 42n5, 43n17, 71–72, 79–80
Schumacher, E. F., 149
September 11, 2001, 139–40
Sharma, Arvind, 66, 76, 83
Sikhism/Sikhs, 15, 23n33, 68–69, 122, 133–34
Sinclair, Murray, 143, 146
Singh, Nikky-Guninder Kaur, 68–69
Singh, Rama, 6, 111, 114, 153
Smith, Gordon, 76
social justice, 41, 45n39, 158; function of truth, 41; requires non-violence, 41; in South Africa, 48. *See also* Gandhi; non-violence/violence
South Asia: cowardice and bravery in, 35–36, 37, 40, 42; cultural ideals, 35, 36–37, 40, 42; immigration to Canada (*see* Canada)
sustainability, 7, 8
swadeshi, 99, 100, 147. *See also* technology
swaraj (including discussion of civilization in India and the West), 6, 7–8, 11, 12, 18, 25n45, 26n52, 27n67, 36, 37, 74, 78, 79, 81, 116, 118n7, 129, 131–32, 147–48, 160; *Shrambharati Khadigram* and, 118n4

Tagore, Rabindranath, 70–71, 75
Tamils/Tamil Canadians, 133
technology, 7, 74, 75–76, 99, 128–29, 135, 147–48, 149
Tolstoy, Leo, 129–30
Torchia, Adela D., 144
"traditionalism," 134–35
Trudeau, Pierre Elliott, 123–24, 125, 133, 134
Truth, 6, 37, 38, 41, 42, 54, 61, 145–46, 147, 149, 161–62; non-violence and, 37, 38, 41, 49, 53–54, 58

University of Calgary, 84
University of Manitoba, 83–84, 144
University of Toronto, 82
University of Victoria, 84
University of Waterloo, 83

Vedanta, 137

Webster, John C. B., 67
Wedderburn, William, 19
Wilfrid Laurier University, 83, 89–108
Wilson, Boyd H., 6
Winnipeg (Man.), 6, 15, 143–44, 150
women, 33, 79–80, 109–19, 117n2, 118n7, 118n8, 130–32, 133. *See also* Gandhi
Wright, Robert A., 81

Young, Katherine, 39
Younger, Paul, 5–6, 78–80, 81–82, 85, 121

www.ingramcontent.com/pod-product-compliance
Lightning Source LLC
Chambersburg PA
CBHW051729020426
42333CB00014B/1218